Joni: The Anthology

EDITED BY BARNEY HOSKYNS

Barney Hoskyns is the cofounder and editorial director of the online rock-journalism library Rock's Backpages (rocksbackpages.com), and the author of several books including *Hotel California: The True-Life Adventures of Crosby, Stills, Nash, Young, Mitchell, Taylor, Browne, Ronstadt, Geffen, the Eagles, and Their Many Friends* (2005), *Lowside of the Road: A Life of Tom Waits* (2009), *Small Town Talk: Bob Dylan, The Band, Van Morrison, Janis Joplin, Jimi Hendrix and Friends in the Wild Years of Woodstock* (2016), and *Never Enough: A Way Through Addiction* (2017). A former U.S. correspondent for *MOJO*, Hoskyns has contributed to *Vogue*, *Rolling Stone*, *The Guardian*, *GQ*, and *Uncut*.

JONI

THE ANTHOLOGY

EDITED BY
BARNEY HOSKYNS

Picador | New York

Picador
120 Broadway, New York 10271

Library of Congress Control Number: 2017027146
Picador Paperback ISBN: 978-1-250-14863-6

Our books may be purchased in bulk for promotional, educational, or business use.
Please contact your local bookseller or the Macmillan Corporate and Premium
Sales Department at 1-800-221-7945, extension 5442, or by email
at MacmillanSpecialMarkets@macmillan.com.

Picador® is a U.S. registered trademark and is used by Macmillan Publishing Group, LLC,
under license from Pan Books Limited.

For book club information, please visit facebook.com/picadorbookclub or
email marketing@picadorusa.com.

picadorusa.com · instagram.com/picador
twitter.com/picadorusa · facebook.com/picadorusa

1 3 5 7 9 10 8 6 4 2

Acknowledgements

With thanks to Andreas Campomar, Lucian Randall and Claire Chesser at Little, Brown, and to Matthew Hamilton and Matias Lopez-Portillo at Aitken Alexander Associates. To my Rock's Backpages colleagues Mark Pringle and Tony Keys for sourcing the articles. Also to Debbie Paitchel at Wenner Media for her assistance with the *Rolling Stone* articles. And last but most to all the contributors to *Joni*: Loraine Alterman, Colman Andrews, Jacoba Atlas, Johnny Black, Caroline Boucher, Stephen M. H. Braitman, Mick Brown, Geoffrey Cannon, Barbara Charone, Martin Colyer, J. D. Considine, the late Karl Dallas, Dave DiMartino, Ian Dove, Robin Eggar, Todd Everett, Helen Fitzgerald, Ben Fong-Torres, Jerry Gilbert, The Writer Formerly Known As Betty Page (Beverley Glick), Fred Goodman, Michael Gross, Nicholas Jennings, Mark Kemp, Larry LeBlanc, Gerrie Lim, Kristine McKenna, Stuart Maconie, John Milward, Tom Nolan, Ian Penman, Sandy Robertson, Wayne Robins, Steven Rosen, Ellen Sander, Joel Selvin, Paul Sexton, Ben Sidran, Dave Simpson, Wesley Strick, Adam Sweeting, Frank Tortorici, Jaan Uhelszki, Michael Watts, Susan Whitall, the late Paul Williams, Richard Williams and Dave Zimmer.

Contents

CONTENTS

CONTENTS

CONTENTS

Our Lady of Sorrows

AN INTRODUCTION

On the afternoon I interviewed her in September 1994 (see 'Conversation' on pages 189–205), Joni Mitchell was in the most infectious of moods: giggly, garrulous, bordering on flirtatious. When we were done talking, she hammed it up for the photographer on the street, just around the corner from her manager Peter Asher's office on West Hollywood's Doheny Drive.

I've always felt privileged to have met this genius of North American music, this Canadian prairie maid turned folk poetess turned canyon confessor turned jazzbo hybridiser turned . . . well, never mind the many shapes Mitchell's shifted over half a century. Let's just agree she's peerless and untouchable as a singer-songwriter of intricate lyrics and swoopingly beautiful melodies.

Her words and her 'weird chords' you can read about at length in the pieces pulled together in this compendium. Included in *Joni* are some of the most open and thoughtful interviews Mitchell has ever given, as well as some of the finest snapshots of her complex, often spiky personality. Here are reviews of (almost) all her albums – the consensus masterworks, the curate's eggs – and of live appearances she's made in tiny clubs and glitzy concert halls. Here are the words of writers who've fallen, as I did, under the spell of her piercing honesty, her tingling musical intimacy, her coolly nuanced moods: Americans and Brits alike, men and women who know how uniquely brilliant she is.

Some would say Mitchell has been her own worst enemy – has too often bitten the journalistic hands that stroked her. I choose to think she's struggled to bear the weight of her talent and intelligence in an arena better disposed to the crass and the facile. True, she might have made life easier by not being quite so savage about the 'three-chord wonder' strummers who identify themselves as her disciples – but then why pretend they aren't mediocrities when so many queue up to crown them the New Jonis? And when an artist has given us 'The Arrangement', 'River', 'Car on a Hill', 'The Boho Dance', 'Amelia', 'Dog Eat Dog', 'My Secret Place', 'The Magdalene Laundries', 'Man from Mars' and 'If I Had a Heart' – to offer a random smattering of marvels that span the length and breadth of her work – who are we to judge her character? Many of Mitchell's songs are great art. Almost all are emotionally complex, musically gripping. From the earliest virginal days of 'Chelsea Morning' to the late, husky despair of *Turbulent Indigo*'s 'Sex Kills', Joni's is a voice that belongs to her alone. So we should excuse her occasional impatience with the received idea that she is godmother to those who do nothing more useful than string together stale chords and trite musings and call them songs.

Granted, Mitchell's own earliest compositions sound somewhat fey today. 'Urge For Going' and 'Both Sides Now' have a kind of fluting, pellucid innocence about them, while even she acknowledges that the winsome 'Circle Game' only has currency these days as a campfire singalong. The first hint of her defining gravitas came with 'Woodstock', a song of starry-eyed hippie faith that, with its shimmery electric piano and curiously yodelled vocals, sounded a simultaneous note of dread. Personally, I go a bundle on the grainy maturity of her vocal persona on such '90s songs as 'Passion Play', 'Come in from the Cold' and 'Nothing Can Be Done', but they're not to everybody's tastes.

In these pages you'll find the late Paul Williams, acknowledged founder of rock criticism, and Ellen Sander, one of the first women to write about pop. You'll find Michael Watts and Geoffrey Cannon, subtle British commentators from rock's first golden age. You'll find keyboard player Ben Sidran on Joni's homage to cantankerous jazz maverick Charles Mingus, as well as considered appreciations – not always raves – of Mitchell's art by Wesley Strick, Susan Whitall, Sandy Robertson, Joel Selvin and others. You'll get the fine words of Tom Nolan, Loraine Alterman, Mick Brown, Ben Fong-Torres, and many other contributors to Rock's Backpages.

Here is most of what you could ever want to know about Joni Mitchell, a towering troubadour and sometimes reckless daughter of America's folk-rock revolution.

Barney Hoskyns, Rock's Backpages
London, January 2016

Part One

Urges for Going (1943–1967)

Beginnings

Nicholas Jennings, from *Before the Gold Rush:
Flashbacks to the Dawn of the Canadian Sound*
(Toronto: Penguin Canada, 1997)

In 1958, Joni Mitchell was still Joan Anderson, a fifteen-year-old living in Saskatoon. That year, she purchased her first instrument – a $36 baritone ukulele – with money she earned from modelling. The ukulele was an alternative to a guitar, which her mother had strictly forbidden. But it enabled her to accompany herself singing Kingston Trio songs and other folk material of the day. Coincidentally, Neil Young also received a ukulele from his parents around the same time, while living in Pickering, Ontario. The thirteen-year-old Young, who, like Mitchell, also suffered a childhood case of polio, had been inspired by seeing Elvis perform on TV's *Ed Sullivan Show*.

As the only child born to William and Myrtle Anderson in Fort McLeod, Alberta, Roberta Joan had grown up in Saskatoon – not far from [Buffy] Sainte-Marie's own birthplace on the Cree Indian Piapot Reserve in the Qu'Appelle Valley. A self-described 'good-time Charlie', Joni first wrecked her stockings dancing to the jukebox jive of Chuck Berry, Elvis Presley and the Coasters. But at a certain point, like many teenagers in the early '60s, she traded rock's 'jungle rhythms' for the more cerebral qualities of folk music. 'Rock'n'roll went through a really dumb, vanilla period,' she recalled. 'And during that period, folk came in to fill the hole.'

At parties, Anderson began to lead singalongs, accompanying herself on baritone ukulele with chords she'd learned from a Pete Seeger instruction record. While performing at a local wiener roast in 1961, the eighteen-year-old caught the fancy of some people connected with Prince Albert's TV station who promptly booked her as a one-time replacement for a late-night moose-hunting show. Two years later, while working as a waitress at Saskatoon's Louis Riel coffee house, Anderson ventured to the stage during one of the Riel's weekly 'hoot nights'. Sitting on a stool, the pigtailed performer screeched into the microphone and plunked away on her ukulele for some puzzled onlookers.

Indeed, her developing taste for folk music left more than a few people bewildered. 'My friends who knew me as a rock'n'roll dancer found this change kind of hard to relate to,' she admitted recently. 'The songs at that time [were] folk songs and English ballads, and English ballads are always [about] "the cruel mother" and there's a lot of sorrow in them. But they had beautiful melodies, that was the thing, and I always loved melody. Melody is generally melancholy and sad and the text that accompanies it must be the same.'

In the fall of '63, Anderson enrolled at the Alberta College of Art in Calgary to pursue her interest in painting. But she continued to entertain thoughts of becoming a folk singer and was soon showing up at Calgary's Depression coffee house. Will Millar, then a budding folk singer and later the leader of the Irish Rovers, recalls: 'Joni came with her uke and tormented us all with a shrill "Sloop John B" and "I With I Wath an Apple on a Twee".' But by the following year, Anderson had improved enough that the Depression paid her

$15 to entertain weekend audiences of mostly fellow art students. She even got hired to perform at Edmonton's Yardbird Suite coffee house, which, along with the Depression and Vancouver's Bunkhouse, was a major stop on the folk circuit in Western Canada.

With a guitar now in hand, Joni Anderson purchased a one-way train ticket from Calgary to Toronto and set out to attend Mariposa in July '64. She'd quit art college and, whether she knew it yet or not, was a couple of months pregnant – the result of a love affair with fellow art student Brad MacMath. Somewhere between the Prairies and the Lakehead, she penned her first song, 'Day by Day', a bluesy piece written to the rhythm of the train wheels that she later described as a 'feeling-sorry-for-myself' song.

Joni arrived in Toronto and took a bus up to Orillia only to find that Mariposa was in trouble. The previous year's festival had attracted such an unexpected flood of people that the town of Orillia had been overwhelmed. Although it was hardly a disaster of Woodstock proportions, there had been complaints of traffic jams, inadequate facilities and well-publicised acts of drunken debauchery. The local police chief claimed that the festival had given Orillia 'the worst forty-eight hours in its history'. So even though Mariposa had been granted permission to use nearby farm-land for the '64 festival, a nervous town council blocked the move at the last minute – and the courts upheld the decision just one day before the festival was scheduled to open.

When Anderson and other early birds showed up, organisers were in complete chaos, faced with the monumental task of packing up and moving several tons of equipment and supplies back to Toronto, where the Maple Leaf baseball stadium had been lined up as a last-minute venue. According to the festival's Martin Onrot, Joni helped to load trucks along with other volunteers. Then, at the stadium by Lake Ontario, she and others braved the rain and cold temperatures to watch performances by blues legends Sonny Terry & Brownie McGhee, Mississippi John Hurt and others. In particular, Anderson studied the distinctive vibrato style of Sainte-Marie, who enjoyed no fewer than four standing ovations.

After the festival, the new girl in town had to find a place to crash. She discovered a rooming house in the Annex neighbourhood of the city and to make ends meet landed herself a sales job in ladies' wear at the Simpson's department store. Although Anderson must have figured it out by then, her pregnancy was still not evident. Eventually, her weekly wage would enable her to pay the dues required to join the Musicians' Union. In the meantime, she settled for playing several non-union coffee houses in Yorkville. The first to hire her was the Penny Farthing, which featured novice folk singers in its basement.

That same month, February '65, Joni Anderson gave birth to a daughter. A month earlier, she had moved out of the Annex rooming house and into an apartment above the nearby Lickin' Chicken restaurant with Vicky Taylor, another folk singer. Taylor remembers that Joni brought the baby girl home for a couple of weeks. But when she realised she could neither support the child financially nor get on with her singing career, she made the wrenching decision to place her daughter with foster parents. 'That really tore her apart,' recalls Taylor. 'She knew that she couldn't be a single mum and do anything with her music. It was a really hard decision for her to make.'

The decision haunted Joni for many years. She left clues about the baby, whom she had named Kelly, in some of her songs, including 'Little Green' from her *Blue* album. In a fairy-tale ending worthy of a Disney movie, Mitchell and her daughter, whose adoptive name is Kilauren Gibb, met each other again in March 1997 in an extraordinary, media-hyped reunion.

Above the Lickin' Chicken Joni began writing songs in earnest. Taylor remembers her getting up in the middle of the night and working, sometimes until dawn. 'One morning,' says Taylor, 'she told me that she'd woken up with a tune going around in her head and couldn't go back to sleep until she worked it all out.' That song turned out to be 'Here Today and Gone Tomorrow', one of several that she later described as 'lost-love pieces for a wandering Australian who really did me in'.

By the spring of '65, Joni Anderson was back struggling to find work as a folk singer. She landed gigs at the Half Beat and the New Gate of Cleve, where Mariposa's Estelle Klein saw her for the first time. 'She wasn't doing all her own material,' recalled Klein, 'but she was a nice singer and had a very charming manner.'

Bernie Fiedler [owner of the Riverboat coffeehouse] was not so quickly impressed, offering the folk singer a job in the kitchen when she first inquired about work at the Riverboat. She turned it down. (Fiedler has always denied this story, but she insists it's true.) Fiedler says he does remember saying to Joni, 'So, Miss Anderson, I see you're going for the Baez sound,' a comment that surely must have rankled her. Truth was, the more she wrote her own material, the less derivative she sounded.

'Once I began to write,' she admitted, 'my vocal style changed. My Joan Baez/Judy Collins influence disappeared. Almost immediately, when I had my own words to sing, my own voice appeared.'

You might say Joni Anderson was on the rebound from losing her daughter or maybe it was the wandering Australian. But when the older and wiser Chuck Mitchell blew into town that June she was clearly vulnerable. He was the 'star' folk singer from Detroit, performing upstairs at the Penny Farthing while she was the local girl on the basement stage. When he turned on the charm, the impressionable Joni found him hard to resist. 'I was at an indecisive time in my life,' she later admitted, 'and he was a strong force. He decided he was gonna marry me. So he dragged me across the border, got me some work and we were quickly married.'

Quickly is right. Vicky Taylor remembers the courtship as lasting all of thirty-six hours. The two were married in Mitchell's parents' backyard in Rochester, Michigan. 'I was totally shocked,' says Taylor, 'but I figured Joni knew what she was doing.' She and Chuck moved into a cheap fifth-floor apartment on Detroit's Wayne university campus and Joni moved into her husband's world. Chuck was well known on the coffee house circuit and soon their apartment became a crash pad for visiting folkies, from Gordon Lightfoot and Buffy Sainte-Marie to Tom Rush and Eric Andersen. Andersen taught Joni some unusual open tunings on the guitar, which she quickly used to write new songs.

Chuck and Joni began touring together, playing Detroit's Chess Mate coffee house and New York's Gaslight Café. Recalled Joni, 'I wasn't very good, and I had a lot of trouble with the audience booing and hissing and saying, "Take your clothes off, sweetheart." Things like that really shook me up because I didn't know how to counter or act. I thought I'd bombed.' Larry LeBlanc, writing in *Rolling Stone* in 1971, described the Chuck and Joni show as a variety act, with him performing very theatrical Brechtian shtick and Joni doing her own folky thing. When they did team up on duets the songs they sang were often Lightfoot's.

During the spring of '65, while Chuck and Joni were touring the 4D Club circuit, Joni started adding some of her own material into her sets, including 'Both Sides Now', a song she'd written about growing up. One night, after playing at Winnipeg's 4D, a tall kid with a Beatle haircut shuffled up, introduced himself as Neil Young and told her he'd written his own coming-of-age song. Later, as the café was closing, Neil played Joni the bittersweet 'Sugar Mountain', which he'd written on his nineteenth birthday. Moved by its tale of a boy too old for the fairground, Joni wrote a response – 'The Circle Game'. In her song, which cleverly echoes the carnival imagery of 'Sugar Mountain', she assures the boy that 'there'll be new dreams, maybe better dreams and plenty'.

In August 1965 Joni took her new material to Mariposa, held for the first time at Innis Lake north-west of Toronto. On a weekend hit by heavy thunderstorms, she made her last appearance as Joni Anderson, sharing the stage with Ian & Sylvia, Phil Ochs, bluesman Son House and the Dirty Shames (during a power failure one night, Ochs had to sing through a megaphone while illuminated by car headlights).

Joni went over well, both in concert and at a songwriters' workshop. But she insisted on singing only her own songs, which at that point were precious few apart from 'Both Sides Now' and 'The Circle Game'. Some people complained, Estelle Klein recalled. 'They said, "She's really nice, but she's singing the same thing over and over again." So when I invited her back for the next year, I said, "Joni, I really like what you do, but could you expand your repertoire a little?"'

In the car ride back to Toronto from Mariposa in August 1965, Joni wrote a new lyric: 'It's like running for a train that left the station hours ago/I've got the urge for going.' Although she has explained that the song was written about the changing folk scene and the need for moving on, it also reflected what was happening in her relationship with Chuck.

'It was not a marriage made in heaven,' she admitted. 'He was relatively well-educated and in contempt of my lack of education. I was developing as an original, unschooled thinker [with] the gift of the blarney [and] the gift of metaphor. But he ridiculed me in the same way that Pierre Trudeau ridiculed his wife Margaret when she wrote her book. [Trudeau] said, "My wife is the only writer I know who's written more books than she's read." So there was this educated pride versus the uneducated and the marriage didn't last very long.' Still, Chuck did give Joni something other than a married name. He advised her to protect her songwriting by forming her own publishing company, something she still gives him credit for.

Her marriage on the rocks, Mitchell ran into more chauvinism in October when she appeared on CTV's *Let's Sing Out* program with US folk singers Dave Van Ronk and Patrick Sky. Mitchell felt inferior alongside these experienced performers and was looking to them for encouragement. But as she recalled, she didn't get it. 'Van Ronk was saying things like, "Joni, you've got groovy taste in clothes, why don't you become a fashion model?"' she said. 'And Sky was saying, "It sucks."' But, she added, 'David did like "Urge for Going" and he asked me for it, I remember. I wondered what ulterior motive he had in mind after saying all those dreadful things to me. I thought, he must just want to laugh at it or something. I was that insecure about my writing.'

Despite that insecurity – or maybe because of it – Mitchell threw herself into songwriting with a vengeance. At the same time, other artists began recording her songs. First 'Urge for Going' got a country treatment by George Hamilton IV, followed by versions by Tom Rush, Judy Collins and Van Ronk. Then Ian & Sylvia and Buffy Sainte-Marie covered 'The Circle Game'. Suddenly, Joni Mitchell's name was known on the US coffee house circuit and her songs were earning her a tidy income to boot.

Joni Mitchell faced a much more receptive crowd at Mariposa that summer (1966). In fact, Mitchell returned to the festival as one of its most popular attractions, joining a line-up that included Gordon Lightfoot, Doc Watson and the New Lost City Ramblers.

Dressed in paisley and accompanied by guitarist David Rea, Mitchell captivated audiences at both her evening and afternoon performances. This time she brought a suitcase full of new songs, including 'Both Sides Now' and 'Night in the City', which she told her audience was inspired by Yorkville. 'Music comes spilling out into the street,' she sang. 'Colours go flashing in time.'

Mitchell's appearance was a resounding triumph. 'This girl has everything,' enthused Ruth Jones (the Mariposa founder) in *Hoot*, the Canadian folk magazine; 'looks, charm, personality, an inventive mind, excellent guitar and, above all, a voice which ranges from gutsy to sublime. My guess is that she will be a name to reckon with – and soon.' Only two years earlier, Mitchell had come to Mariposa to hear her heroine Buffy Sainte-Marie. Now she was one of the festival's major stars.

In November '66, Joni Mitchell made her debut at Bernie Fiedler's Riverboat – on the stage, not in the kitchen. It was a triumphant performance, establishing Mitchell as an artist in her own right and a songwriter whose material possessed a distinct Canadian quality. Songs like 'Urge for Going', 'Winter Lady' and 'Come to the Sunshine' that she performed that week were rich in imagery. Each painted a vivid portrait of the changing seasons and owed much to her origins on the Saskatchewan Prairies. Like Tyson and Lightfoot before her, Mitchell was writing songs with a unique sense of place.

Her Riverboat performance was a turning point. Afterwards, Mitchell left her husband and moved to New York where, she hoped, bigger things lay in store. Settling in Manhattan's Chelsea district, she turned her one-bedroom apartment into what she called her 'magic princess' retreat, with bedroom walls covered in tinfoil and door frames lined with crepe paper. There she began writing as many as four songs a week, including the buoyant 'Chelsea Morning' (for which US president Bill Clinton and his wife Hillary later named their daughter). 'I Had a King' detailed her marriage break-up with its lines about the man who 'carried me off to his country for marriage too soon'. With $400 in the bank, she told *Rolling Stone* she thought she was 'filthy rich'.

But Mitchell was about to become much richer, very quickly. While performing for $15 a night at New York's Café Au Go Go, then the hottest club in the city, her new friend Buffy Sainte-Marie brought along her manager Elliot Roberts to see her. Although Roberts remembers Mitchell as 'a jumble of creative clutter with a guitar case full of napkins, road maps and scraps of paper all covered with lyrics,' he was astonished at her talent – so much so that he promptly quit managing Buffy to handle Joni exclusively.

Leonard Cohen, who would not record his debut album *Songs of Leonard Cohen* until later that year, stole the show at Newport from Joan Baez and Pete Seeger with his poetic ballads of romantic despair. Meanwhile, backstage, there was an instant attraction between Cohen and Mitchell. Their love affair lasted for part of the summer as their paths crisscrossed on the festival circuit. Ultimately Mitchell would write two songs about their brief affair – 'The Gallery' and 'That Song About the Midway' – both of which would appear on her *Clouds* album. On 'Midway', Mitchell wrote of Cohen, 'You stood out like a ruby in a black man's ear'. She would later refer to

Cohen, along with Dylan, as her only real 'pace-runners' when it came to songwriting.

Mariposa was something of a love-in itself that summer. Joni Mitchell and Leonard Cohen continued their not-so-secret affair there at Innis Lake north of Toronto. With Mitchell, Cohen, Buffy Sainte-Marie and Murray McLauchlan (making his Mariposa debut), there was a heavy emphasis on Canadian singer-songwriters, now becoming a strong national tradition.

After the summer of '67, Joni Mitchell left behind her 'magic princess' castle in Chelsea to become a lady of California's Laurel Canyon. Immediately, she began work on her first album with singer David Crosby producing. Crosby remembers 'a willowy blonde with blue eyes and high cheekbones, singing art songs in a bell-like soprano with a Canadian accent and accompanying herself on acoustic guitar and dulcimer . . . not anyone's idea of the next big thing.'

But Joni surprised everyone. The self-titled album was a quiet, sparsely produced chronicle of the past year of her life. Side one was titled 'I Came to the City' (meaning New York) while side two, featuring songs like 'The Dawntreader' – about life on Crosby's boat – was called 'Out of the City and Down to the Seaside' (presumably the Pacific Ocean). The album established Mitchell as an artist in her own right. In December she performed at the Miami Pop Festival before a hundred thousand people, on a bill with Marvin Gaye, Fleetwood Mac, Canned Heat and Three Dog Night. The same month, Judy Collins's version of Mitchell's 'Both Sides Now' became a major hit.

Part Two

Our Lady of the Canyon (1968–1972)

Joni Mitchell Sings Own Songs in Debut at Troubadour Nitery

Stephen M. H. Braitman, *Van Nuys News* (Los Angeles), 7 June 1968

Many of the current crop of popular folk singers today have used the songs of Joni Mitchell in their rise to the top. Now young Miss Mitchell has taken it upon herself to show how her songs should be sung.

On Tuesday evening, she made her performing debut at Doug Weston's Troubadour and proved herself emotionally and stylistically impressive in her approach to her own numbers.

The Canadian-born songstress has a distinctly individual vocal quality that can be either powerful or gentle, depending on the song she's singing or the interpretation she places upon it.

Accompanying herself on guitar, Joni rendered the simple melody of her 'Circle Game' with tenderness befitting the lyrics, which describe a children's game.

Other tunes which found the audience highly receptive included 'Marcie', 'Roses Blue', 'Michael from Mountains', 'I Don't Know Where I Stand', 'Slowing Down' and 'Clouds'.

Review of *Joni Mitchell* (aka *Song to a Seagull*)

Paul Williams, from 'The Way We Are Today', included in
The Age of Rock, ed. Jonathan Eisen (New York: Vintage, 1969)

J oni Mitchell is a young lady from Saskatchewan, simply an adventurer, off to seek her fortune in the States and meeting all these people and living in these places and having things happen to her. She is very much a peer of the young, of you or me who did or didn't go to college but anyway were looking for something and also finding things out at the same time – 'I came to the city and lived like old Crusoe' – and bumping up against people, which is the part that seemed to make a difference.

I describe her as a peer and will do the same for Pete Rowan of Earth Opera, not because I think I know who you are but because it is unusual these days that 'rock' people actually sing about themselves and particularly unusual that they do it in a manner so mixing the general and the specific that it is comfortable and natural to 'identify' with them in their songs. It is easy to see what and why Pete Rowan sees in the world he encounters in his album; it seems natural to feel how and what Joni feels of the things that happen in her songs. The very best music can be related to as an immediate reflection of the listener's life (just as the *I Ching* is the most personal of books), and even better music is that which reflects you and yet tells you of me.

Joni Mitchell's particular triumph is that girl singers or girl artists of any kind who have really gotten at what it is to be a woman can be counted on the fingers of one hand (if you're generous, use some fingers twice) and this record is a profound expression of 'I, a woman' – I have yet to meet a girl who doesn't feel that Joni speaks for her. Most girls think and speak on a fairly simple level but feel on a deeply complex one; a song like 'Cactus Tree' may say what anyone would be clever enough to say of themselves ('but she's so busy being free'), but in its entirety – the mounting impact of the verses and the change in that line as it is repeated, the way the vocal struts and fumbles the defensiveness and pride, the sound of all those notes and thoughts (have you ever noticed how much more important is the sound of a woman's voice than what she says with it?) – 'Cactus Tree' holds all the fullness and complexity of 'this is where I am now', this is what I feel I know, a feeling one achieves in an afternoon alone and might not be able to begin to express in a month of conversations.

Joni, well, she's a thousand different people and knows it: she understands everything just up to here and knows nothing at all beyond this point, which is just as it should be. She disclaims nothing, demands no credit, spends her present walking unswervingly into the future, in harmony with her world because she has accepted nothing without first understanding it and has never rejected that part of herself that she did understand; what I'm getting at is she hasn't tried to choose who she is or who she will be. So she writes

songs that are simple and straightforward and enormously perceptive, she makes no presumptions, she really likes people and is quite
cautious – careful not to like them for the wrong reasons.

In 'Michael from Mountains', she really conveys how and sort of
why a woman could love a man and desire a man and that's no
everyday achievement. A great many ladies have their heads so full
of all they've read and heard and seen about why a man loves a
woman that they can think of little save how lovable they are. But
Joni even knows that a woman can have a will ('know that I will
know you') without being unfeminine or unyielding herself. She is
also most sensitive to other women ('Marcie' is not a song about
herself; but you can see her seeing herself in her friend – empathy.
Wonderful) and she even knows that there's no one to blame. No
one to name as a traitor here. Harmony. Peace and beauty. Five
stars for good vibrations.

———

Joni Mitchell's album (which has a name, *Song to a Seagull*) is divided
in two parts – 'I Came to the City' and 'Out of the City and Down
to the Seaside' – and ten parts: her songs. Each song has a consciousness, each has its clockwork, its secrets, its soul. 'I Had a King' tells
of a particular old man, a particular event in the history of a life and
also a general state in the relationship between men and women:

> *You know my keys won't fit the door*
> *You know my thoughts won't fit the man*

– and aren't those words clever and charming and right? 'He
lives in another time.' She really perceives things; her words are a
delight to be hit over the head with. And the games are played so

unobtrusively . . . 'the queen's in the [Coconut] Grove till the end of the year' . . . everything you want is there – and more – and seldom too much, and for all the words you're still most impressed by the music.

The songs are singable. The melodies are so specific you know she knew just what she wanted and found it every time and was delighted. Everything is a whole, a painting in which paints and colours and subject matter and movement and forms all are one in the act of creation, united through clarity of vision and will. Phrases return, are altered, sing across each other, simple patterns move their quiet movements and leave the touch of fingers on guitar to make announcements. Embellishment is the work of the performer; the composer has done the jobs of framework and appeal. Joni-as-performer appreciates and makes full use of the achievements of her composing self; as a team, these Jonies are as efficient and effective as any playwright-actor team could be.

She plays guitar like someone smiling at you; she knows the communicating impact of every movement each speaking finger makes. Her singing is not quite so clarion; it is harder to listen to your own voice, it takes more years to know; she is learning; she explores and, oh, so often she succeeds. And she is trying, and knows how to try; where to make the effort which means half the battle won. The listener can hear that, cannot help but be pleased, cannot help feeling more-than-content.

And she is pretty, which means her words and voice and face and music and she's alive, which means the album; it is something you should welcome in your world.

Joni, the Seagull from Saskatoon

Karl Dallas, *Melody Maker*,
28 September 1968

---

alking to Joni Mitchell about her songs is rather like talking to someone you just met about the most intimate secrets of her life. Like peeping in a window on someone and then discussing with her what you have seen. Her songs are so personal.

They're honest, too. The girl in the songs on her Reprise album isn't all sweetness and light and she doesn't seem to win the wholehearted approval of the writer herself.

'Her heart is full and hollow like a cactus tree/While she's so busy being free,' she sings, in a full round voice that has a lot of Judy Collins in it – which is interesting, since Judy has recorded two of [Joni's] songs and is putting more on her next album.

'I've always admired Judy ever since I first started singing in Saskatoon, Canada, where I come from. Now we are close friends. But in those days I think I sounded more like Joan Baez. Since I started writing songs the range of my voice has extended downwards something like two octaves, which gives me a lot more freedom in the sort of melodies I'm writing.'

She certainly uses that freedom with long, free-ranging tunes that swoop down and soar up in ways that few except perhaps mesdames Baez and Collins could handle. In this they are unlike the deadpan, almost banal melodies used by her fellow Canadian, Leonard Cohen.

'My lyrics are influenced by Leonard,' she admits. 'We never knew each other in Canada, but after we met at Newport last year we saw a lot of each other. My song "Marcie" has a lot of him in it, and some of Leonard's religious imagery, which comes from being a Jew in a predominantly Catholic city, seems to have rubbed off on me, too.'

'Marcie' is about a girl waiting for a letter that never comes and who walks out of the last verse to go west again. Is Marcie Joni?

'I suppose so, really. Marcie is a real girl, she lives in London. I used her name because I wanted a two-syllable name. But I'm the girl in all these songs. And the first song in the album, "I Had a King", is about the breakup of my marriage.'

The album is one of the few I can think of – the others that spring to mind are *Sgt. Pepper* and the Mothers of Invention LPs – which successfully hangs together as a complete whole.

The title, written so subtly by the wings of flying seagulls on the cover that few people notice it, is *Song to a Seagull*. The first side is called 'I Came To The City' and the second side is called 'Out of the City and Down to the Seaside'. Both are lines from songs on the second side.

'The album does tell a story, though not necessarily in chronological order. Certainly the songs aren't placed in the chronological order that I wrote them. As we were working on it, songs came up that would fit in. And, since it was finished, I've written others that could go into the sequence too.'

Joni is not doing too much writing at the moment. 'I'm too hung up about what's going on in America politically. I keep thinking, how can I sing "Night in the city looks pretty to me" when I know it's not pretty at all, with people living in slums and being beaten up by police?

'It was what happened in Chicago during the Democratic convention that really got me thinking. All those kids being clubbed. If I'd been wearing these Levis, they'd have clubbed me – not for doing anything, but this is the uniform of the enemy. That's what they are beginning to call the kids today: the enemy. I keep trying to put what I feel into words, but it's all been said so much better by other people. Strangely enough, a song I wrote at the end of last year, "The Fiddler and the Drum", expresses what I feel now, though I wasn't conscious of feeling that way then.'

Because Joni Mitchell was originally a painter – she designed the sleeve for her own album – the things that stick in the mind from her songs are all visual: the king she lost, painting the pastel walls of her home brown thinking of ladies in gingham while she is a girl dressed in leather. Michael, stirring puddles with a stick to change the taffeta patterns of an oil slick. Neon sign colours in the city 'waltzing in time'. Traffic lights that are red for anger and green for envy. And all through this album, the seagull that wheels above you cries and then is suddenly gone.

I think Joni Mitchell is that seagull.

Memories of Joni

Ellen Sander, Rock's Backpages, October 2012

I was driving Stephen Stills to a Crosby, Stills & Nash recording session. It must've been 1969 and the subject of Joni Mitchell came up. Nothing unusual about that: 'everyone' was talking about her. 'Every man within fifty feet falls in love with her,' Stills let loose with that gravelly chortle, and his sideways grin told me that he was probably one of them.

I had occasion to listen to a private collection of some live tracks of Joni Mitchell recently and her voice was just soaring, rippling, traversing octaves, hitting that little yodelly break. From deep in a spiral of memories I fell into the same thrall as when her music was a frequent visitor in the air around me, as sweet as it gets, like seeing a sun rise just for you, pouring through backlit clouds in billowing hues.

I remember when I met her in New York (in Chelsea) and her first album, with that breathy folksy sound. And later exploring her lower register in the second album. After a couple of tours – and she'd moved to LA by then, to Laurel Canyon – she held her sides and told me she felt the muscles around her ribs bulking and remarked that she now understood why opera singers are so barrel-chested.

When I reviewed her first album, *Song to a Seagull*, for the *New York Times* (published 29 December 1968), I wrote that 'Joni Mitchell's songs are the product of her fascination with changes of heart, changes of mind, changes of season and changes of self . . . The songs about herself are songs for today's independent young woman . . . "I Had a King" is a sad, backward glance at the artist's broken marriage, without bitterness or self-reproach. "Cactus Tree" speaks of today's young divorcee on the rebound "so busy being free".'

What actually intrigued me, which I didn't put in writing (because I didn't know how to admit it), was how she handled a litany of relationships in her songs with such class and unapologetic confessional. Not to mention gorgeous melodies, exquisite lyrics. Nobody ever painted womanhood in such lithe watercolour strokes.

Her loves were also the fodder for reprehensibly gauche notice: Warner Brothers came out with a print ad for the first album with the headline of 'Joni Mitchell is 100 per cent virgin'. Mitchell's manager hit the roof and they pulled it immediately. I'm not sure where I actually saw it – perhaps in the trades? *Rolling Stone*, with a chart identifying her lovers, from rumour and from inference, once named her 'old lady of the year'. Crude, rude and lewd. A woman articulating the nuances of relationships in explicit detail? And no remorse? I guess no groundbreaking work goes unpunished, even works executed with such poetic skill, dignity and insight.

I know for a fact it upset her very much. But it didn't faze her, not one bit. Because in addition to her stunning, understated beauty, her extraordinary talents and taste, she's got courage and lots of it. Personally and musically. She composes in modes few musicians can name, plies vocal lines with unexpected shifts and intervals and has forged a career that is unique.

People analyse her songs all the time to figure out who they are about. I happen to know exactly who 'stood out like a ruby in a black man's ear' in 'That Song About the Midway', one of my favourites. And he certainly does. Even now.

She once told me the smartest thing anyone ever said about songwriting. People ask her all the time if a certain song is about such and so a person. She said that if you never tell whom the song is about, everybody thinks it's them.

And I do. Joni Mitchell writes my life, the part of my life that connects with nature and romantic misadventure and womanhood and language and wondering under the night sky. And yours. What a gift.

Joni Mitchell

Uncredited writer, *Rolling Stone*,
17 May 1969

F olk music, which pushed rock'n'roll into the arena of the serious with protest lyrics and blendings of Dylan and the Byrds back in 1964, has re-entered the pop music cycle. Once again, with a new crop of guitar-toting composer-singers at the vanguard, folk is 'in'.

As with country, jazz, and other rock music satellites, it is not 100 per cent pure. Joan Baez is completely off of her abortive rock-album trip, but there's a solid country beat to her Dylan LP. Peter, Paul, and Mary couldn't have been serious singing 'I Dig Rock and Roll Music'; nevertheless, they used a full complement of session men (and even backup voices) in their *Late Again* album. Dylan is back to the basics, leaving electronics largely to the boys in The Band, but his next LP – as with his *John Wesley Harding* – is Nashville-twanged.

The old names are back but in more commercial regalia. Judy Collins, softened, orchestrated, countrified (and even, on national TV, mini-skirted), is a regular chart item now, after years of limited success.

The music (someone called it 'Art Rock', but that can be ignored) features a lighter, more lyrical style of writing, as exemplified by Leonard Cohen. As if in aural backlash to psy-ky-delick acid rock and to the all-hell-has-broken-loose styles of Aretha Franklin and Janis Joplin, the music is gentle, sensitive, and graceful. Nowadays it's the personal and the poetic, rather than a message, that dominates.

Into this newly re-ploughed field has stepped Joni Mitchell, composer, singer, guitarist, painter, and poetess from Alberta, Canada.

Miss Mitchell, a wispy 25-year-old blonde, is best known for her compositions, 'Michael from Mountains' and 'Both Sides Now', as recorded by Judy Collins, and 'The Circle Game', cut by Tom Rush.

She has a first LP out (on Reprise). A second album – recorded during successful concerts at UC Berkeley and at Carnegie Hall – is ready for release, and another studio album has already been recorded. She is editing a book of poetry and artwork; a volume of her compositions will follow shortly. And she has received a movie offer (to conceive, script and score a film).

Not bad for a girl who had no voice training, hated to read in school, and learned guitar from a Pete Seeger instruction record.

Just who – and what – is Joni Mitchell, this girl who's so obviously perched on the verge?

To those who don't spend hours in audio labs studying the shades, tones and nuances of the human voice, Miss Mitchell is just a singer who sounds like Joan Baez or Judy Collins. She has that fluttery but controlled kind of soprano, the kind that can slide effortlessly from the middle register to piercing highs in mid-word.

Like Baez, Miss Mitchell plays a fluid acoustic guitar; like Collins, she can switch to the piano once in a while. And her compositions reflect the influences of Cohen.

On stage, however, she is her own woman. Where Joan Baez is the embattled but still charming Joan of Arc of the non-violence crusade, and where Judy Collins is the regal, long-time lady-in-waiting of the folk-pop world, Joni Mitchell is a fresh, incredibly beautiful innocent/experienced girl/woman.

She can charm the applause out of audience by breaking a guitar string, then apologising by singing her next number a cappella, wounded guitar at a limp parade rest. And when she talks, words stumble out of her mouth to form candid little quasi-anecdotes that are completely antithetical to her carefully constructed, contrived songs. But they knock the audience out almost every time. In Berkeley, she destroyed Dino Valente's beautiful 'Get Together' by trying to turn it into a rousing singalong. It was a lost cause, but the audience made a valiant try at following. For one night, for Joni Mitchell, they were glad to be sheep.

In Laurel Canyon, where she shares a newly purchased house with Graham Nash, Joni sits on an antique sofa and bemusedly shrugs her shoulders. She is talking about an offer from a giant Hollywood film company to write a movie – 'on any theme I want to choose' for a huge amount of money. She is talking about her book of poetry: 'The poems are already written. It's just an eclectic collection of all kinds of things I've done that I don't know what else to do with. I'm putting them into a book because I don't like to lose anything.' And she is showing her artwork – fine pen-and-ink drawing; felt-pen watercolours; a self-portrait for her second LP cover. Some of these, too, will find their way into a Joni Mitchell book.

Whatever she's going to say next will be an understatement.

'I have so many irons in the fire now,' she says. Joni lives in a house filled with the things she loves. Antique pieces crowd tables, mantels and shelves. There are antique handbags hung on a bathroom wall, a hand-carved hat rack at the door; there are castle-style doors and Tiffany stained-glass windows; a grandfather clock and a Priestley piano. Nash is perched on an English church chair and Joni is in the kitchen, using the only electric lights on in the house. She's making the crust for a rhubarb pie.

'Lately, life has been constantly filled with interruptions. I don't have five hours in a row to myself. I think I'm less prolific now, but I'm also more demanding of myself. I have many melodies in my mind at all times, but the words are different now. It's mainly because I rely on my own experiences for lyrics.'

The difference in experiences is the difference between the urban centres of the east – Detroit, Boston, Philadelphia, New York – and California, where she arrived late last summer.

'In New York, the street adventures are incredible. There are a thousand stories in a single block. You see the stories in the people's faces. You hear the songs immediately. Here in Los Angeles, there are less characters because they're all inside automobiles. You don't see them on park benches or peeing in the gutter or any of that.'

Joni Mitchell, after schooling in Saskatoon, Saskatchewan, wanted to be a commercial artist. She attended the Alberta College of Art in Calgary. While studying art, she took up the ukelele.

The guitar – with the Pete Seeger record – followed shortly. 'But I didn't have the patience to copy a style that was already known.' Joni dumped the record and learned guitar by experimentation so that today she re-tunes her guitar after almost every song, and she plays direct harmony to her own singing.

Her vocal training was no less informal. 'I had none. I used to be a breathy little soprano. Then one day I found that I could sing low.

At first I thought I had lost my voice forever. I could sing either a breathy high part or a raspy low part. Then the two came together by themselves. It was uncomfortable for a while, but I worked on it, and now I've got this voice.'

But the poetry – the writing. There must have been a solid literary background; some early influences and guiding lights.

'The only time I read in school was when it was compulsory, like for a book report.'

Miss Mitchell reads more now than ever before. Herman Hesse is a favourite author; Leonard Cohen her favourite poet, with Rod McKuen also on her shelf.

In short, Joni Mitchell seemed almost totally unprepared for her jump into the United States folk circuit in 1966. Further, 'I started at a time when folk clubs were folding all over the place. It was rock'n'roll everywhere, except for a small underground current of clubs.'

But Joni had been making the Toronto scene for more than a year by the time she hit Detroit, and she had written a number of good tunes. Tom Rush, in Detroit for a gig at the Chess Mate, heard some of them and decided to record 'Urge for Going' and 'The Circle Game'. Joni Mitchell had broken water.

She drifted to New York where in the fall of 1967 she met her manager, Elliot Roberts. There, too, she met Andy Wickham. He signed her to Reprise.

Now, despite the current clamour for her time, Joni Mitchell looks forward to writing songs about 'peaceful things'.

In concert, she does a number called 'Song for America' and her first LP was produced by David Crosby, the politically aroused ex-Byrd. 'So I can't help but know what's happening. But I also know that I can't do a thing about it. It's good to be exposed to politics and what's going down here, but it does damage to me. Too much of it can cripple me. And if I really let myself think about it – the violence, the sickness, all of it – I think I'd flip out.'

Joni Mitchell has arrived in America.

Review of *Clouds*

Geoffrey Cannon, *Guardian*,
24 June 1969

Joni Mitchell has written songs for Tom Rush, and the Fairport Convention have used her songs on both their albums.

In each case, I'd had the idea of an intricate delicacy; but tiny intonations in both interpretations indicated that the singers didn't own the songs they'd chosen. Rush is one of those singers whose songs lose tautness through musing, and Judy Dyble, the original Fairport singer, although she feels her songs, fails to charge them. An English girl singing 'All alone in Carolina and talking to you', for example, loses a crucial sense of place. Fairport Convention, however, are a beautiful band, with a light, tactful thoughtfulness that is good for moments of waking or drowsiness.

All the songs on *Clouds*, Joni Mitchell's album, are her own. Her voice is pure and she sings with spare acoustic guitar accompaniment. When I say that her songs are her own, I don't merely mean that she wrote them. She owns them, because each of them, different from the others, concerns herself – and she paints in a different part of the mind of a valuable person, unique in place and time, who affects us and enters us precisely because she will tell only her own story.

She is Canadian, from Alberta. Her background is placed into her songs by means of names and nouns used because of what they mean to her.

Without wishing to be alone, she has become accustomed to herself. She has the absorption of childhood and – with self-consciousness informing her emotional traceries – an ability to look at herself and the other person which makes truth mandatory, even at the cost of loss. 'What will happen if I try/To put another heart in him?' 'Picked up a pencil and wrote "I love you" in my finest hand/Wanted to send it, but I don't know where I stand.' 'It's love's illusions I recall/I really don't know love at all.'

She can't grab and so may appear passive. Because she can describe herself as well as others, she can be a spectator of herself. Now she's in another land, the contacts that once she made face-to-face are available to her by long-distance communication. 'Telephone, even the sound of your voice is still new/All alone in California and talking to you.'

Life seems a gallery of mementos, infecting her and her landscape. She has songs which have a Carson McCullers flavour: she gazes at objects so long and avidly that they become more charged with meaning than the people who are now gone, who placed them where they are. Her mind resembles that of the American south, is fed intently upon itself. Nevertheless, she is young. She'll not find love by seeking it out but by it embracing her with an entirely personal magic.

Because she thinks and feels and means every item in her good songs ('The Fiddle and the Drum' is her only failure, because its metaphors don't have her living in them), her faintest inflexion of voice or guitar can clearly indicate miles and years of particular emotion.

Coarsening her voice with 'reflections of love's memories' shows many failed offers. The high guitar, held that way, with her voice singing above and below it in 'Chelsea Morning', has the mood of one single day held pure and joyful. She refers to Dionne Warwick, delicately, in 'I Don't Know Where I Stand', giving the song a poignancy not in the words. The odd slang word in 'Roses Blue', concerning a lady lost in mysticism, makes the song clearly about a real person and not just a pretty story.

'It's life's illusions I recall/I really don't know life at all'. But she knows herself and fills the images of her illusion with herself.

Joni Mitchell is extraordinarily talented and moving, because she is herself, and her self is beautiful.

'My Personal Life is in a Shambles'

Caroline Boucher, *Disc and Music Echo*,
10 January 1970

Gentle, shy Joni Mitchell flew into London last week with her friends, Crosby, Stills, Nash & Young, to do her last concert for a long, long time.

Since fame caught up with her and propelled her to become one of America's top three female folk-singers – along with Joan Baez and Judy Collins – Joni has been fighting a losing battle against time. With constant touring she finds she has no time for her home or for her writing and a long rest is vastly overdue.

'I would like the luxury of a day with nothing to do, so I could wake up and say, "What shall I do today?" It's been years since I could do that,' said Joni, smiling nervously.

She was talking at a party given in her honour by her record company in London. Dressed in a long green skirt with a green velvet top and her long fair hair in pigtails, Joni looked ten years younger than her official twenty-six. On her left hand was a collection of cameo rings which she twisted as she apologised for smiling ('I always smile when I'm nervous'). Her manager, a hippy happy American named Elliot, kept popping up at her elbow to help out and bring ginger wine.

'I need a rest,' explained Joni. 'I'm going through a change as an artist. I'm beginning to write on the piano, which is a much freer instrument and I want to learn the concertina and the violin. True, I've had two weeks off between three weeks of touring but when you know you're going back on the road there's so many things to do – every minute becomes vital – and my writing suffers. As a woman I have a responsibility to my home and it takes me a week to get the house re-perking [*sic*]. My personal life is in a shambles, and it's hard on me knowing I'm not giving anything to people I love.'

Home for Joni is a house of her own in Laurel Canyon, near Los Angeles.

'Most of my friends are musicians – I'm not very social. I'm a very solitary person; even in a room full of people I feel completely alone. You need solitude to make anything artistic. You need the focus which you can't have surrounded by people.'

Nevertheless, between tours Joni has managed to write many beautiful songs that have been recorded by so many other people that – even if you don't know Joni Mitchell – you will certainly know some of her songs. One that she should be justifiably proud of is 'Both Sides Now', sung by many – most notably Judy Collins.

'When I first started, Judy Collins was a great influence on me so of course I was so pleased when she sang that. But she was really beautiful to me two years ago at the Newport Festival. She was singing one of my songs, so she asked me down as her guest, which was so generous.'

Unlike Judy, who now appears in concert with a small backing group, Joni still prefers to accompany herself. 'I think a backing only waters it down,' she says. 'Other people onstage take some of the responsibility from you and I also think it takes some of the dynamics from you. I'm very possessive about my own art – I think everyone is. I know how I want it to be and I have a very total picture of it. It's expanding now and I can see other instruments. I can't write music, though. I sing different parts into a tape recorder. If I had two years off I'd probably go back and learn composition.'

Unlike Joan Baez and Judy Collins, Joni is not a great demonstrator for peace. 'I'm interested – everyone wants peace – but it's like some people go to church on Sundays and some don't, but they're still Christians. I feel that a lot of people actively working for peace do it for the wrong reasons – they are saying, "Look at me, I'm working towards peace", and they are abusing the word.'

Joni's concert is at London's Albert Hall on 17 January. Try to go. Her spirit is refreshing.

Joni Still Feels
the Pull of the Country

Jerry Gilbert, *Melody Maker*,
10 January 1970

Canadian singer Joni Mitchell this week denied rumours that she would be retiring after her Royal Festival Hall concert on 17 January.

But Joni, who can scarcely be described as a folk singer anymore and has no current connections with Canada either, will be a good deal more withdrawn in the future.

Joni flew into London from Los Angeles last week, and at a Warner-Reprise reception she told *Melody Maker*: 'It's true I've postponed all bookings indefinitely but that's just to catch my breath. I really need to get some new material together and I also want to learn to play more instruments and find some time to do some painting.'

Joni, far from taking things easy, is going to have her time cut out in the next few months. She made it quite apparent that she is going through a transitional stage in her career; expressing herself through a wider range of media, but at the same time delving deeper into her own distinctive musical bag.

'I've got a hard-core of fans who follow me around from one concert to another and it's for them I feel I ought to produce some new songs. I come from Saskatoon, Canada, originally and I'll probably move back there, but at this point in my life I would rather live in Los Angeles as it's right in the middle of change, and therefore far more stimulating. There are a lot of artists in LA at the moment and the exchange between artists is tremendous.'

Joni took a trip back to her previous two visits to England. The first she remembers specifically as her first taste of English folk clubs and the second for her appearance at the Festival of Contemporary Song in September 1968, with Al Stewart, Jackson C. Frank, and the Johnstons. It was this concert that really established her as a major artist in Britain, and she is still more than enthusiastic about it. 'I'd sure like to meet the Johnstons again while I'm here,' she added.

But songs like 'Chelsea Morning', 'Marcie' and 'Both Sides Now', which acted as her springboard, have now made way for slightly more complex numbers, perhaps brought about by the change of environment.

'I want my music to get more involved and more sophisticated. Right now I'm learning how to play a lot of new instruments. In the last month I've managed to write three new songs, including a couple of Christmas songs. I've also written a song for a film score that hasn't been used and "Woodstock", which is the next Crosby, Stills, Nash & Young single.'

Joni emphasised that she will not be playing any folk clubs while in Britain. She will make only one concert appearance, and will be telerecording a guest spot on the Tom Jones show. 'I shall then take a couple of weeks' holiday in Britain before returning. I want to get out into the country and in particular to Scotland.'

Country and city life both play prominent, but entirely different roles in Joni Mitchell's life. And it is the latter that is currently influencing her writing.

'I've a feeling that America may suddenly get very strange. In Los Angeles the air is very bad and it's not good to breathe city air all the time. But it's not just this environment that influences me. Any kind of music that moves me in any way, has some effect on my writing.'

Joni is more than enthusiastic about her next album, which is almost completed. A couple of tunes she picked out for special attention: 'They Paved Paradise and put up a Parking Lot' and 'He Played Real Good for Free', the latter being about a sidewalk musician.

Review of Show at the Royal Festival Hall, London

Geoffrey Cannon, *Guardian*, 28 April 1970

'**W**ell, thank you,' said Joni Mitchell, on stage at the Festival Hall last January. And she began a second encore, minutes of applause in her ears. I'd never before experienced such a close communion between a singer and an audience. On that day, Joni accomplished the dream of every singer: to be the heart's spokesman of everyone in the audience.

And, after the second encore, a great raucous shout, as loud as a football barracking, but yet – in the closeness Joni had created – as if from across a room: 'Joni, please: do it again.' And she smiled and sang again.

Joni Mitchell's fourth album, *Ladies of the Canyon* (Warner Brothers), is about to be released here. I believe that Joni Mitchell is better able to describe, and celebrate, what it means, and should mean, to be alive today, than any other singer. She tells us what we already know, but have felt obliged through life's circumstances, to forget: that we are free. That we have love. And she does this by scrupulous observation and thought only of what she herself has heard and seen and felt.

The difference between her and other singers who search themselves, like Davey Graham, Tim Hardin or Nico, is that they are wandering in the spaces of their mind, finding waste, purposeless patterns, and fragments of different personalities. Each of these three outmatches all but a few other singers. But compared with them, Joni has arrived: not at a fixed point, but in a country where she may live. For her, nothing is accomplished until she makes sense of it for herself.

She says what she sees. She sings of the lady who hurts a man she cares for. She sings of the man she loves, who wishes to be able properly to love her but who is bruised by previous emotional blows.

Each of her songs she sings clearly with her own guitar accompaniment and also with some augmentation. The meaning of her music is so large – because so personal – that clarity is crucial. I would think that any lady, hearing Joni sing, would feel herself love. Joni could sadden only a man who was irreversibly alone.

Joni Mitchell's New Album Will Mean More to Some Than to Others

Reprise Records ad for *Ladies of the Canyon*, May 1970

Amy Foster, twenty-three years old and quietly beautiful, was sitting in her orange inflatable chair listening to Neil Young's second album and toying indifferently with the enormous antique ring on the index finger of her left hand. Mostly she was trying with the usual lack of success to avoid lapsing into that state of bored listlessness she'd found herself in so frequently of late as she waited for the Country Store delivery boy to arrive with her groceries and Rit, with which she planned to pass the evening by tie-dying some curtains for her '64 Chevy camper.

To say simply that she had been under the weather these past few days would have been to wildly understate the case. Indeed, ever since she had been told on Saturday night by a mutual acquaintance that David, who had left her a month ago in favour of some chick he had met at the Jeans West shop he managed, had up and married, Amy had been more than a little inclined to chucking everything in the back of her camper and taking off for indefinite points north to try to get her head back together. Today, of course, was no exception:

'I'm incredibly down, man,' she observed to herself as the turntable's arm lifted quietly off 'Down by the River' and someone began knocking impatiently at the back door.

It was the delivery boy. After depositing her groceries on the kitchen table, he stopped to admire the Van Morrison collage she had made, so Amy offered him some tea. He accepted with a gracious and endearing toothy smile.

As they sat in the living room sipping Constant Comment with orange honey mixed in and listening to side one of *Déjà Vu* he, whose name turned out to be Barry, took out a concise little joint, lit it and took a couple of polite hits and passed it over to Amy. 'Mellow,' she responded, her spirits lifting slightly.

'Hey, you have a really far-out system here,' Barry commented in reference to her stereo set-up as she handed the joint back. 'Do you think we could listen to some of Joni Mitchell's new album on it?' for he had purchased *Ladies of the Canyon* at the Music Hall just that afternoon. 'Hey, groovy,' agreed Amy, who had not even realised that the album had been released.

So Barry brought it in and placed it on the turntable. By the time 'For Free' was over they were both quite mellow indeed. As much as they downed her by reminding her all too vividly of her now-irrevocably-consummated relationship with David, 'Willy' and 'Conversation' were somehow reassuring – there was someone else, even another canyon lady, who really knew. Amy began to feel a little better.

By the time 'Circle Game' had finished, Amy was no longer dejectedly contemplating splitting for Oregon. In fact, she could scarcely wait for the sun to get through setting so she could drive up to the top of Lookout and watch Los Angeles twinkle beneath the indigo April sky.

'Let's Make Life More Romantic'

Jacoba Atlas, *Melody Maker*, 20 June 1970

Joni Mitchell is a poet whose time has come. Because she uses the vehicle of music, her words and thoughts reach out to countless minds. With Joni, there is no restriction of reading or schooling; she sings her poetry and brings it to the people.

In the past year, Joni has emerged as a major force in music. Her songs, once the exclusive property of a few, have become the catchword of many. No longer is she only known to the few connoisseurs who read album credits; instead her creations are sought after and her work applauded. Her songs are reflections of a very feminine way of looking at life. All too seldom in music and, indeed, in any art form, is the female view of the world set down. Joni does just that.

One critic suggested that women think in a complicated manner and speak in simple terms. This could certainly be said of Joni's material; but her simplicity reveals a sensitivity and awareness that few composers possess today. With phrases like 'Know that I will know you' and 'While she's so busy being free', we are given an entire picture of a woman's mind and heart at work.

Joni has been seeing situations and storing them in her memory and in her music since her birth in Canada some twenty-five years ago.

She originally wanted to be an artist, a desire she still retains. Interestingly enough, most of her musical adjectives relate directly to a painter's vocabulary: 'Umbrellas bright on a grey background'. Joni describes her home as 'a musical one' and her interest in writing 'was there since I was nine'.

In the mid-'60s Joni came to America and played in clubs, travelling the folk circuit in the east, bravely waiting out her turn to make the mark. But the single folk singer was on the way out – rock was coming in and managers figured that, with Joan Baez and Judy Collins, who needed a Joni Mitchell?

Fortunately, fellow folk singer Tom Rush heard Joni's songs and introduced her material to his following and the writer to Judy Collins. The result was an invitation to sing at the Newport Folk Festival and Miss Collins' recordings of 'Both Sides Now' and 'Michael From Mountains'.

Her present manager, Elliot Roberts, brought her to the attention of Reprise records. Her first album was *Song to a Seagull*. It sold only moderately but she became an underground 'find'. With *Clouds*, Joni's second album, it was evident that she had arrived; with *Ladies of the Canyon*, her third album, it is evident that she is exalted. With each album there has been more music, more of an effort to bring in other musicians but, despite added instruments and group singing on various stages, Joni remains forcefully a loner.

'I used to be in a duo and that was the last time I played with anyone else except for my friends. I like to play with Graham [Nash] and Judy [Collins], but we sing together for fun. I flat-pick my music and I know there are places to be filled in. There could be more texture to it. When I finger-pick, I play the melody line and in many cases that's the way it stays. When I've finished a song, I've honed it to a point where it's a completed song to me. And anything that is added . . . might to other people sound better and more complete but to me it sounds extraneous.

'I'm very serious about my music and so I like that seriousness to remain. When I play with other people I like that to be for fun. It's on another level . . . a looser level where a sense of my own imperfections doesn't enter into it because it's just for my own pleasure. It would be difficult for me now to learn to play with other people, like teaching an old dog new tricks.'

Until *Ladies of the Canyon*, Joni's melodies emphasised her past association with folk music: simple and straightforward, they encompassed little of what rock has brought to the music scene. However, her present association with rock musicians has somewhat liberated Joni from the confines of the folk idiom and you can hear that change in *Ladies*. 'I guess there will just come a time when I'm hearing more music than I'm able to play and then the change will come about naturally.'

Joni does not see adding musicians as back-up men as a step toward co-writing. 'I don't think I could do that for the same reasons I can't play professionally with other people. I know what colours I want to use, I'm too opinionated . . . no, that's not the word I want. It's just that I feel too strongly about what the finished thing should be, whether it's music or a painting. I mean, how many times do you hear about painters working together? The Fool are three painters who paint together, but how many times do you hear of that? I feel very much about my music like I feel about my painting. If I were working for a master and he came up to me and said, "Well, if you put a brush stroke of red in that corner, you'll save it,"

I would have to reject his way of saving it or improving it until I could find a solution of my own which was equally right.'

Joni's strong desire to be independent and an entity unto herself can seem at times a contradiction with her own gentleness and music. However, it somehow isn't. Early on, Joni was criticised for being too feminine, too romantic ('secrets and sharing sodas, that's how our time began').

But just how a woman can be too feminine isn't really clear to Joni, who sees the lack of womanliness in her contemporaries as one of the worst aspects of progress.

'I think there's a lack of romance in everything today. I went to see the film version of *Romeo and Juliet*, which is supposed to be the epitome of romance, and I thought it was very unromantic. Everything was too perfect. I think that women are getting a bum deal. I think we are being misguided. It's just, follow the leader. Like, for a long time I wouldn't go out without wearing my false eyelashes, because I thought that without them I was plain. You know, that's really silly, isn't it? But that's what happened.'

'There's the fear of the big hurt, we're taught to be very cool. And be noncommittal. That's the thing about places like Italy. Like they're encouraged to say, "Oh, I love you, my darling," and then if it doesn't work out they all say, "Poor little Emilio, his heart is breaking," and nobody puts him down. You know, they're all very kind, they shelter him because he's mourning openly for the loss of someone. Whereas in America you stifle that so much . . . well, anything that's repressed and goes underground really gets distorted. You don't know what you want after a while if it's repressed.'

'Even if I'm writing about myself, I try to stand back and write about myself as if I were writing about another person. From a perspective. I wrote this one song – I can't remember the name of it now – a triangular story where I wrote about myself from the point of another woman. It's written about one person and myself, and still another rolled into one. To give the person more dimensions. It's really tough because I want to explain to you how I write, but I can't. It's just standing back and getting another perspective on it. I step back and carry on a conversation with myself. It's almost schizophrenic. You lay out a case and argue with yourself about it and with no conclusions. But I have to write a long time after something has happened, because when I'm in the middle of something I'm totally emotional and blind. I can't get a perspective on it.'

Like many poets, Joni insists that her lyrics be worked over until every word is absolutely necessary and cannot be altered. She admires both Dylan and Leonard Cohen, although each for their differences.

'Leonard's economical, he never wastes a word. I can go through Leonard's work and it's just like silk. Dylan is coarse and beautiful in a rougher way. I love that in him. I think I'm a belated fan, at least my enthusiasm is growing the more I live in urban places. The last two years have made me a very strong fan, but before I lived in cities I couldn't see what he meant. I'd never know what the street meant. I was sheltered, I hadn't seen the injustices. Now I can understand him.'

Her ability to understand and transform has made her almost a legend in the United States. Critics and listeners alike rhapsodise over her songs and her psyche. She is fulfilling something of a 'goddess' need in American rock, a woman who is more than a woman; a poet who expresses a full range of emotions without embarrassment.

Her legend is beginning to obscure her work; because she is virtually without competition (Joan Baez and Judy Collins don't have the output; Buffy Sainte-Marie doesn't have the immediate newness), she is without comparison. Her work, for now, goes almost totally without question, without debate.

Success has worked its hardships on Joni's life as well. With sold-out concerts come demands on personal time and involvement. After *Ladies of the Canyon* she split to Greece for sun and silence. She said she needed the time to be alone and find her creativity again.

Her house, redwood and hand-honed, high in Laurel Canyon, stands empty and waiting. One of her many treasures within the house is a grandfather clock which refuses to tick . . . it's too old to be repaired . . . it stands idle, useless, and beautiful.

That in itself tells us as much about the lady as anything she might write.

Glimpses of Joni

Michael Watts, *Melody Maker*,
19 September 1970

Scene in a television studio: a girl, in a long pink shift which catches at her ankles when she walks, picks hesitantly at a few bars on the piano, reluctantly gives up, and asks for a glass of something hot, maybe tea.

Her manager, looking like a thinner, less ebullient version of David Crosby, brings her a drink and she tells the audience sitting out there in the darkness of the television theatre that she must have picked up a cold in London – she always gets colds when she is in England; does everybody get colds when they go to America? Gives a nervous little giggle.

She resumes the song, unfolds it carefully like a love letter written on finest paper, pouring out its lines with a peculiar little sob in her voice, as if she cannot bear to let the words slip away. And they are deep, genuine words, about the lover who, 'when he's gone, the bed's too big, the pan's too wide', which says it all so simply yet so fully.

Still in the same low key, she moves into the lyrics of 'Woodstock' and the line about the 'bombers in the sky turning into butterflies above the nation', which is tremendous imagery, and then 'Willy':

'He is my child, he is my father, I would be his lady all my life.' No other contemporary songwriter could compose lyrics the equal of these in tenderness and innocence, a sweet combination.

She plucks at a couple of tunes on a dulcimer, which she has only been playing since February, and then picks up her guitar to sing 'Big Yellow Taxi', which gets great applause, of course, as does 'Clouds'. She falters a bit on it and cannot quite reach the pitch at times, but it is the final number and she has made it through all right.

Short pause while she stands timidly in the centre of the stage, looking vulnerable and dreamy, then fade-out.

Cut to the dressing room, and a typical dressing room scene, with a few friends, one or two press, a lot of record company representatives, and the usual well-known visitor.

In appearance, she seems rather severe in an attractive sort of way, with her fine blond hair scraped back from her tanned face, which has large bones around the cheeks and forehead and a wide, generous mouth. It's a pleasant, open face that sits on top of a body whose seeming fragility inspires a feeling of instinctive protectiveness.

Joni Mitchell is not her real name. At Fort McCloud in Alberta, Canada, she is known as Roberta Joan Anderson but in 1965 she got married to one Chuck Mitchell, a marriage dissolved about twelve months later. Her first album, *Song to a Seagull*, reflects the sadness of this marital split and, indeed, the motions that have inspired many of her songs are always tangible, beating like veins near the surface of her work.

'Willy', for instance, refers to her association with Graham Nash, now ended, while the impetus for writing 'For Free' came from a clarinettist she saw playing on a London street – 'nobody stopped to hear him, though he played so sweet and high', one line goes wistfully.

'There is a certain amount of my life in all my songs,' she told me softly. 'They are honest and personal and based on truth but I exercise a writer's licence to change details. Honesty is important to me. If I have any personal philosophy it is that I like the truth. I like to be straight with people and them with me. But it is not easy to do this all the time, especially in this business where there is so much falsity.'

Her first album was not released until late 1968, but she had been singing for five years then in clubs and bars while her name was attracting public attention through other artists' interpretations of her songs: Judy Collins' version of 'Both Sides Now' is probably the best example.

More recently too, Crosby, Stills, Nash & Young cut their interpretation of her lovely, floating song 'Woodstock', whipping it up in the process into something fierce and pounding, far removed from the original in tone and execution.

'I liked their performance too, in its way,' she said. 'They were seeing Woodstock from the point of view of the performers while my version is concerned with the spirit of the festival. I never did actually get to Woodstock itself, you see, because the traffic jams to the site were nine miles long, so I sat in my New York hotel room and saw it on television.'

If anyone has helped her, though, in popularising her work it has been the cowboy rock'n'roll singer Tom Rush who, she said, had got her to leave Michigan, where she was doing the round of folk clubs and secured her a gig at the Gaslight in New York.

This was not a total success, but Rush put out a version of her 'Urge for Going' after it had been turned down by Judy Collins and this became a favourite on the club circuits, opening doors for her in consequence.

'Yes, he was the first to help. Until he played that and "Circle Game", nobody really wanted to know; they would time me when I went on as an opening act so you can see that I have had to work my way up. It has all been very gradual. Tom helped me as well in that period because I was unsure about my writing and didn't think it was very good. But there have been a lot of people who have been good to me.'

Count among these David Crosby, who produced her first album. He has given her lots of hints on recording techniques, she says, and has captured in the studio her stage presence – 'he helped to keep the music simple and basic'.

'No one paid much attention to folk music three years ago,' she remarked quietly, 'and the record companies wanted to change my music, so I had to wait until I was in a position so that I could play as I wanted.'

The Judy Collins' album *Wild Flowers*, which included some Mitchell compositions, allowed her to bargain, and the subsequent albums have been made completely under her direction, even down to the sleeves.

All of the album covers she has painted herself, from the rather plain but expressively poignant self-portrait on *Clouds* to the stark simplicity of the sketch on *Ladies Of The Canyon*. But it is the songs within the covers that are important and they are tender and sensitive and as spare in construction as the line drawings on the sleeves.

Her great quality is her spirit of humanity: the compassion for the solitary clarinettist on the street corner, the unalloyed romanticism of 'Willy', or the comradely feelings for the half-million gathered at 'Woodstock'.

At the same time as being deeply emotional – though they manage to avoid the clingings of nostalgia – her work shows no signs of being mushy. Rather, it is built of sturdy bones and in – 'Big Yellow Taxi', for instance – shows humour, as she herself does ('Clean linen and funk is my idea of a good life,' she told me with a laugh).

For those who saw her on the Isle of Wight or will be able to see the TV programme on BBC2, it was a brief glimpse of an American artist who bids fair to have the same impact in the '70s on the popular musical consciousness that Dylan and Baez had in the '60s. For those who miss her . . .

You don't know what you've got till it's gone.

Joni Takes a Break

Larry LeBlanc, *Rolling Stone*, 4 March 1971

anadians are stunned by the vague, awesome level that Joni
Mitchell has reached. She was the least known of the Toronto
group of folksingers of the '60s.

Joni returned to Toronto, this summer, to appear at the annual
Mariposa folk festival on Toronto Island (fifteen minutes by ferry
from downtown) – her first public performance in more than six
months. She has an undisputable genuine affection for the Mariposa
event. One reason is that it is possible to find a degree of privacy
here among old friends. In the afternoon workshop she freely doo-
dled a dulcimer, smiled, and hummed in rhythm with her hands.

She appeared shortly before eight, backstage, dressed in a short
robe belted loosely around the middle that hung without tightness
to all of her. In the shelter of the trees along the lagoon we
talked. The sun was gone, there was a shadow all across the grassy
prairie-like opening and a small cloud of insects hovered over.

A few feet away, Gordon Lightfoot sat on a park bench and said
how great it was to be a spectator for a change. David Rea, who at
last is emerging from the relative obscurity of being the guitarist
for Lightfoot, Ian & Sylvia and Joni, were there, cheerier than
ever. Jack Elliott, with significantly smiling eyes, pulled his

broad-brimmed cowboy hat over his forehead, put his thumbs in pockets and waited his turn at the bottle being shared by Mississippi Fred McDowell, J. B. Hutto and Lightfoot.

Joni sat watching, curiously and quiet, nodding 'Hello' now and then. With her chin resting on her crossed legs, she seemed just a little self-conscious but most inwardly serene. So perfect with high soft cheekbones, great bright blue eyes, bittersweet blonde hair dribbling down past her shoulders; she has a broad smile worth waiting for and a tremendous vanilla grin which makes her always magical.

Carefully, almost cautiously, she picked the words to describe self-exile from the pop scene.

'In January, I did my last concert. I played in London and I came home. In February I finished up my record. I gave my last concert with the idea I'd take this year off because I need new material. I need new things to say in order to perform, so there's something in it for me. You just can't sing the same songs.

'I was being isolated, starting to feel like a bird in a gilded cage. I wasn't getting a chance to meet people. A certain amount of success cuts you off in a lot of ways. You can't move freely. I like to live, be on the streets, to be in a crowd and moving freely.'

She confirmed that she was still uneasy about the great army of photographers scrambling around her, the crowds fawning on her at every turn, wanting something, wanting to touch her. In the centre she worked hard to smile constantly, answer the seemingly endless questions, and make that magic.

'It's a weird thing,' she said solemnly. 'You lose all your peripheral view of things. It has its rewards but I don't know what the balance is – how much good and how much damage there is in my position. From where I stand it sometimes gets absurd and yet I must remain smiles, come out of a mood where maybe I don't feel very pleasant and say, "Smile." Inside, I'm thinking, You're being phony. You're smiling phony. You're being a star.

'I was very frightened last year,' she said quite directly, wiping some hair out of her eyes. 'But if you're watching yourself over your own shoulder all of the time and if you're too critical of what you're doing, you can make yourself so unhappy. As a human you're always messing up, always hurting people's feelings quite innocently. I'll find it difficult, even here. There's a lot of people you want to talk to all at once. I get confused and maybe I'll turn away and leave someone standing and I'll think, Oh, dear.

'I've changed a lot,' she said. 'I'm getting very defensive. I'm afraid. You really have to struggle.' She paused, frowned and laughed. She leaned forward suddenly and said, 'I feel like I'm going to be an ornery old lady.'

Last January she made the surprise announcement of her self-imposed retirement, and cancelled two important gigs – in New York's Carnegie Hall and Constitution Hall in Washington. She took a vacation instead.

'I've been to Greece, Spain, France, and from Jamaica to Panama, through the canal. Some of my friends were moving their boat from Fort Lauderdale up to San Francisco. I joined them in Jamaica and sailed down through the canal. It was really an experience.

'On the plane to Greece we – I travelled with a friend, a poetess from Ottawa – met a man who was studying in Berkeley. He was a fairly wealthy Greek, very into the family. They're very family-oriented people. He invited us to his home for supper. In that tradition, his sister, cousins and aunts were there. It was very formal. They had a maid who brought the dinner and prepared all the national dishes of Greece kinda in our honour.

'From the peasant on up, when they have guests in the house, they're hospitable and lay on their best feed. Then he took us to a couple of nightclubs with Greek musicians playing. It was a very sophisticated introduction to Athens. Not sophisticated like New York sophistication but on that level of their culture.

'He would always say, "We must be spontaneous. The Greek is spontaneous. Let us dance, drink some wine, throw the gardenia to the singer."'

She giggled, bringing to her freckled and tanned face a smile that almost closed her eyes. She remarked she was delighted with Crete. It was a beautiful country, she said. 'I hiked in boots through the fields. It's very rugged, very simple, so basic. People live from the land much more. The seas are very small, very countryish. Peasants walked donkeys. There were very few cars.

'Even the poorest people seem to eat well: cucumbers and tomatoes, oranges and potatoes and bread. They ate that well. They lived in concrete huts with maybe one or two chairs, a bed where the family slept and a couple of burrows and chickens.'

After a brief pause, she added, 'To me, it was a lovely life, far better than being middle class in America. I lived for five weeks in a cave there. The only trouble was it was very commercialised. The magazines were writing it up. As a result, you had a lot of prying tourists all of the time. Even that was kinda funny, because most of the people living in the caves were Canadians, Americans, Swiss and French. They'd say, "Oh, here come the tourists." It was kinda funny, the Greeks being the tourists.'

Then she described the Matala surroundings: 'It was a very small bay with cliffs on two sides. And between the two cliffs, on the beach, there were about four or five small buildings. There were also a few fishermen's huts. The caves were on high sedimentary cliffs, sandstone, a lot of seashells in it. The caves were carved out by the Minoans hundreds of years ago. Then they were used later on for leper caves. Then after that the Romans came and they used them for burial crypts. Then some of them were filled in and sealed up for a long time. People began living there, beatniks, in the '50s. Kids gradually dug out more rooms. There were some people there who were wearing human teeth necklaces around their necks,' she said with a slight frown. 'We all put on a lot of weight. We were eating a lot of apple pies, good bacon. We were eating really well, good wholesome food.

'The village pretty well survived from the tourist trade, which was the kids that lived in the caves. I don't know what their business was before people came. There were a couple of fishing boats that went out, that got enough fish to supply the two restaurants there. The bakery lady who had the grocery store there had fresh bread, fresh rice pudding, made nice yogurt every day, did a thriving business and ended up, just before I left, she installed a refrigerator. She had the only cold drinks in town. It was all chrome and glass. It was a symbol of her success.

'Then the cops came and kicked everyone out of the caves but it was getting a little crazy there. Everybody was getting a little crazy there. Everybody was getting more and more into open nudity. They were really going back to the caveman. They were wearing little loincloths. The Greeks couldn't understand what was happening.'

Sadly, she confirmed she didn't find much privacy there.

'I just kinda took it anyway. Well, because the people living in the caves were all Canadians and Americans and young. So it wasn't there. I didn't meet any Greeks. When I first got there I found I was carrying around a sketch pad, pens, paper. I was all prepared should inspiration strike in any shape or form – I'm going to do something with my time.'

She agreed things rarely happen that way. 'Well, I somehow felt like I do sometimes about photographers. When I was in Jamaica with my friends, we went up into the mountains, and suddenly we stopped in this village. It was beautiful and primitive. We all got out, jumped around, cameras up to our eyes. I thought from their point of view we must've looked like creatures from outer space, real monsters. I got into "capturing the moment" as kind of a rape. Even with a pencil or a brush. It was just an attitude I had at that time. I couldn't do anything really until I got away from Crete. When I got to Paris and back into the city, with time to reflect, I began to realise differently.'

Like most Canadian artists she was discovered only after other artists began recording her material. A much-needed punch was given to her early reputation (mostly Canadian) when Tom Rush picked up on 'Urge for Going' during a gig in Detroit.

Judy Collins noticed a distinct Canadian feel, a more old-fashioned bouquet than American. Canadian composers seem to write closer to nature, away from the competitive rush. Commented Judy: 'There are lots of writers who write good material but there seems to be a feeling about Canadian writers that is a very special feeling. I sing Joni's songs because I like them immensely. There doesn't seem to be anyone quite as good. Her lyrics are exquisite and it all fits together.'

As the composer of strange autobiographical songs like 'Urge for Going', 'Michael from Mountains', 'Both Sides Now', 'The Circle Game' and 'Chelsea Morning', she gained the respect, friendship and endorsement of the music world before recording them herself.

New York gave her the inspiration to write the songs on her first album *Songs to a Seagull*, produced by David Crosby. The cover had fine pen-and-ink drawings and Joni's picture was on the back, from a fisheye lens on a New York backstreet.

The songs inside had lots of grace notes, showed trickling light and beautiful melodies. They dealt with people like Nathan LaFrenier, the crass, hard-bitten cabdriver; Marcie, Joni's Canadian girlfriend, who moved to New York the same time as her and Chuck Mitchell, Joni's old man who carried her off to the country for marriage too soon.

The original cover for *Clouds* showed seasons with a castle and a moat. She had become depressed with it, left it and only finished it when boyfriend Graham Nash encouraged her.

Song structures were simpler, more reminiscent. *Clouds* came on in 'Both Sides Now' as 'rows and flows of angel hair/And ice cream castles in the air/and feather canyons everywhere'. 'The Fiddle and the Drum' offered subtle comment on war.

Ladies of The Canyon is the most overtly autobiographical of all Joni's albums. 'For Free' expresses thoughts on the way her musical life has been rolling.

She wasn't at Woodstock but her song shows she was alive to what went down there. 'Willy', the soft, still, brooding ballad, was written about her relationship with Graham Nash. 'Big Yellow Taxi' received saturation airplay in Canada and was covered stateside by the Neighbourhood. And she finally recorded 'The Circle Game', which she'd written years ago in Toronto.

The cover of *Ladies of The Canyon* is the simplest of the three albums. There is a fine, one-line profile of Joni and a homely watercolour of Laurel Canyon. Like the other illustrations, its mood perfectly fits the contents of the album. 'The drawings, the music and the words are very much tied together,' she agreed, coiling and uncoiling the ends of her belt, occasionally looking at the ground and slowly rolling the pebbly earth. 'It's like taste. It changes and reflects in everything you do creatively. I never get frustrated to where I'll say, "Quit writing." I come to dry periods where either I feel I don't have anything new to say or feel like I'm repeating patterns.'

Her expression became serious when she spoke of the kind of material she wants to sing now: 'Like, now I don't really want to write. The kind of material I want to write – I want it to be brighter, to get people up, to grab people. So I'm stifling any feelings of solitude or certain moods I might ordinarily develop into a song. I steer away from that now because I don't want that kind of material to perform.'

Has her writing passed its complicated stage?

'Well,' she answered, 'I don't notice what I'm doing so much until I've done it and then look back at it. At the time, you're really not aware you're doing it. In order to be simplified it has to be honed down more. It takes a lot more polishing for that simplicity than it did for anything complicated. I do a lot of night writing. I need solitude to write. I used to be able to write under almost any condition but not anymore 'cause I have to go inside myself so far, to search through a theme.

'First of all I'll write something down and then I think, Oh, I like how the words sound together but it doesn't say anything. When I finish a new song I take it and play it for my friends, who are fine musicians and writers. I'm very impressed by their reaction to it. If they like it, I'm knocked out. I guess I write for those people. They're really my audience.

'My music now is becoming more rhythmic. It's because I'm in Los Angeles and my friends are mostly rock'n'roll people . . . and being influenced by that rhythm ... I've always liked it. When I was in Saskatchewan, I loved to dance.'

Joni's father, in the Royal Canadian Air Force, was stationed in Fort Macleod during the war. Joni was born there as Roberta Joan Anderson. The Anderson family moved when her father was transferred to bases in Calgary and then Yorkton. Following the war, her father worked for a grocery chain in North Battleford. Her mother taught school. Joni was about six and started school there.

Joni's loving memory of the fresh prairie air and budding things stems from the prairie kingdom that stretched at her feet. The flat prairie of Saskatchewan, a have-not province plagued by droughts and wavering wheat prices, holds things that must be seen and touched: crocuses spreading a mauve mist along railway ties before the last patch of snow was melted; wheat fields merging into a wave-surfaced golden ocean and telephone wires strung like popcorn.

The family finally settled in Saskatoon – a small, dry, proud town right in the middle of the sea of wheat and atop the potash swells sprawled pleasantly along the high east bank of the South Saskatchewan river. The town is sober to the point of dullness. It was founded eighty-eight years ago by the Ontario Methodist Colonization Society which dreamed of creating a teetotaller's paradise far from the corrupting influences of civilisation.

Joni grew up straight: won trophies for bowling, liked to swim and dance. She took art lessons and, for drama presentations or dances, Joni always pitched in to provide the decorations. Polio at age ten brought her close to her mother, who taught her at home for a few months before she was well enough to return to school.

At Mariposa, she looked back and gave credit to her seventh grade teacher at Queen Elizabeth public school for getting her interested in writing.

'He encouraged us to write in any form that we liked,' she said. 'Even at that age I enjoyed poetry, the structure of it, the dance of it, to essays or any other form. His assignments were very free like that. He'd just tell us to write something.'

The teacher, Dr Kratzman, is surprised that Joni dedicated her first album to him. He remembers her as 'a blonde, bright-eyed kid. Very receptive to ideas. I can see her now, in the back seat of the second row.'

'Later on, in the tenth grade,' Joni reminisced, 'I joined an extra-curricular writer's club. Again I wrote poetry, because there wasn't much poetry assigned in the writing class. I really haven't read too much except for assigned reading in school. Even then, I only read the quota of books on the programme. I've been more of a doer, especially painting. Any free time I have, I'd rather make something.'

And she loved to dance and listen to music: 'I guess I liked the hit parade in those days 'cause I was looking at it from the view: "Can you dance to it?" There wasn't much to the lyrics although, "Get out in the kitchen and rattle those pots and pans" – that's great music, great. I love "Shake, Rattle and Roll", the Coasters, Chuck Berry. I've been with rock and roll from the beginning and it's just starting to come out now.'

In Saskatoon she didn't show much interest in playing until her last year in high school. She bought herself a ukulele, taught herself the rudiments of guitar playing from a Pete Seeger do-it-yourself manual and took to hanging out at a coffee house called the Louis Riel.

In the Saskatoon club Joni met up-and-comers like Joe & Eddie and Bonnie Dobson, who wrote 'Morning Dew'. She began playing a baritone uke, taking it everywhere and going plunk-a-plunk every time she learned a new change.

At a weiner roast, a TV announcer from nearby Prince Albert heard her sing and asked her to appear on his programme. She only knew four or five songs, but it came off all right.

Then she went to the art school of Calgary because she wanted to become a professional illustrator. She worked for nothing at the Depression, the local coffee house.

'She looked just tremendous,' John Uren, the club's owner recalls, 'with all that blonde hair. I brought Peter Elbing in from Toronto. And he listened to Joni and said she could sing. She met a lot of people. Will Millar was around. He's one of the Irish Rovers. It was a good scene in those days. And Joni was part of it. She did more for the uke than Tiny Tim.'

She migrated east at the end of the first school year to see a Mariposa festival. Although intending to return to college, she found work in Toronto and stayed with only a hint of what she would find. She worked as a salesgirl to earn the $140 union fee so she could perform. She began writing her own songs (about four a week) and made the rounds of long-shuttered clubs.

She was hired at the Penny Farthing, one of several clubs in Yorkville Village, which has been the early training grounds for José Feliciano, the Irish Rovers and Neil Young. While she was playing in the basement section, Chuck Mitchell and Loring James came into town and played upstairs.

Joni was a strange young girl in those days – an all-around golden girl, running around discovering life for the first time. Playing and singing on Yorkville Avenue, she was part of the early scene. Walk down the street, during an evening then, and you'd hear David Clayton-Thomas, Bonnie Dobson, Jack London and the Sparrows (later Steppenwolf), Gordon Lightfoot, the Dirty Shames, the Stormy Clovers, Elyse Weinberg or Adam

Mitchell (who joined the Paupers). Buffy Sainte-Marie wrote 'The Universal Soldier' in Yorkville. Phil Ochs wrote 'Changes' there, too.

Her short marriage with Chuck Mitchell was described in 'I Had a King'. Their show was pasted together like a collage. Chuck played heavy Brechtian material ('while he sings them of wars and wine'). They did a handful of Gordon Lightfoot songs. But basically, Joni did her own thing and Chuck did his.

With help from friends, the two broke New York, worked the Gaslight Café on MacDougal [Street] in the Village and gained some recognition. Next they made the Toronto-Philadelphia-Detroit circuit.

Gradually, the breaks started to unfold. Bernie Fiedler at the Riverboat coffee house booked her and other clubs followed. Canadian Broadcast Corporation producer Ross McLean got her to compose the title theme of CBC's *The Way It Is*. Television and radio engagements followed.

After Tom Rush and Judy Collins performed her material, her own career moved in full swing. She moved to New York, where she met her managers Elliot Roberts and Joel Dean. They put the finishing polish on her act, got her a Reprise recording contract, and sent her out on tour.

Her personal life became a series of interruptions. But she accepted it with a certain quiet gratitude even when it bore down on her with an overpowering weight.

She retreated to her isolated, wood-hewed home in Laurel Canyon about three miles north of Hollywood's Sunset Strip and immeasurable social light years away from Canada. Surrounded by stained Tiffany glass windows, oak-beam wooden floors, a Priestley piano, a grandfather clock and a black cat named Hunter – a nine-year-old tom – she read her rave record reviews and equally enthusiastic stories about her public appearances.

But, she said, just about every songwriter reaches a point where he feels uncomfortable.

'The experiences I was having were so related to my work. It was reflected in the music. I thought I'd like to write on other themes. In order to do this, I had to have other experiences.'

Review of *Blue*

Geoffrey Cannon, *Guardian*,
29 June 1971

Joni Mitchell's new album, *Blue*, is about to be released here by Warner Brothers. A large proportion of Joni's most notable songs, to date, have been intensely visual. What she's seen she has refined: but the songs' images have been those of the eye.

The lyrics of *Blue* are less adventurous than in her previous three albums; on the other hand, its music is less careful. This is a fair exchange. The album is much more about Joni herself, less of scenes she's observed. The songs that stand out, at least at first, are earthy. In 'All I Want', Joni wants to 'wreck my stockings in some juke-box dive'.

She makes it clear that she doesn't care to be construed as dependable. Instead, she insists on being able to be wilful. *Blue* is, I suppose, less representative of women than Joni's previous albums; but its songs are as marvellously singular, if more relaxed.

Graham Nash is the 'Willy' of the Joni song of that name. His style is openly confessional. There's a group of singers in California, including Joni, James Taylor, Stephen Stills, and Neil Young, at least some of whose songs are letters to one another. Nash has just released his first album, *Songs for Beginners* (Atlantic).

Songs for Beginners is yet another album recorded at Wally Heider's studio, with the mandatory star musicians as backers. This over-population helped to make David Crosby's solo album a swamp of unresolved sound. By contrast, Nash uses his musicians with focus and economy.

Review of Show at the Royal Festival Hall, London

Michael Watts, *Melody Maker*,
13 May 1972

There was Jackson Browne, Joni Mitchell and this third, malignant presence on stage at the Festival Hall on Friday. With no sense of regard for the crowded audience, this unwanted addition manifested itself by a series of whistles, screeches and hoots in the PA system, whose volume level was skittish to the point of perversity.

Poor old Jackson Browne. As soon as he got stuck into a song the sound would die on him and he'd be left mouthing into the mike like some caricature from a silent movie. The mood of the audience passed from annoyance to bewilderment to slight amusement and then through to pity as the kid wrestled with the problem of getting himself across.

What I actually heard of him was great. The numbers were mainly off his album. His roots seem to be very firmly in the folk field, not rock'n'roll, and his songs are almost without exception quiet, introspective and extremely personal. It would be interesting, however, to hear him with a band backing up, as I understand he works in the States.

For Joni Mitchell, the house PA replaced the one used on his set, but even so she sounded muffled in the higher registers. However . . . it's difficult to see how anybody can actively dislike Joni Mitchell. Her writing touches peaks of sensitivity, particularly on *Ladies of the Canyon*, that no other songwriter can currently compare with. Her playing is direct and evocative and her voice is magnificent, especially when she soars on those high notes.

To those who attend her concerts, however, she's much more than a singer and a songwriter. She's some kind of high priestess, virginal and vulnerable, not to be vilified. The effect was heightened on Friday by her appearance in long flowing culottes that dazzled white in the spotlights. It seems almost like heresy to criticise her, but one fault to my mind is that the mood of her performances tends to be excessively devotional. When she sits down at the piano she knows the song is going to be melancholic and when she takes up the guitar only slightly less downbeat. She becomes not just a performer but a kind of icon.

On Friday she sang more new songs than old, although there was the obligatory 'Big Yellow Taxi' and 'Clouds', and a beautiful version of 'For Free', which she explained was written about a New York street clarinettist. There were not the obvious songs about the men in her life. There was 'Blue' but not 'Willy'. Among the new songs was a comparatively light number inspired by a meal at Trader Joe's, and one called 'Song for Ludwig' (dedicated to Beethoven), which had lovely rolling piano lines.

The highlight of her act was a song whose title I didn't get but whose inspiration she went into at length.

That's exactly it. One wonders what so many of her compositions are like in their raw state. It would be interesting to hear them.

Part Three

A Dream to Fly (1972–1977)

Review of *For The Roses*

Richard Williams, *Melody Maker*,
9 December 1972

More songs of transient euphoria and stabbing loss, played out against an ambiguous background of relentless fatalism and constant hope, mingled in approximately equal proportions, from the poorest little rich girl in Laurel Canyon.

The difference between Joni and most of her male-balladeer companions, and the reason I respect her and not them, is that she writes her diary with an uncompromising honesty; alone among them, she knows herself and describes her psychodramas with a cool, clear brain. Not for her is self-pity and her task is made easier by an almost total command of poetic device. Her images and metaphors are the result of thought, never the first incomplete ideas of a lazy writer who grasps the first phrase which comes to hand. Add to this a considerable and ever-developing musician-ship, and a voice flexible enough to avoid the blandness this genre so often attracts and you have a talent that, for once, justifies the acclaim it receives.

For The Roses is mostly about loss: in many of these songs, she caresses her precious yesterdays like the cover of an old, well-thumbed leather-bound book. 'See You Sometime' and 'Lesson in

Survival' are such but 'Woman of Heart and Mind' is the best because she stands outside herself, painting a portrait as dispassionately as one can in such circumstances of a quixotic demanding man – both a putdown and a come-on, it winds up as catharsis. She's at her best like most modern poets, when she's least explicit: 'Electricity' uses a marvellous metaphor to illuminate the breakdown of a relationship, while 'Lesson In Survival' contains the only jarring moment when she sings 'Oh, baby, I can't seem to make it with you socially'; she didn't need to say that because she's already made the point in more subtly powerful ways. In 'Blonde in the Bleachers' she speaks from bitter experience of another girl who may be herself, and even 'You Turn Me On, I'm A Radio', which sounds like a shout of joy, is really an uncertain plea.

Her expanding talents as a musician are illustrated on the two most ambitious pieces. 'Cold Blue Steel and Sweet Fire' is a smack song and has her most finely poised writing: 'A wristwatch, a ring, a downstairs screamer/Edgy – blade cracks of the sky/Pin-cushdreamer!' 'Judgement of the Moon and Stars' is addressed to Beethoven, writing symphonies in his deafness. It demonstrates how she's now thinking of songs in terms of unbroken development rather than as simple repetitions of a specific format, and I'm sure this is where her future lies.

Lastly, I should mention her voice. There will always be that mildly uncomfortable break between the contralto and soprano registers but sometimes she can enunciate a word or phrase in a way that comes straight from heaven. The way she sings 'movie queen', in 'Let The Wind Carry Me' is the perfect mating of a rigorous intelligence and an earthy sensuality. The product of these two qualities is a third: grace, which suffuses the album.

Review of Live Show at the Troubadour, Los Angeles

Steven Rosen, *Sounds*, 9 December 1972

When Joni Mitchell makes one of her rare appearances at the Los Angeles Troubadour, there are sure to be sold-out shows throughout her engagement, and indeed capacity audiences filled the club every night of her recent four-day stay.

When a performer of any calibre stays out of the public (and critics') eyes, the immediate reaction of the press is to pounce, criticise and crucify. (A point in case is the recent re-emergence of Joe Cocker.)

Miss Mitchell defies negative criticism and garners favourable critiques with every project she pursues, be it her successful return to the stage or her creative knack of producing timeless and poignant albums. And Sunday evening (her final show) was no exception: two and a half hours of the only substitute for Joni on record – Joni in person.

As soon as Joni Mitchell stepped on stage, she was presented with a glorious bouquet of roses and it was for the roses that she turned in a set of warm, tender and sensitive music.

'Big Yellow Taxi' sparked immediate recognition in the Troub audience, as Miss Mitchell's humorous but brutal lines, 'Took all the trees, put 'em in a tree museum/And charged the people a dollar and a half just to see 'em,' etched grins on all her listeners' faces.

Joni's uncanny use of double entendre metaphors, unquestionably clever rhyme schemes and poignant lyrics make every Mitchell composition a challenge and pleasure to listen to. Unlike her contemporaries, whose newer material has none of the vitality or freshness of their earlier material – notably James Taylor and Carole King – Joni is consistent in producing noteworthy and valuable albums.

'Sometimes it takes a personal crisis to turn you on the spiritual path. During your childhood and your teens you go through many crises. Everybody should go through it: it's a good experience. After a crisis you go through a re-evaluation of yourself. Anybody with a smile on their face is enlightened. Everybody knows more than you! I walked into a restaurant a while back and I saw three waitresses and thought they were the Trinity. I moved closer to see what they were talking about and maybe see what it was all about, and I saw they were all wearing black diamond earrings. While going through some guru books, it said that some people look to Mecca, some to the cross and some to the City National Bank. But I decided they were all wrong. It was happening right here in the restaurant.'

Her enlightening introduction over with, she launched into 'Barangrill' off her newest album, *For The Roses*. Not knowing where to turn or find an answer, Joni sees her salvation in her three waitress friends: 'And you think she knows something/By the second refill/You think she's enlightened as she totals your bill/You say, "Show me the way to Barangrill".'

Joni's approach to music is an honest and sincere one. Her songs are personal appeals that find their ways into universal hearts. Like Joan Baez, who has likewise been faithful to her cause, Joni is a living example of how truth may be translated into beauty.

'While looking for the guru, I found a book on the spiritual development of Beethoven. I wrote him a song and was gonna call it "Roll Over Beethoven Revisited", but I decided to call it "Ludwig's Tune". No disrespect intended.'

This was her first piece on the ivories and immediately Miss Mitchell's flowing, bubbly playing could be heard ringing through the club. Besides listening to her delicate lyrics, it is possible to understand what she is trying to say by simply listening to her music. One line from 'Ludwig's Tune', 'Strike every chord that you feel', sums up this non-verbal communication between artist and audience.

The lady from the canyon performed 'For Free' with some instrumental (clarinet) backup by Tommy Scott, who plays woodwinds and reeds on the *Roses* LP and turned in a delightful solo while sitting incognito somewhere in the audience. He then joined Joni on stage for 'Let The Wind Carry Me' – another new composition.

'Cold Blue Steel and Sweet Fire' was Joni's comment on heroin addicts, a lyrical pinnacle in her career. 'Bashing in veins for peace/ Cold blue steel and sweet fire/Fall into lady release,' Joni sang as the audience sat hushed while her crystal voice pierced the silence of the hall.

Dressed in her classic floor-length dress, sunshine hair spilling onto her shoulders, and snowy white teeth reflecting from the stage lights, Joni delved into a little bit of 'pop' talk. 'I always wanted to have a hit. I never had a hit, you know, so I made one up. I decided there were some ways to make a hit, increase the chances. The DJs have to like it, so you put a long part at the beginning and the end so the DJs can talk over it. Take a tender situation and translate it into commonly appealing songs for the DJs. It'd have to be a bit corny, so I wrote this little song called "Oh, Honey, You Turn Me On, I'm a Radio".'

This number, in particular, showcases the Mitchell-esque use of double-meaning metaphors: 'Who needs the static?/It hurts the head,' and 'Call me at the station/The lines are open' are two clever examples in the song.

This was Joni's final number but the Troubadour audience didn't think so. She was brought back accompanied by abandoned applause with everybody shouting out their favourites. 'I know what I'll do. OK, if I sing "Circle Game", you all have to sing with me, OK?'

Three hundred voices joined the pleased singer for the chorus of the song, and coaxed her into one more number, 'For The Roses', title track of her latest album.

Review of
Court and Spark

Loraine Alterman, *New York Times*,
6 January 1974

Joni Mitchell doesn't write love songs. She writes songs about love. And she is the premier explorer of the terrain. Romance and reality both work within her sensibility so that her songs honestly express the range of feelings involved in love. In *Court and Spark* (Asylum), her sixth album in as many years, Mitchell continues to probe this vital life force and, as always, she couches her keen insights in poetry that moves both the heart and the mind.

Although she is wise enough to know there can be no final answers, she understands the tension between love and freedom, something every thinking person feels but can't – or won't – always articulate with honesty.

What makes Mitchell's work so fascinating is how perfectly she expresses the continuing psychic struggle. By now she has had her share of the downs as well as the ups of love. She knows that she's got to find fulfilment as a person in her art – and, indeed, she wants to – yet she's still looking for that one love, that one man who will 'court and spark' her, even though she realises that the 'spark' probably won't last for long. There are no double standards for her because she knows that both women and men feel that urge to be unfettered just as much as both have the desire for commitment.

'Help Me' relates this frankly. There's a breezy sense of irony in her voice and music that gives a sharper edge to the last two lines, 'We love our lovin'/But not like we love our freedom.' 'Car on a Hill' is a moving recreation of what it's like waiting for one's lover to show up. He's three hours late – has he been hurt? Has he met someone else? Why does the delight of love turn into this? She expresses all these feelings quite simply in images that stick and the music echoes the sense of impatience turning into despair. 'The Same Situation' emphasises the continuing presence of the conflict between the 'I' and the 'We' with its last lines about being 'Caught in my struggle for higher achievements/And my search for love/That don't seem to cease.'

Not all of Mitchell's songs focus solely and inwardly on love. She's fine at telling tales too, like the fast and racy 'Raised on Robbery', about a prostitute vainly attempting to make a sale in a bar. 'Free Man in Paris' shows her awareness that the success drive, just like the love drive, can be at odds with freedom. Just as love makes demands, so does business. This particular song is about the businessmen she knows best, those in the record industry.

For the first time on any of her albums, Mitchell has recorded a song written by someone else, 'Twisted' by Annie Ross and Wardell Gray. For some reason 'Twisted', originally performed by one of Mitchell's early favourites, Lambert, Hendricks and Ross, over a decade ago, is enjoying a mini-renaissance. Bette Midler just did it on her new album, but Mitchell's version is much better: she sings with a wide-eyed innocence similar to Annie Ross's and that gives the surprise ending more impact than Midler's somewhat campy rendition.

Musically, *Court and Spark* offers no directions different from Mitchell's previous work. There are traces of 'Cold Blue Steel and Sweet Fire' in 'Car on a Hill' and of 'Judgment of the Moon and Stars' in 'Court and Spark'. However, what she lacks in musical surprises she makes up for in arrangements and productions that become more sophisticated with each album; the drama of the soul that unfolds in her lyrics is now matched by the drama of the music.

The instrumental break before the final verse of 'Down to You' is an example of how she can build up emotion with superb taste, contrasting the lone and rather defiant piano part with warm, romantic strings. The bridge sets the stage for the conflicts in the final verse with its lines like 'Just when you're thinking/You've finally got it made/Bad news comes knocking/At your garden gate.'

There's no doubt that men as well as women can relate to Mitchell's songs; but because she is a woman her work does have a special meaning to all women who are caught in the basic dilemma of knowing they must realise their own potential at the same time they still want to find that one love. As a friend of mine, who is very deeply involved in the feminist movement, said rather wistfully one day – 'all the theory is great but you can't share your bed with it'.

Mitchell's songs are very personal, in that they have roots within her own experience. It's impossible to fake the intense reality of her perceptions, but that doesn't mean that each song is to be interpreted as strict autobiography. Like all great artists she can turn her own experiences into truths that touch everyone.

How 'Free Man in Paris' Came Along

Johnny Black, *Blender*,
September 2004

When Joni Mitchell played the finished tapes of her 1974 album *Court and Spark* for her Asylum Records label-mate Bob Dylan, the venerated spokesman of his generation fell asleep. 'I think Bobby was just being cute,' is how Mitchell figured it.

It's certainly hard to imagine that Dylan was bored because the album included what turned out to be Mitchell's biggest hit singles: 'Help Me' and 'Free Man in Paris'. Had Dylan paid a bit more attention, he might have realised that the subject of the latter tune was standing in the room beside him.

'I wrote that in Paris for David Geffen,' Mitchell has explained, 'taking a lot of it from the things he said.' Geffen and Mitchell went a long way back. He had been her agent at the start of her rise to fame in the '60s, and by the time she wrote 'Free Man in Paris' he owned the record label for which she (along with the Eagles, Jackson Browne and Dylan) was recording. The pair were such close friends that they even shared a house, but despite wide speculation about a romantic entanglement, theirs was more akin to a *Will & Grace* relationship.

Ned Doheny, another guitarist-songwriter who was managed by Geffen at that time, has characterised the dynamic young executive as an unhappy man despite his wealth and power. 'There was always something kind of desperate and sad about David,' he told author Fred Goodman, noting that Geffen paid an unusual amount of attention to the progress of his clients' romantic affairs.

'People assume everything I write is autobiographical,' Mitchell complains. 'If I sing in the first person, they assume it's all about me. With a song like "Free Man in Paris", they attribute almost every word of the song to my personal life, somehow missing the setups of "He said" and "She said".'

Geffen, then, is the one who, in the words of the song, 'felt unfettered and alive' in Paris because 'there was nobody calling me up for favours'. The song articulates his desire to rid himself of the 'dreamers and telephone screamers' and other hassles of being a music-industry mover-and-shaker and return to the freedom he had felt while strolling down the Champs Élysées.

Although Mitchell's early career was founded in folk rock, by 1973 she was having trouble finding rock musicians who were sensitive to the way she structured her songs and phrased her melodies. 'I had no choice but to go with jazz musicians,' she says. 'I tried to play with all of the rock bands that were the usual sections for James Taylor when we made our transition from folk to folk rock. They couldn't play my music because it's so eccentric. They would try, but the straight-ahead 2/4 rock'n'roll running through would steamroller right over it.'

Mitchell had started moving toward jazz on her 1972 album *For the Roses* by bringing in woodwind player Tom Scott. She then hired his entire band, the L.A. Express, for the recording of *Court and Spark* in 1973 at A&M's suite of studios in Los Angeles.

'When Joni gets musicians in the studio,' noted her engineer and co-producer, Henry Lewy, 'the first three or four takes are usually just for listening. She doesn't really want to think too much about them – she just wants to play and frequently you get some real magic happening in those takes.'

The breezy 'Free Man in Paris' opens with guitar, percussion and Tom Scott's flute. 'I refer to our experience together as a real ping-pong match,' he says, 'where I'm out in the studio and she's in the booth and I play this and she'll say, "That's great; why don't we try this?" It's back and forth. We were co-creators of that aspect of her records.'

The track was already evolving nicely when fate lent a hand. 'I was working with John Lennon in a studio along the corridor,' recalls guitarist José Feliciano. 'We were doing his back-to-roots album *Rock'n'Roll*, but things weren't going too well. John had got very drunk so I got bored and walked out into the corridor.'

Hearing 'Free Man in Paris' wafting out of Mitchell's studio, Feliciano recognised it as something that fit nicely with his own style. 'I already knew Joni from when we both worked in Canada,' he explains, 'so I walked in and said I thought I could play some good electric guitar for it. The great guitarist Larry Carlton of the L. A. Express was already on the track but I knew I could hold my own with him. Joni didn't try to direct me at all, just let me do what I do, and it turned out really good.'

His contribution in the can, Feliciano then favoured Mitchell with some advice. 'She was playing with her guitar in an open tuning,' he recalls, 'so I pointed out that although open tunings are nice, they can be restrictive. I said that she'd be better off just to tune her guitar in the normal way. She didn't like that. I think it put her off me a little.'

Although Mitchell was pleased with the song, which features David Crosby and Graham Nash on backing vocals, Geffen was not so sure. 'He didn't like it at the time,' she says. 'He begged me to take it off the record. I think he felt uncomfortable being shown in that light.'

Court and Spark was released in January 1974 to glowing reviews, but its eventual multiplatinum success has been a two-edged sword for Mitchell. '*Court and Spark* was about as popular as it got,' she says. 'Everything after that was compared unfavourably to it.'

It's responsible for influencing subsequent generations of musicians, including Madonna, who once noted, 'In high school, I worshipped Joni Mitchell and sang everything from *Court and Spark*, my coming-of-age record.'

The album's first single, 'Help Me', hit No. 7 on the *Billboard* charts and when the time came for a follow-up, Mitchell's thoughts turned to the forlorn love song 'Car on a Hill'. 'I wanted to release it as a single and [Asylum Records] fought me on it. Instead, "Free Man in Paris" was released, which never sounded like a single to me.'

The public, however, thought otherwise, pushing it to No. 22 in the US and giving Mitchell her biggest international hit to date. The song has also become one of her most-covered compositions, with Elton John, Neil Diamond and Shawn Colvin among the many who have taken it to heart.

As for Geffen, he never did manage to quit the music industry. He's now a billionaire and part owner – the G – of the vast multinational entertainment conglomerate DreamWorks SKG.

Lost Innocence with a Rock'n'Roll Band

Barbara Charone, *New Musical Express*,
9 February 1974

J oni Mitchell, no longer an innocent folkie, has turned her back on the garden for rockier pastures. Yep, the times certainly are changing.

The first lady of the acoustic guitar is now backed by a real live, real loud electric band – namely Tom Scott and his L. A. Express. And Ms. Mitchell's present American jaunt with the outfit has audiences begging for more. Maybe Asylum records boss David Geffen really does own the world? First Bob Dylan's majestic tour and now this . . .

While the Dylan tour flies about in Starship One, the ultimate in rock luxury, Joni and gang are getting to gigs on a comfortable bus decked out with colour TV and eight-track stereo. More than a few parallels exist as Joni hits cities Dylan's just left. Asylum's silent partner, Mr Elliot Roberts, travels with Joni, just to make sure everything is all right. And damn if it isn't a coincidence that both Dylan's and Joni's brand new albums are released simultaneously.

Anyway, how did Joni discover veteran jazzer Tom Scott and his all-star friends?

'I met her through a weird quirk of fate,' Scott smiles, relaxing after a Chicago concert. About four years ago, Quincy Jones started a record company and I was one of the artists. Quincy suggested that I record "Woodstock" and I said "Oh, yeah, the one CSN&Y do." Well, Quincy played me Joni's version and I was floored. Especially with her voice. So I did the tune using a recorder, kind of imitating Joni's voice. She heard the track and asked me if I'd like to play on her new album, which at the time was *For The Roses*. A few nights later we went to the studio and struck up a very rewarding relationship.'

But before there was *For The Roses*, Scott was learning a thing or two about every kind of reed instrument you've ever heard. He's played clarinet since eight and took up baritone sax in high school as it was the only vacant chair in the dance band. A modern jazz fanatic, he cites people like Miles Davis and Gerry Mulligan as inspirations.

Tom Scott is what you'd call into playing and play anywhere he did, from weddings to bar mitzvahs. Eventually he started playing with everyone from Oliver Nelson, Lalo Schifrin and Wayne Newton to David Cassidy. How's that for variety?

And the L.A. Express contains a few surprises; like lead guitarist Robben Ford, fresh from a year-long stint with Jimmy Witherspoon, drummer John Guerin, who's worked with everyone from Roger McGuinn to veteran jazzers, as has bassist Max Bennett and keyboard player Roger Calloway.

But back to Joni . . .

'One day this summer Joni came to see the band at the Baked Potato, a North Hollywood club. She asked us to play on a couple of tracks on her next album. Immediately I knew it was going to be more than a coupla tracks,' Scott smiles.

When the L.A. Express recorded *Court and Spark*, the new Mitchell delicacy, Larry Carlton and Joe Sample were on lead guitar and piano respectively, but other commitments prevented them from touring.

'The L.A. Express had just made an album for Lou Adler's label, Ode, when Lou informed me one day that Joni had passed down word that she'd like to go out on tour with us, and would we consider. "I said, 'Yes, we'd consider',"' he laughs. 'Up until the tour we weren't sure if Larry Carlton was going to come. It looked like we'd need a guitarist. So we went to see Robben Ford. Now it just so happened that Robben was on the verge of quitting Witherspoon. So he took the L.A. Express and Joni Mitchell albums home with him. A week later he called us up and said, "Yeah, it looks interesting!"'

Pretty crazy story: one princess of folk music surrounded by a harem of veteran blues, jazz and rock fanatics. Not your typical get-it-together-in-the-country band.

In concert, the L.A. Express kick things off with forty minutes of steaming rhythm and virtuoso solos ranging from original compositions to stuff by John Coltrane. And when Tom Scott introduces Joni, the crowd goes crazy. It happens every night.

In Madison, Wisconsin, one dedicated fan waited most of the day to give Joni a present with a personal note: 'I give you apples and cheese, you give me songs.' They love her all right, no doubt about it.

The first few dates had people screaming out for solo Joni, but that was to be expected. Those kids came to see a lady and one acoustic guitar. They got all that and more. In Chicago, someone yelled out, 'Turn down the volume.' Joni's reply was: 'What's the matter, do we have a hall full of purists? I thought Chicago liked to boogie.' This speech was delivered all innocent-like, emphasizing the 'oogie', so it sounded real cute.

'There were a few hard moments in the beginning,' Scott recalls. 'In St. Louis someone screamed out, "Let's hear her without the band." But a minute later someone hollered, "Let's hear her with the band." But audiences have been receptive to us generally speaking. We couldn't ask for anything more. We're practically an unknown group.'

It's a new woman up there on stage this time around. Quick with the jokes, lightning fast with the riffs, as always in amazing voice. '"White Rabbit"', one crazy man requests and Joni answers, much to everyone's amusement, 'I'm slick but not that slick.'

What with both Joni and the L.A. Express getting solo spots, then coming together for the bulk of the show, everyone seems to be satisfied. Show stealers like 'Raised on Robbery' (imagine Joni Mitchell doing rock'n'roll) or a very rhythmic, jazzed-up 'Woodstock' keep the place jumping.

Says Scott: 'We rehearsed for ten days before the tour, mostly learning Joni's material because it's so intricate. Her music is very delicate and needs to be treated very carefully. We worked hard to be as true to her tunes as we could. It evolved very spontaneously. Maybe instead of just playing the melody on sax we'd try guitar and sax. That really seemed to click so we've done several tunes constructed around that tension. Joni's lyrics aren't as easily accessible as Dylan's. Dylan's lyrics are universal messages at his best but Joni's are more transparent – you have to look a little deeper.'

Meanwhile, remembering Joni on stage, I have this picture of her putting on this very sophisticated cabaret routine for a rousing encore of 'Twisted'. As she stands there, swaying to the sleazy beat, she looks like no folkie you've ever seen.

'Singing without her own instrument is revolutionary for Joni,' Scott goes on. 'The first time we rehearsed "Twisted" she said, "Oh, I feel like Helen Reddy." But she's getting into it. She's been trying to record that song for over two years. It's merely coincidental that Bette Midler put it out. It's funny that after all these years, when the tune has been sitting on that Annie Ross record, two heavy lady singers release it in the same month.'

Memories of another gig: two hours, twenty-one tunes, and several shouts of 'Joni, you're beautiful' later, the show is over.

Backstage, Joni Mitchell looks radiant, even prettier with the spotlights off. A few brave fans gather the courage to mumble 'nice show' or 'I like the record'. She sits there in a big, floppy hat and grins thank-yous.

'There's a certain amount of polish in the show that you won't find from your average folkie,' Scott quips. 'Now, she defies categorisation altogether. Don't know what she is except a very talented lady.'

Review of Show at
Avery Fisher Hall, New York City

Ian Dove, *New York Times*, 9 February 1974

Joni Mitchell has in previous performances stood, flaxen-haired and frail, alone in the spotlight. On Tuesday at Avery Fisher Hall, however, she threw this sedate image aside as she crashed into her first song, backed by the L.A. Express group, a jazz-rock unit dominated by the tough saxophone (both tenor and soprano) of its leader, Tom Scott. Later a largish string section materialised to take Miss Mitchell farther away from her earlier environs. But the impact of the violins was somewhat lessened by sound problems.

This is not to say that Miss Mitchell has turned rocker – just that she has sewn her folkishness right onto a gutsier framework, sweet and sour working together.

Miss Mitchell remains earnest in approach, highly serious, a singer of editorials for herself through which a tune may – or may not – be threaded. She is now including songs about being a star (which she is) and feeling guilty about the whole thing.

The Mitchell voice, seemingly delicate, can still cut through the energetic arrangements of L.A. Express, making her folk-rock's Ethel Merman.

Review of *Miles of Aisles*

Tom Nolan, *Phonograph Record*,
January 1975

The two most annoying things (to me) about Joni Mitchell in the early years of her career were her songs, which often seemed impersonal, shallow and written by formula (remember that oft-played opus about the surly New York cabbie?) and her voice, which leapt all over the place in a shrill demonstration of technique. ('Congratulations to Joni Mitchell upon her conquest of the octave,' Richard Goldstein wrote sarcastically of her first album.)

Voice and songs! Two big strikes against a budding singer-songwriter. It's no wonder many checked out after her second or third record and refused to listen anymore, despite rumours of artistic maturity and increased sophistication.

This two-record live album, then, is an ideal introduction to this artist and her 'recent' work: that body of songs in which Mitchell has found her proper subject matter, come into power as an artist and deservedly increased her audience to star proportions. All but two or three of these selections are about men and women, their games, roles, cynicisms and optimisms, despairs and new beginnings. When she strays from the country of the heart, as in 'Real Good for Free' [sic] and 'Woodstock', she wanders toward an Aquarian age-*Redbook* magazine soppiness, but when she charts the geometry of emotion and makes pictures of full-dimensioned human beings, she's as effective, intelligent and entertaining a writer as anyone around.

These are marvellous short stories she creates; her touch is sure and literate. Listen, for instance, to the artful and economical beginning of 'Peoples' Parties'; how easily she sets a scene and draws one into it. The talent she always had for summoning and adapting situations – a commercial quality – has in recent years acquired a toughness of mind necessary if her work was to be elevated above the merely clever.

Mitchell's sound here is not at all jarring. The harsh, brittle attack present on much of her recorded work is replaced by a breathier, free-flowing approach. While she plays around with her voice, the result is not the undisciplined self-indulgence I was dreading but soft, rhythmic and pleasantly blurred. The melodies and tempos are treated with a welcome lack of inhibition and these songs so familiar to the audience seem to blend into a many-faceted suite. The effect is satisfying rather than monotonous with much credit due the L.A. Express, who provide imaginative coloration for a variety of moods. Especially well served is 'The Circle Game', pumped along by a catchy blues riff which salvages it from its dated past. Although apparently absent for almost two whole sides of this double album, [the Express'] influence and memory seem to linger until their return.

Two new songs, 'Jericho' and 'Love or Money', round off this collection of previously released material and are fine enough to deserve more attentive studio versions.

Besides the very generous amount of music included here and the most agreeable manner in which it's performed, there is another factor making this the perfect record with which to become acquainted with Joni Mitchell: the opportunity it allows for her personality to show through. In contrast to the somewhat aloof impression that has accrued to her in her years of not granting interviews, there is much good humour here: in her pleasant handling of request-shouters; in her perfect Lily Tomlin waitress one-liner in the middle of 'The Last Time I Saw Richard'; and in her acknowledgement of Bob Dylan's hilarious alternate verse of 'Big Yellow Taxi' by incorporating it into the text. In fact, in a year when the fashion is for performers to erect a cool space between themselves and the first row of seats, the good feelings emanating from this set are positively inspiring.

Review of
The Hissing of Summer Lawns

Michael Watts, *Melody Maker*,
29 November 1975

O n the inside sleeve of this album Joni has a short, cryptic liner note stating that the record is 'graphically, musically, lyrically and accidentally' a total work, but adding that she is not about to unravel its mystery for anyone.

With almost any other artist I'd be tempted to think this kind of riddle-me-ree was crap, but since Joni is a writer of such great sensibilities, with a fierce conscience at that, I feel drawn inescapably into her game.

And yet I confess it is difficult. Always a lyricist of exquisite subtlety, preferring to suggest rather than interpret meanings, she has devised a delightful torture. Unlike the past three studio albums – and particularly the last one, *Court and Spark* – she is not concerned with the conflict between the private and public artist and that business of 'the star-maker machinery behind the popular song'. There is no obvious theme, just as there are no longer any obvious melodies but songs and singing that exhibit a great interest in the shifting inflections of jazz, which one can surely attribute in part to the influence of her good friend, the drummer John Guerin of the L.A. Express.

I can only hazard the thought that she is making a statement this time about a far less specific but much deeper fascination. As is implied by the album cover (self-drawn, of course), with its depiction of African natives dragging a huge snake across what could be Central Park, with New York skyscrapers in the distance, there is a theme juxtaposing the primitive and sophisticated, an idea borne out by the album title with its evocation of sprinklers on suburban lawns . . . and yet something else. This Pinterish construction would certainly be supported by several tracks. 'The Jungle Line', which almost certainly has given rise to the African tableau and was assuredly inspired by Henri Rousseau's turn-of-the-century picture *Virgin Forest at Sunset*, has her singing over a tape of the booming warrior drums of Burundi, about 'Rousseau's vines steaming up to Brooklyn Bridge' and develops an analogy between nature and the feral quality of New York's own jungle. There are other clues.

In 'Harry's House/Centerpiece' – the 'Centerpiece' of which was written by Johnny Mandel and Jon Hendricks – she describes a businessman checking into his New York hotel suite and drifting off, as he looks out the window, into a fantasy of his wife as he first met her in school; the fantasy, represented by the Mandel-Hendricks tune, is then rudely shattered at the song's end by the voice of a virago telling Harry 'just what he could do with Harry's house and Harry's take-home pay'.

This theme of uneasy urban life is expanded upon in 'Edith and the Kingpin', with its tale of the seduction of a small-town girl by 'the big man', and more sinisterly, in the title-track which, as in Hockney's Californian paintings, contrives to make the fact of 'blue pools in the squinting sun' unreal and intriguing.

In all these songs she seems to be commenting on 'life's illusions' that she wrote about in 'Both Sides Now' – Rousseau, a sophisticated man, yearns for a red-blooded primitivism – and she uses 'The Boho Dance', a Tom Wolfe term for would-be artists making a virtue out of suffering in garrets, to further illustrate her idea of the self-deluding quest for 'real' experience by over-civilised people. It's the most overtly autobiographical number on the album, and she reveals her own unromantic position in relation to the theme when she says 'the streets were never really mine, not mine these glamour gowns'.

Doubtless the exact drift of Ms Mitchell's lyrics will become evident in time, but for now I can only enthuse about the quality of her writing. No other popular artist I can think of writes with such a polished, well-balanced and economical style.

She has clipped away all adjectival excess, and every word is weighted in the line. As indicated before, the nature of her music is now leagues away from the generally straightforward folk songs of the past and she has forged a form of personal expression that is beyond imitation. This, her most mysterious and ambitious record, breathes with her cool and damaged beauty that lingers long after the last playing.

Review of Show at
Nassau Coliseum, Long Island

Michael Gross, *Swank*, June 1976

From the moment I walked into the Nassau Coliseum, a block-house-like structure surrounded by a no-man's-land of lights, fences and police, I knew I'd found the answer to a question that's been puzzling me for a long time. Joni Mitchell's concert that night, part of a massive world tour, was to my mind a pleasant diversion. But to the thousands of young kids (especially teenage girls) in the audience, the two hours they'd spend with Joni were more a pilgrimage; a visit to Maharaj Ji, a chance to peek into their own dreams.

The question was seemingly a simple one: Where are all the world's beautiful, ripe fourteen-year-old girls? Where are all those Lolitas we've all heard so much about, with their pert tits, hard bums, yadda, yadda yadda? The answer? They're home listening to Joni Mitchell albums, of course.

Thinking about this revelation for a moment, it all seems too clear. These are the girls of the suburbs. No one can convince me that pretty girls live in the cities anymore. Their parents have all high-tailed it to suburbia or Vermont. These girls are living in the old plastic waste-land and the older boys they crave move so fast when freed that Lolita and her sisters have nowhere to go but home to the Sony system, where even their parents are soothed by Joni's delightful voice, her stirring sentiment, her touching inability to stay in love.

Joni's songs have always been the stuff of which adolescent dreams are made. 'I Had a King' from her very first album was the romanticism of the girl from Freeport who finds love at an IND stop and moves into a railroad flat on East Fifth Street. Joni may have found a king; most girls from Freeport find speed-freaks. Then there were 'Clouds' and 'Chelsea Morning' and the now-momentous 'Ladies of the Canyon', which pointed to LA as the place where the streets were paved with female fulfilment for all Joni's growing listeners. By the time of her third album, Joni had grown, if not to complete womanhood, to at least an inkling of her own self-sufficiency, couched as it was in the counter-cultural garbage of making cookies in the canyon.

After that came *Blue*. As more people than you can imagine already know, *Blue* is the best album ever to help you rationalise utter romantic defeat. It's the perfect 'just got home from a one-night stand and the bastard/bitch didn't even cook me eggs' LP. *For The Roses* followed on a new label, David Geffen's Asylum, and people began to assume that Joni was caught up in the frantic El Lay life of pop stars and lollipop swimming pools. What a fantasy figure Joni Mitchell had become! Her cheekbones haunted every college boy's heart. Her songs of grown-up disillusionment wormed their way into the psyches of the nymphet brigade. And she put it all together into such a class act that no one, but no one, could dump on it. You had to know that none of the men she allegedly played with could hold a candle to her in the class stakes.

If *Court and Spark*, *Miles of Aisles* and *The Hissing of Summer Lawns* then proved a bit confusing to those hung up on pretty melodies and sad lyrics, it was only because Joni had abandoned her little-girlishness to become a woman with the same romantic notions and the same musical ability to get dumped on. This was the Joni who took the stage that night at Nassau.

The opening set by the L.A. Express (minus Tom Scott) would have been commendable in a midwestern cocktail lounge. At Nassau it provided the kids with an excuse to cruise the aisles. Overwhelmingly female, they seemed somehow subdued; well-behaved compared to the city audiences most performers face. One girl let out a freedom-seeking yodel and six cops' heads snapped to alert. No one picked up her cry. It was clean-teen night at Nassau, marred only by the predominance of emaciated young men in open-to-the-pupik Dacron shirts and hanging brass zodiac medallions.

Impatient stomps died out in ten seconds, changing to shrill screams as the lights around the black-wreathed stage went down and Joni stepped out to sing. She wore mandatory El Lay hip garb: black slacks, padded-shoulder jacket and slouchy hat. She opened with 'Help Me', looking like a soft David Bowie, singing in the best voice I've heard her in since Newport in the '60s. The set covered her career well, though it was heavy with her recent work. She seemed in total control and the crowd sat munching her words and images like special, sweet Hostess Twinkies of the heart. Her between-song chatter was more coherent and less generous than in the past. All in all, she came off as a self-assured woman, a masterful entertainer, an eclectically brilliant composer, and the possessor of two of the finest instruments in popular music: a great set of pipes and those wonderful, vulnerable cheekbones.

The little girls went home, back to wherever the crunchy granola set go between MOR pop concerts. Their dreams were intact. It was all that mattered.

Review of *Hejira*

Colman Andrews, *Phonograph Record*,
December 1976

Very few of Joni Mitchell's songs since the *Ladies of the Canyon* LP have been recorded by other artists, and I suppose that must be because with every passing album her work has grown increasingly personal while showing her own sensibility more fiercely and unequivocally. It is very difficult to imagine anyone else singing most of the songs on *For The Roses*, *Court and Spark*, *The Hissing of Summer Lawns* or even, for that matter, *Blue*. Or on this new album.

Mitchell's songs and Mitchell's singing seem so close together, and she herself so close to both, that it is almost as if – to paraphrase what someone once said of Van Morrison (in the days of *Astral Weeks*) – she were simply standing up in front of a microphone and spilling her soul. She almost seems to be making the words up as she goes along — ad-libbing her funny, asymmetrical, sometimes heart-rending poetry, fashioning her phrases (alternately Byzantine and blunt) with brilliant care and casual, almost flippant elegance.

Hejira is something of a theme album, though the theme involved doesn't take one as thrillingly (and terribly) by the throat as did the theme of *Summer Lawns*. It might be said, in fact, that *Hejira* succeeds in spite of its thematic unity and not necessarily because of it.

The theme, of course, is travel – moving, running, changing places. Flight, in several senses of the word. Rigs that pass in the night. Fortunately, the 'free, free way' and its many relations (I started counting references to travel and uses of the word 'road' in the lyrics, but I had to go somewhere so I lost track) are used on many levels, and the metaphors are rich and deep enough so that neither 'touring's such a drag' nor 'you can't run away from yourself' ever rear their boring little heads. (*Hejira* seems an ironic title, by the way, since at the end of a hejira there is presumably a Mecca, and no such haven is in sight here – the stances of 'Refuge of the Roads' notwithstanding.)

The music on *Hejira*, as usual with Mitchell, feels a lot like calypso (with the exception of 'Blue Motel Room' and maybe 'A Strange Boy'), both in the lilt of the rhythm section and in Mitchell's own concept of phrasing – the way she makes words fit into patches of time. (There is also merest taunting of a reggae beat on one track.) Musically, certainly, much of *Hejira* will sound familiar. The artist creates his or her own clichés but can get away with it when they are this deliberate and this obviously the artist's own.

Mitchell's songwriting is as good as ever. Her almost accidental eroticism in lines like 'He picks up my scent on his fingers/While he's watching the waitresses' legs' or 'And I went running down a white sand road/I was running like a white-assed deer' or 'Still sometimes the slightest touch of a stranger/Can set up trembling in my bones' is most efficient. At other times, the tristful precision of her descriptive phrases recalls no less a master of that mode than Philip Larkin.

More important even than Mitchell's words, though, is the way she sings what she writes, the way she binds her words to her music. Her manner of shaping phrases is daringly histrionic at times, daringly plain at other times. Her voice knows when to soar and when to grumble, when to waver and when to hold firm. Listen to a song of hers two dozen times, with a good ear and a good voice, and it will still be nearly impossible to match her risings and fallings the twenty-fifth time through. Both her tonal and her dramatic modulations are quite stunning, quite unexpected. She has the eerie ability to make the most incidental audience not only listen to a phrase but care about listening to it. Her readings of short pieces of song like 'no regrets, Coyote' (the first time), 'the next thing I know', 'eighteen bucks went up in smoke', 'honey, tell 'em you got germs', 'or me here least of all' and even just the second syllable of the word 'lover' in 'Song for Sharon' are nearly impossible to forget.

When she sings 'Amelia, it was just a false alarm', she captures a feeling of tired longing that a generation of neo-folkies, many of them extremely talented, have been trying, and failing, to reproduce in a few words for years. And when she curls into her jazz voice on 'Blue Motel Room', she is fire through smoky glass, as good as Helen Humes.

A digression: One distrusted Mitchell as a jazz singer when she tried 'Twisted' on *Court and Spark*, but the distrust disappeared when she did 'Centerpiece' on *Summer Lawns*. 'Motel Room' is so good, and so unusually but genuinely jazz, that one almost wishes Mitchell would, as a one-time thing, try a pure, straight jazz album, with other people's compositions and with pure, straight jazz musicians of the sort who had their cabaret cards before Tom Scott was even born. Mitchell has an obvious love for the King Pleasure/Eddie Jefferson/Annie Ross/Jon Hendricks axis and she could also have fun with things like '720 in the Books', 'I've Got Your Number', or 'Sunday in Savannah' but she could *also* probably do chillingly successful things with serious songs like 'Lush Life', 'The Ballad of the Sad Young Men', or 'Some Other Time' . . .

Some of Mitchell's usual backup musicians are present on *Hejira*, including Max Bennett, John Guerin, Victor Feldman, Tom Scott and Bobbye Hall; they are as firm as ever. Abe Most on clarinet, Chuck Domenico on bass and Neil Young on harmonica (!) guest-star on one track each. But the most impressive player here is Jaco Pastorius (of Weather Report and Al DiMeola's group) on four tracks. His cool, lanky lines on the title song sometimes match Mitchell's own with unerringly accurate inflections, and on 'Refuge of the Roads' his bass is a finely lyrical lead instrument. Larry Carlton's guitar is also a delight, especially on 'A Strange Boy', where his strong, intelligent *obbligati* are reminiscent of Ollie Halsall.

There can be no doubt that Joni Mitchell is a major artist, as both writer and performer – one who seems already mature but still willing to mature further, to polish her considerable talents without wearing them away. Long may she run.

An Evening with
Joni Mitchell

Martin Colyer, martincolyer.wordpress.com,
24 October 2009

It was 1977 and I was at art school in London on a graphics course. To supplement the student grant, some of us were involved with an ill-fated magazine venture. Supposedly a British answer to *Billboard, Record & Radio News* (or something like that) was keeping costs down by hiring students to do the design and paste-up. This resulted in lucrative evenings and weekends, albeit at a cost to our education.

A friend who spent a lot of time working there came across two tickets for a Weather Report concert at the Hammersmith Odeon, and attached were two invites to the post-concert party. The attraction was not so much the prospect of seeing Weather Report as the fact that the party was at a club called the Speakeasy. 'The Speak' was one of those legendary London basement rock'n'roll joints, situated in an unprepossessing street north of Oxford Street. It was supposedly the hangout of 'rock stars' but in reality probably only played host to Rod Stewart's roadies. In the heyday of punk, the Speak's days were numbered . . .

The invites were, however, for the publisher and editor by name. So, looking rather too fresh-faced for our job titles, Tim and I presented ourselves at the Speakeasy's door. To our horror we had to pass down a presentation line of record label executives, being introduced by our assumed names to the managing director of CBS, the head of European sales, and so on. I don't quite know how we survived this ordeal and I'm sure I can remember a couple of quizzical looks passing between recipients of our clammy handshakes, but the free bar helped us recover some of our lost cool. In a slight state of relaxation we helped ourselves to the lavish spread on offer.

We took a table next to Wayne Shorter, after a failed attempt to congratulate Joe Zawinul on the performance (failed since he looked straight through me as I spoke – in retrospect I don't blame him at all). We were eating and trying to eavesdrop on Wayne's conversation when a tall, willowy, long-haired woman, followed by two men – one in his late fifties, one about our age – swept up to our table and asked if the rest of the seats were vacant. We said they were. They sat down and proceeded to strike up a conversation. Joni Mitchell wanted to ask Wayne Shorter to overdub saxophone on a track she'd recorded in LA and the men with her were Henry Lewy, her legendary recording engineer, and his assistant.

As Wayne Shorter was deep in conversation, Joni turned to us and asked what we were doing there. We ruefully admitted that we were there under false pretences but in our defence said that it made a change from the generally poverty-stricken art school life. Upon hearing the magic words 'art student', Ms Mitchell began animatedly talking about art, artists, paint and all manner of things. We in turn asked about guitar tunings and Jaco Pastorius (*Hejira* had been released a couple of months before and we had already worn down the grooves).

Henry Lewy, who had engineered classic albums by the Byrds and the Flying Burrito Brothers, was an extremely courteous man and looked the spitting image of the film director Sam Fuller, only without the cigar. Suddenly next to our table was the whirling dervish that was Pastorius, bobbing manically and muttering cryptic phrases such as 'the nose knows', as well as being accompanied to the men's room by various party members. The conversation flowed freely for the next two hours, various dignitaries dropped by our table, and Wayne Shorter agreed to do the overdub.

There are now only two things that I recall really clearly from the conversation with Joni. One is that she said that I looked like Bud Cort, the actor from *Harold And Maud* (I was pathetically flattered by this not-obviously-flattering comparison). The other was that I gave her directions to the patisserie that had supplied the beautiful pastries for the party, telling her the buses to catch, which – as was pointed out by incredulous friends – was a fairly huge misreading of how Joni Mitchell would travel around town.

In the early-morning hours we all stumbled out of the club together, saying our fond farewells under the streetlights of the West End. And needless to say we dined out for years on the brief encounter – to the point where many friends thought twice before mentioning Joni's name.

Part Four

Singing Clear Notes Without Fear
(1978–1988)

Joni Mitchell Meets
Don Juan's Reckless Daughter

Wesley Strick, *Circus*,
2 March 1978

Nineteen-seventy-eight is a watershed year for Joni Mitchell; *Don Juan's Reckless Daughter* (Asylum) is the superlative singer-songwriter's tenth album; its release marks the tenth year of her association with 'personal manager' Elliot Roberts.

While last year's European tour was cancelled on account of exhaustion, sources close to Roberts claim that Joni 'just may' play the States in '78. But whether Our Lady of the Canyon opts for seclusion or the road, her new deluxe double-set crowns a decade of ambitious record making.

She was born Roberta Joan Anderson in 1943 in Fort Macleod, Canada. Her early inspirations, like those of Jackson Browne and Linda Ronstadt, were drawn from the well of folk music. Like them, she travelled the folk festival and concert route during the early and mid-'60s. Primarily she began as a songwriter, only incidentally plucking a guitar and singing her tunes. In those days it was virtually impossible to get anyone to 'do' your songs. So you sang them yourself.

Curiously, it was the opposite of this formula that became the foundation for Joni's recognition. Married to American folk singer Chuck Mitchell and then divorced, she continued to ply her trade in the States while, almost without effort, other performers began to include Mitchell material in their programs. Among others, Tom Rush and Buffy Sainte-Marie recorded Joni's 'Circle Game' in 1967. Buffy's version, with its rockabilly background, became a hit and listeners began to wonder about the name behind the song. In 1968, Judy Collins' version of 'Both Sides Now' sold a million copies. Joni was poised and ready for public acceptance as a performer in her own right.

And circumstances were in her favour. Buffy's manager, Elliot Roberts, was so taken with Joni's presence on stage that he left his management position to devote himself full time to her career. He signed her to Reprise Records in 1967 and then, when he joined with partner David Geffen, brought her to Geffen's fledgling label Asylum.

Joni eventually settled in LA's fashionably rustic Laurel Canyon where, for many years, she shared the company of peers Crosby, Young, Nash, Browne and assorted Eagles. Most of the material for the series of albums that followed, though gathered through her travels, was formulated there.

Don Juan is an all-studio double – but, at just under an hour, it runs only six minutes longer than 1977's stunning *Hejira* single LP. *Don Juan* is only one song bigger than *Hejira's* nine, *but what a song*: the seventeen-minute autobiographical epic sprawled across side two, complete with full symphony orchestra, called 'Paprika Plains': 'I would tie on coloured feathers and I'd beat the drums like war . . .' Joni sings, forecasting side three's 'Tenth World', the pop poetess's first instrumental track, a conga jam featuring ace Brazilian percussionist Airto Moreira.

There's much more: an all-rhythm (cowbells, congas, shakers, snare drum, sandpaper block) back-up on 'Dreamland', Joni's gem-like contribution to Roger McGuinn's 1976 *Cardiff Rose* LP. Mitchell's rendition evokes her '75 *Hissing Of Summer Lawns* set, with its startling 'Jungle Line' track courtesy of the warrior drums of Burundi.

'Jericho', on the other hand, is a straight studio remake of the delicate tune that Joni debuted on her live *Miles of Aisles* package with Tom Scott's L.A. Express. Here, drummer and sometime lover John Guerin is the only Express holdover, cooking with the likes of Weather Report's Wayne Shorter on sax. Report veteran Jaco Pastorius, who shared bass duties with Max Bennett on *Hejira*, defines *Don Juan*'s moody sophistication with a haunting, single-handed vibrato.

Around Elliot Roberts' office, they're calling *Don Juan* 'Joni's best album in years,' adding that 'she's grown from the jazz proficiency of the Express to the sheer virtuosity of Weather Report.' And, more to the point, '*DJRD* was the highest FM add-on the last week in December.'

Three months and 'lots of money' in the making, *Don Juan* assumed many names – including 'some really long, weird ones that nobody remembers' – before taking its title from 'the song with the ankle bells'. According to a studio assistant, Mitchell decided, mid-session, that she really needed ankle bells for 'tempo and atmosphere'. Long-time engineer Henry Lewy put out a frantic call, with no luck. 'Finally,' the assistant laughs, 'somebody came up with a dancer named Alejandro Acuna. They dimmed the lights, stuck her on a little stage and ran the tapes. I think they got her from the Screen Actors Guild, actually. But she is a real Indian.'

Real Indians – the North American kind – tend to recur ('they cut off their braids and lost some link with nature') throughout the lyric, as do Black Men, mostly pimps with dizzy, adoring White Broads. All three prototypes figure on the cover photograph – and all three are Miss Mitchell in degrees of disguise. 'Norman Seeff took a bunch of pictures,' tut-tuts a friend, 'and Joni happened to like these the best. So they cut 'em up and stuck 'em on the sleeve.' What the friend fails to mention is that, among her ten album covers – all designed by Mitchell, who once studied at Alberta College – *Don Juan* may sport her most provocative image. Joni goes Jolson: how could it miss?

It couldn't. Between her professional family of Roberts, Lewy, Steve Katz, David Geffen and what *Billboard* calls 'her steady legion of fans', Joni has carved a comfortable, serious and significant niche in the barracuda-heavy record biz. Her smoky, folky jazz will always make money for Mitchell and Asylum, even should *Don Juan* take a tailspin in the year of 'You Light Up My Life'. But what's she like to work with, this auteurist who hires orchestras, handles graphics, disdains the press and rarely performs? Is Joni a sublime Barbra Streisand?

'Believe it or not,' the studio assistant swears, 'she's always running around hugging and kissing everybody between takes. She's real affectionate, isn't temperamental because she surrounds herself with friends and pros. There's always David Crosby hanging out, and Henry Lewy getting skinny. Joni doesn't have to be "demanding", either, because she always knows exactly what she wants.' Pause. 'And she always gets it.'

The Underdog Meets
Joni Mitchell

CHARLES MINGUS FINDS A NEW VOICE

Ben Sidran, *Rolling Stone*, 28 December 1978

'This is a very dramatic life lesson,' says Joni Mitchell. 'It's a great opportunity to study a classical form and to breathe new life into it.'

The 'dramatic life lesson' is the album on which Mitchell is collaborating with legendary jazz bassist/composer Charles Mingus, 56, who, according to sources close to him, is fighting amyotrophic lateral sclerosis (a.k.a. Lou Gehrig's disease) [known as motor neuron disease in the UK], which is usually terminal.

Mitchell's album, as yet untitled and, she says, about half-finished, features her lyrics set to six tunes Mingus wrote for her and two Mingus chestnuts ('Goodbye Pork Pie Hat' and 'Self-Portrait in Three Colors') that Mitchell selected. Mingus was present at some early New York sessions that will not be used; the bulk of the album work has been done in Los Angeles, with Herbie Hancock on Fender Rhodes piano and Weather Report's saxophonist Wayne Shorter, drummer Peter Erskine and bass guitarist Jaco Pastorius.

Mingus either will not or – because of his illness – cannot be interviewed at this time. (His management tries to minimise the severity of his condition, and says Mingus is 'vacationing and visiting friends'. Those who have worked with him over the last year, however, confirm that he is gravely ill.) Ironically, Joni Mitchell, who rarely grants interviews, is more than willing to talk about the project.

Mingus, already 'reclusive with the illness', as Mitchell puts it, sent word in May this year that he was interested in working with the singer-songwriter.

'Originally,' Mitchell explains, 'he had an idea for T. S. Eliot's *Four Quartets* to be read, a symphony playing one kind of music and a small combo – an acoustic guitar, maybe myself, and a bass player doing an overlay of another kind of music. He wanted a formal, literary voice reading T. S. Eliot and he saw me coming in as the colloquial voice of T. S. Eliot. In the tradition of the Baptist church, they have a reader reading the Bible in the old way and somebody translating it into the colloquial.'

That project never got off the ground. 'I got the T. S. Eliot book,' Mitchell recalls. 'I called him back and said I couldn't do the project because, first of all, I would rather distil the Bible than T. S. Eliot.' She assumed this was the end of the working relationship, but weeks later received another call from Mingus. 'He said he had written six melodies for me to set words to. He called them "Joni One", "Joni Two", "Joni Three", up to six.'

Mitchell flew to New York to meet Mingus and hear the music for the first time. 'He has a reputation for being a very violent and ornery person,' she says, 'but I seem to like those kind of people. I always suspect that there's a heart beating under there that's very sensitive, which turned out to be true. He has a wide emotional spectrum. Our relationship has been very sweet.'

The ironies of this unique student/teacher collaboration will undoubtedly be more apparent to Charles Mingus' fans than to Joni Mitchell's. Mingus' reputation in the music world is based not only on his musical virtuosity but also on his unrelenting criticism of whites. He hasn't simply been voluble on the subject; he has been volcanic. To think that now, so late in Mingus' life, his music will be heard in hundreds of thousands of homes interpreted by a leading white female pop singer is perhaps the ultimate twist to an extremely stormy career.

Born on 22 April 1922, Charles Mingus grew up in Watts, a few miles from downtown Los Angeles, where he spent most of his first thirty years. Although he studied bass with a classical musician – H. Rheinschagen, formerly with the New York Philharmonic – his Baptist church upbringing and his studies with a music teacher named Lloyd Reese appear to have shaped his ideas most profoundly. Reese, a legend within the Watts community, taught his students formal composition, but he also insisted that they consider all the world as musical and include natural sounds – birds, animals, street noises – as part of their conception of music. Mingus, of all of Reese's students with the possible exception of Eric Dolphy, seems to have taken this lesson most to heart.

His first gigs in Los Angeles included work with Louis Armstrong and Kid Ory in the early '40s, but after some pressure from his friends, Mingus left the old-timers and became part of the bebop vanguard. His career as a bass player advanced steadily during the '40s, particularly after he did some West Coast gigs with Charlie Parker. But Mingus' first fame came as a leader and composer after his move to New York in 1951. He led a series of experimental combos, which included players like Thad Jones, Teo Macero, J. J. Johnson and Kai Winding, and in the late '50s he established the revolutionary Jazz Workshop.

In the workshop, Mingus led various aggregations of handpicked players through exercises in spontaneous combustion, drawing on such diverse sources as the gospel church, Yiddish, Spanish and Arabic music and adding literary and historical references. He ignited this mixture with a volatile personal style that often seemed more newsworthy than the music itself. Mingus fast developed the reputation of being a genius who either freed a player's spirit or busted his jaw. Or both.

'A lot of people didn't understand the concept of the Jazz Workshop,' recalls drummer Dannie Richmond, one of its earliest members and a man who has performed with Mingus across three decades, from 1957 until the latter's retirement from bass playing nearly one year ago. 'Mingus always insisted on rehearsing, even on the gig. People thought he was "out" doing this: stopping the band, explaining something to a musician onstage, starting over again, maybe even stopping again.'

Perhaps it was the way Mingus did it: swearing at players, even putting his bass down to push the pianist aside and physically demonstrate the proper voicing of a chord. Musicians didn't seem to mind, but the press had a field day.

'There wasn't any bullshit in Mingus' bands,' recalls Richmond. 'Musicians would always be on their very best. I saw a lot of musicians get opened up through him. They'd come into the band afraid to venture out and try new things, and over a period they'd stretch out.'

Even an abbreviated list of just the horn players who were schooled in Mingus' bands is staggering: Booker Ervin, John Handy, Eric Dolphy, Roland Kirk, Jackie McLean, Benny Golson, Jimmy Knepper, Clifford Jordan, Charles Mariano, Jerome Richardson, Ted Curson and George Adams.

Mingus developed an organic approach to leading these musicians through the labyrinths of what he called his 'extended form' compositions. He preferred to sing parts to players rather than write out even a basic chord chart: he made musicians rely on their ears and musical memories rather than on their eyes and intellectual capabilities. The result was an emotional brew that was often thematic in structure. One early composition, a 1956 piece called 'Pithecanthropus Erectus', was a half-hour excursion that retold the story of proto-man in music rather than words.

During the '50s, the accepted jazz formula was either straight-ahead bop or west coast cool jazz. Mingus' accelerating and decelerating tempos and his multiple horn players' bending notes and shouting responses to Mingus' chants (what Richmond calls 'moanful-type ingredients') brought a whole new dynamic and emotional range to the music.

Equally important in Mingus' music was the sound of protest. 'In the beginning, the race thing was daily, every day,' says Dannie Richmond. 'Going to a gig, we would stop at a restaurant and couldn't go in to eat. We would go around to the back and get some food. And we *had* to eat, man. But it got to Charles so badly that he said, "Okay, you all eat, but I can't." And so when Mingus had the excuse to get back at the people he thought had done all of these injustices to him and other black people, he took full advantage of it, each and every time it presented itself. When he wasn't doing battle with them in person, then the music was the vehicle. That was the protest part.'

While Art Blakey and Horace Silver and their Jazz Messengers made hit records riding the wave of what was then called soul jazz, Mingus remained known only to a relatively elite audience. He continued to lead various permutations of the Jazz Workshop in the first half of the '60s, but the audience for jazz, especially 'protest' jazz, was dwindling. And in retrospect, it appears that Mingus' refusal to be fashionable and ingratiate himself with 'important people' on the music scene – the A&R men, the press, the agents – only furthered his deepening obscurity. As time went on, he developed a more and more negative reputation and became an oddity, an eccentric, and was less and less marketable.

Mingus entered a period of semi-retirement in 1966. He didn't record again until 1970; instead, he worked on his autobiography. He was treated briefly at Bellevue hospital in New York for depression and exhaustion. He wasn't sleeping, and he told friends that he had perfected the art of 'just looking at himself in the mirror and just wishing he would die and doing it long enough so that he got to the point where he could see himself leaving his body'. He even boarded up the windows to his apartment because he found it was 'easier to leave himself' that way.

Mingus' records continued to circulate the marketplace, but mostly as cut-outs. His two landmark CBS records, *Mingus Ah Um* and *Dynasty,* and his best work on Atlantic, such as *The Clown* and *Mingus/Oh Yeah,* as well as the bulk of his work on Impulse, which included some of his best recordings with Eric Dolphy, all disappeared from the shelves. And his LPs on Candid, which had distributed Mingus' own Debut label, seemed to evaporate from the stores so fast that they were more like rumours than recordings.

In 1972, he went to Europe for some brief engagements a year after his long-awaited autobiography, *Beneath The Underdog,* was published. The, book, which Mingus had been writing for almost twenty years, contained very little information about his musical career, focusing instead on his sexual excesses and his on-and-off associations with pimps and whores. It, too, failed to make much commercial headway.

But at least Mingus was back and performing again in the early '70s, if not with his old fire. In 1974 Dannie Richmond told me, 'Mingus is sad, man. He's drug [sic] about the things he's been the innovator of – other people are getting the credit. Mingus is saying that he's seen it all, done it all. I'll ask about certain records we'll hear on the radio and he'll just say, "Oh, I did that," and name a date, a time and the sidemen.'

In the mid-'70s, Mingus and Richmond put together a critically-acclaimed band that recorded several albums for Atlantic (*Mingus Moves* and *Changes 1* and *Changes 2*). Each album barely sold 15,000 copies.

'Even people at Atlantic weren't listening to it,' admits Raymond Silver, currently Atlantic's East Coast head of A&R. 'People here felt he wasn't giving them the product they needed, and little by little his albums started getting lost.'

It was Silver's involvement with Mingus, starting in 1976, that began to turn the situation around. 'I did it slowly,' Silver says. 'People said, "If you can get him to listen to you, you have accomplished a great deal." So I went to see him at a club one night about two years ago. He was eating an apple, cutting it with a knife. Dannie Richmond was there. He was offering Dannie slices. Mingus' wife said, "Charles, this is Raymond Silver from Atlantic. He wants to help." He ignored me. I was standing there for half an hour and he didn't acknowledge me. Later, somebody was talking about music and I came out with an intelligent remark. Mingus looked straight at me and offered me a slice of the apple.

'So I talked to him. I said, "Listen, I'm a young man. I listen to your music, I have some ideas, so if you want some help, here I am."'

One of those ideas was for Mingus to record with a large group of contemporary big-name players, including sessionmen like Randy and Michael Brecker, as well as Larry Coryell, Sonny Fortune and George Colman. Further, suggested Silver, why not use *three* guitars? He added Phillip Catherine and John Scofield to the list. 'Just before the album came out,' Silver says, 'he sent me a telex from Brazil, saying he didn't like the album, but I could put it out anyway if I thought it would sell.'

The LP, released in 1977 as *Three or Four Shades of Blues*, sold well over 50,000 copies, Mingus' best-selling record ever. It received five stars in *DownBeat* and, more important, it received airplay. 'For the first time,' says Silver, 'Mingus crossed over. They were playing Mingus music on the radio again! It surprised us. Even Mingus.'

And then, suddenly, tours were cancelled and Mingus became reclusive again. News trickled out that he was not well. In fact, it was serious – *very* serious.

'My mind couldn't accept it,' recalls Richmond. 'Always, through the years, when we got together, we would give each other a big hug. This time he was sitting and when I extended my hand, ready for our embrace, I noticed that he could hardly bring his hand to mine. Still, I refused to believe it.'

Biding time, Atlantic released *Cumbia and Jazz Fusion* in early 1978. 'Cumbia' was a long piece left over from the previous album and the flip side was a soundtrack to an Italian movie that Mingus had recorded earlier with his working band. Album sales were disappointing, given the success of *Three or Four Shades of Blues*. So when Silver got news around then that Mingus was feeling somewhat better and was actively composing again, he jumped at the chance to record a follow-up to the original session.

Mingus said he had an idea for an extended suite called 'Three Worlds of Drums' which would incorporate the entire history of drumming, from the backbeat through swing and into free jazz. Mingus and Silver settled on a format, which included a forty-piece orchestra and employed most of the players from *Three or Four Shades of Blues*, plus such jazz luminaries as Lee Konitz and Pepper Adams, and using drummers Joe Chambers and Steve Gadd along with Richmond. At times, both Eddie Gomez and George Mraz played bass.

'Mingus didn't play,' admits Silver, 'but he was there through the whole recording. He was sitting in a wheelchair, conducting, yelling, "No!", "Yes!" I mean, his spirit was right there.' Recorded last April and tentatively titled *Me, Myself an Eye*, the LP is scheduled for release in January 1979.

———

After those sessions, Mingus first contacted Joni Mitchell and the two agreed on a plan of action.

'Initially, he just gave me the melodies,' Mitchell says, 'and it was my job to set words to them. I asked what each of the moods suggested to him. The first one, he said, was, "the things I'm going to miss". There's some hope that he will live, though it's a long shot – but at that point, I don't think there was any hope. He was preparing to die and he was in a very reflective state. His wife turned to him and said, "Oh Charlie, you know you've done everything." He looked at me and in that look I knew that no matter how much you've done in a life, when you're confronted with the possible finality of it, there are a million things you've left undone. So I simply became him in my imagination and wrote what he would miss.'

But how could she know these things?

'I cut myself off from everything and meditated on it,' Mitchell says. 'And I have a very powerful imagination. It's not too hard for me to imagine myself in his position. We all have some things in common, experientially. And there are things in common musically. We both have a broad range of feeling. And there's a literariness to his writing. And within his idiom he's an eccentric: some of the eccentricities are parallel to mine.'

Does she feel the collaboration is primarily a nostalgic effort or is it part of her own current direction?

'It seems to me that art forms are passed over and disposed of too quickly,' she replies. 'Music like this [Mingus' music and bebop in general] has more power than a decade in it. I think there's still a lot more to be done. I mean, there weren't a lot of great lyrics in that idiom, that's for sure – the singer was kind of the low man on the totem pole. And in some ways, rightfully so, because the horn is imitating the human voice and the singer is then imitating the horn and doesn't have the technical advantages of the horn.'

How does she write lyrics for that kind of music, then?

'I'm like a jeweller. I have a piece of metal and I'm setting stones into it. And yet when the things are finished, the result is a very liquid kind of lyric, where word for word it suits the inflections of the notes and seems completely natural.'

Has it been difficult to adapt her singing to the style of Mingus' melody lines?

'It's melody with a lot of movement to it,' Mitchell concedes. 'It's a different kind of breathing. And, ironically, it's a more natural form of music for me as a singer than my own music because you have such creative liberty within the bar. In rock'n'roll you're hitting tight to the downbeat and you don't have a lot of space for musical freedom. And a rock'n'roll singer is wide-throated, with a lot of scratch to the voice, a lot of volume and really strong, simple rhythm. My instrument is better at a moderate volume, using the dynamics of range, phrasing and slurring and holding straight lines. Like Miles [Davis].'

What was it like to work out Mingus' compositions with Herbie Hancock, Wayne Shorter, Jaco Pastorius and Peter Erskine?

'Our sessions for this project have been very free,' Mitchell says. 'It's almost like an *Our Gang* movie. There've been thrills of different kinds along the way, but nothing like this. Coming together with these players over this music, it's like a handicap has been removed.'

Add one more musician liberated by the music of Mingus. Permanently?

'I think so. Definitely. After this, rock'n'roll is like a metronome.'

―――――――

And what of Mingus?

Most probably, he will never play again. Perhaps, through his enormous inner strength and the ministrations of the various holistic approaches he's enlisting, he will survive his ordeal. The odds, however, are not all that good.

The final irony, of course, is that his recorded work is about to flourish. Even now, his old labels are preparing reissues and when Joni Mitchell's album hits the streets we can expect a flood of Mingus' music to surface.

'I'll tell you this,' says Raymond Silver. 'There's a new interest in him over here at Atlantic. They are interested in pushing him with ads. Everybody's concerned now about when the new album's coming out and how great the cover looks, things like that. Even if he, God forbid, passes away, Mingus will still be here.' [Note: Charles Mingus died on 5 January 1979 in Cuernavaca, Mexico.]

Review of *Mingus*

Sandy Robertson, *Sounds*, 30 June 1979

NOTE: The second sentence of the second paragraph was amended by the writer to correct garbled text that existed in the published version. The words 'Laurel Canyon whimsy, but she sold records via catchy tunes and concise lyrics that avoided her . . . ' originally read as 'Laurel Canyon and concise lyrics'. Also the phrase 'black classical music' was wrongly printed as 'black classic music'. – Ed.

If intention automatically equalled success, then this would be one hell of an album. As it is, it's beautifully recorded, self-consciously precious, a maddeningly white attempt at blackness. Wolves howl and worlds sprawl in these 'audio-paintings'.

Of course, Joni has never really known what's good for her. Her early albums occasionally became victims of critical salvos for being cute, dippy, Laurel Canyon whimsy, but she sold records via catchy tunes and concise lyrics that avoided her campus-girl folkiness by virtue of hooks and sharp observation, like 'Big Yellow Taxi' and 'Both Sides Now'.

In the last few years, mainly subsequent to her live history book *Miles of Aisles*, Joni has lost her little-girl-with-big-acoustic appeal and has pared her increasingly mature physical appearance with a move towards a looser, jazzier style. The trouble with the idiomatic logic that goes on in her head is that Joni still sounds as if she should be singing folk songs in coffee houses: technically perfect, but lacking in abandon. Too nice to be nasty.

The present album is the result of a collaboration between Mitchell and famed black jazzman Charles Mingus, which the latter didn't live to see completed. Five of the six songs are Mitchell's words married to Mingus's music, the other being an all-Mitchell composition.

The liner notes reveal how much Joni held Mingus to be some kind of mystical black saint figure; the typical dizzy white people's view of black people, the stupid idea that they're privy to some inner secrets that us poor honkies will never understand. She talks of him 'laughing at me dog-paddling around the currents of black classical music' and the album sounds just as I anticipated it would: moaning acoustic bass, strangled Mitchell guitar and her slight vocals, her meaningful watercolour phrases: 'Dangerous clowns/ Balancing dreadful and wonderful perceptions'.

Interspersed here and there are tapes of Mingus, talking about this 'n' that, an attempt at injecting poignancy as he jives about his own death. Joni says that she cut each song three or four times; combine that striving for perfection with the services of the likes of Herbie Hancock and Jaco Pastorius and you get a too-clean machine.

Joni's cover paintings have more intensity than the music. There's even a list of the musos who played on the sessions that didn't make it onto the album: Tony Williams, Stanley Clarke, John McLaughlin ad infinitum. Compare Mitchell's album with that of her pal Neil Young – straight off the mixing desk, that's the way to capture the fire. Only the sad 'Sweet Sucker Dance' approaches truth, an obvious one at that.

I find no illuminations on this record – it's merely pleasant, something one wouldn't expect after reading the Mingus autobiography *Beneath The Underdog*, a book filled with rough, violent, vibrant images of crude sex and self-mythologising. Mingus was an artist, but he was always a bullshit artist too.

When Mitchell gets anally retentive the only difference is that she doesn't seem to realise she's doing it, from 'The Dry Cleaner from Des Moines' to her interpretations of 'Goodbye Pork Pie Hat', through 'The Wolf that Lives in Lindsey' and 'A Chair in the Sky' – oh, that reverential tone! Thankfully, Mitchell and Mingus never got round to their proposed musical version of the work of that arch-wanker T. S. Eliot.

The title of one song here tells it all: 'God Must Be a Boogie Man': Joni Mitchell the little white girl in awe of the big black man. Ultimately, in art as in life, that's the stuff of which disappointment is fashioned. Sincerity is the one virtue *Mingus* holds on to.

Review of
Shadows and Light

Ian Penman, *New Musical Express*,
27 September 1980

L ike a *Rolling Stone* picnic or something more in touch with these
headachey contemporary days? *Shadows and Light* is, like
1975's *Miles of Aisles*, a double live album slide show – sliding
from past to present, sketching evolution and revolutions, travels
and emotions.

In the five years separating *Miles* from *Shadows*, the mercurial
all-American (or Canadian) girl has moved on, sometimes drasti-
cally, progressed through four albums and an array of metaphors.
She hasn't worked a way forward in the backward, somnambulist
manner of some old peers who also started the(ir) 'trip' in the '60s;
Shadows ends with 'Woodstock', but it isn't a spot she has returned
to in order to settle down.

Mitchell, I'd say, can be precisely set against such tired old
troupers as Dylan and Young – the former has well and truly
settled down in the righteous heart of today's middle America as a
sold-again Christian soldier and Neil is the same ol' rock'n'roll
conservative, rusty as all get out.

Where the boys' muse has snoozed off in some tattered and homely hammock, gently rocking out a limited series of pat phrases – by now all but meaningless through repetition and reputation – Ms Mitchell has expanded all her ranges, often to excess. In the more disciplined and deluxe Mitchell catalogue we find contradictions and movements stolen from a number of genres, from Torchy to more archaeological avenues – *recherché du vamps perdu!* She's in love with certain subjects and it's not at all true that the favourite one is herself. America and Love are the primary mythological reservoirs – and Travel links them, land in land: States of mind. There's seldom heard the maudlin self-inspection so rightly associated with the singer-songwriter club.

Pull down the blinds. *Shadows and Light* is – with the exception of 'Woodstock' and a frothy 'Why Do Fools Fall in Love?' – a list of the last five years, overlapping *Miles of Aisles* through the inclusion of one song from *Court and Spark* ('Free Man In Paris'): after that, we get three from *Hissing of Summer Lawns*, five from *Hejira*, one from *Don Juan's Reckless Daughter* and three from last year's *Mingus*.

So it's on to the perennial ponderable: what joy – bar the fanatic's – in a two-record live set? If this is a 'documentary', should we edit out all the drifting and skidding? Sometimes, is probably the answer. *Shadows and Light* is sometimes lazy. No matter how 'tight' a musician is, how necessary is it to solo (for so long)? God made little green ECM labels for those kinds of things.

There are points where the skid and drift are irresistible. Where Mitchell's vocal changes course – off cue – and takes the long way round a phrase, letting technical control over phrasing slip up on a moment. The same thing – improvisation kept under control – can be said of the musicians she employed, which were Jaco Pastorius (bass – the best he's played for a while and no solo!), Don Alias (drums), Pat Metheny (guitar), Lyle Mays (keyboards) and Michael Brecker (sax).

There are points where they don't steer so clearly – where 'Black Crow' dives into Don's solo and 'Amelia' bumps into Pat's, for instance. I could really have done without sides three and four entirely, as it happens – but then I'm just a borderline case: my heart only goes as far out as the jazzy blonde in her.

Shadows and Light is a trail of clues, a blaze of sights seen, an on-the-road exhibition of her favourite (?) bits and pieces. She keeps on being busy, she's pretty pithy, she's often lousy. But more like a strolling player than a rolling stone . . .

Shadows and Light is Mitchell for memory. Blonde or blind spots.

Review of
Wild Things Run Fast

Dave Zimmer, *BAM*, 3 December 1982

Joni Mitchell's in love. At least she was while writing and recording *Wild Things Run Fast*. You can hear it in the loose and easy nature of her vocal performances and the generally hopeful, positive music and lyrics.

Sure, Joni makes her usual references to romance's darker sides ('Since love has two faces – hope and despair/And pleasure always turns to fear' from 'Moon at the Window'); more often, though, she gets positively giddy ('Yes I do – I love you! I swear by the stars above I do!' from 'Underneath the Streetlight') and blissful ('No demands/Just pleasurable sensations/Hand in hand' from 'Man to Man'), but it's been a while since she openly bared her heart in her music.

After *Court and Spark* ('74), Joni started looking outward rather than inward, and got more daring with her music, sometimes abandoning familiar song forms in favour of unorthodox, experimental jazz pieces, especially on *Don Juan's Reckless Daughter* ('77) and *Mingus* ('79). This was very engaging stuff, but also often difficult to fathom – unless you sat back and really studied the words and flowed with her curling, sax-like vocals. *Hejira* ('76) was closer to the ground, filled with hollow-body electric guitar lines over Mitchell's lyrical journeys across dreams and human lives, but there was a certain detachment, more reflection than personal insight. *Shadows and Light*, Joni's 1980 double live album, served as a coda for this period, with bassist Jaco Pastorius, guitarist Pat Metheny, keyboardist Lyle Mays, etc. caressing and carroming around Mitchell's vocals. Beautiful sounds, but still, Joni's fans in Peoria were waiting for more 'accessible' tunes.

On *Wild Things Run Fast*, she sails back into striking pop-jazz-rock territory, but without diluting her muse. If anything, she broadens it and uses more of the colours on her musical palette. The title track burns into gear with a blistering Steve Lukather electric guitar rhythm (it's kind of jolting the first time through), then cruises and percolates underneath Joni's swinging vocals. There are clear *Court and Spark* echoes, her cover of '(You're So Square) Baby I Don't Care' matching the reckless frivolity of 'Raised on Robbery' and the chorus in 'Solid Love' harking back to 'Help Me'.

There are still plenty of Mitchell jazz strokes on the LP – seductive, personal ones, expertly interpreted by bassist Larry Klein, saxophonist Wayne Shorter, synthesist Larry Williams and drummer Vinnie Colaiuta. 'Be Cool' scats along rhythmically with a lazy, Marvin Gaye-esque feel. 'Ladies Man' pumps and swirls, with Joni vocalising *à la* David Crosby. And on 'You Dream Flat Tires' (containing Joni's most obtuse lyrics on the record), criss-crossing dissonances set up a playful, conversational exchange between Mitchell and Lionel Richie.

There is a tremendous quotient of youthful exuberance on this LP. Joni addresses the issues of ageing and the passage of time with a shrug instead of despair. She recognises in 'Chinese Café' (fused with some lyrics from 'Unchained Melody') that 'we're middle-aged' and 'nothing lasts for long'; but she sings the lines without a trace of urgency. She just gets dreamy. And during 'Love' (including biblical passages from Corinthians II:13), Joni examines her emotions of love. Ah, Joni, may you stay in love forever.

The Dream Girl Wakes Up

Kristine McKenna, *New Musical Express*,
4 December 1982

I used to love Joni Mitchell's music, but I stopped listening to it once I realised The Dream that girls get raised on wasn't good for me. I can't say that I've replaced it with a better dream, but that one was a definite dead end and it was all I was hearing in Mitchell's music. So, around 1972 – after *Blue* – I shifted my allegiance elsewhere.

Then, over the next ten years, while I wasn't watching, Joni made some drastic revisions in her telling of The Dream. Her thoughts on the white-picket-fence happy ending became increasingly convoluted and oblique and a lot more interesting.

One of the major stars to emerge from the '60s, Mitchell was the quintessential folk-rock old lady of the Woodstock era; her persona as a sweet beauty on a quest for spiritual growth sent her reeling in and out of ill-fated romances.

Simplicity and candour were limited qualities in the Dylanesque '60s, and Mitchell's confessional writing style coupled with her imaginative melodic ear yielded some of the most popular standards of the folk-rock canon. An exquisitely controlled vocalist capable of yodelling octave leaps, Mitchell accompanied herself on exotically tuned guitars. She sounded unique and pretty so that when her debut collection of dainty warblings from the battlefront of love come out in 1968, she was an instant star. The sunny childhood of Mitchell's career culminated in 1971 with *Blue*, considered by many to be her finest work. Although she scored three hit singles with her 1974 release *Court and Spark*, she'd already begun to tinker with the lucrative song formula she'd perfected and was edging out of the glaring pop spotlight and into the world of jazz.

Her music began to stretch out and took on more air and space. Structurally her albums evolved from being collections of songs into fluid, interwoven symphonic compositions with a cinematic feel; ethereal music embellished with ethnic rhythms and flourishes of jazz, floating around a loosely sketched storyline.

Her melodies were now fragile hothouse creatures that required special handling to survive. Her contemporaries stopped covering her compositions, because who else could sing them? Her voice, too, had become so elegant and rich it was downright air-conditioned.

This phase began in 1975 with *The Hissing of Summer Lawns*, Mitchell's last album to reach the Top 10. The musical equivalent of a story by Ann Beattie, *Hissing* was an essay on the spiritual bankruptcy of America's upper-middle class and a work of jarring disillusionment. The wide-eyed lass of the '60s who'd penned such anthems of hope as 'Woodstock' had clearly seen a lot in the intervening years.

Mitchell's involvement in jazz deepened, while the cynicism she expressed on *The Hissing of Summer Lawns* subsided into just plain weariness on her next albums, *Hejira* and *Don Juan's Reckless Daughter*, which dealt with escape, lost innocence and the parched purity of the American Southwest.

Mitchell completed her transition from pop singer to jazz vocalist in 1978, when she collaborated on an album with jazz great Charles Mingus that was his last work prior to his death in 1979.

Gone rambling across the musical map for nigh on seven years, Mitchell had let that white picket fence get a mite run down and had completely estranged herself from her early fans. Joni, we hardly knew ye, they moaned. Mitchell's new album *Wild Things Run Fast* should help quiet the grumblings of fans who've been anxiously awaiting her return to the pop song format. It's easily the most mainstream record she's done in years, including a vocal duet with Lionel Richie and a version of Leiber and Stoller's '(You're So Square) Baby I Don't Care', which has been released as a single. She's presently in the midst of preparing for an extensive tour – her first in three years – which kicks off in Japan in February, takes her through New Zealand, Australia, Europe and concludes in America in mid-'83.

As Mitchell herself puts it, she's most definitely 'back in the harness'. I interviewed her one afternoon at her manager's office on Sunset Boulevard. Expecting a cool, aloof rock star, I was pleasantly surprised to find a warm and open woman of impressive intelligence. Mitchell admits that The Dream didn't turn out to be as simple as we'd once hoped but, even better, she laughs about it.

Yes! Joni Mitchell, legendary for her incurably sick heart, actually has a terrific sense of humour.

Kristine: *You have a reputation for being reluctant to meet with the press. Why do you dislike being interviewed?*

Joni: There are many reasons. First of all, the form doesn't bring out what I feel are the most interesting parts of me. I'm full of vignettes and stories but it takes the associative process that's at work in a conversation to bring them out. In an interview you're fielding questions about ideas and feelings that you probably haven't thought through and your initial responses aren't always accurate. Then you're held to these improvisational comments that are often very stupid. And the relationship between the interviewer and interviewee is sometimes kind of like a trial. I don't know what kind of peer group pressure journalists are subjected to, but it seems they often look on the celebrated person with animosity. You feel like you're going into enemy camp, as if it's a heavy competitive sport or something and you've got to be on guard all the time – which obviously doesn't lead to a very good exchange.

I've been in this business a long time and have noticed this recurring pattern that goes: if nice things were said about you last year, then this year it's your turn to get attacked. I happen to be at the point in the cycle where I'm due for nice things.

As I recall, your last record, Mingus, *got fairly good reviews.*

They were mixed. There was a lot of controversy around the record, which is good. The European press and the jazz press seemed to have a fairly good understanding of it, although some jazz circles thought it was presumptuous for a white woman to work with Charles, who had a reputation for being racist – which wasn't true at all. He was just outspoken about black problems.

The pop press didn't know what to do with the record so they either ignored it or treated it as some kind of breach of orthodoxy, as if I'd been a Catholic and suddenly became a Baptist. They called it pretentious and [used] a lot of the kinds of adjectives that imply, 'Don't you *know* what you are?!' It just seems to be human nature to typecast. Friends even do it to one another, so it's not just the press or record buyers. For an artist, once your audience realises that change is part of your style, they assume an attitude of, 'What will he do next?' – and then you're home free.

I think that finally, after fifteen years of making records, people have adjusted to the fact that I change and my changes are more comfortable now.

Many people see your music as being very much intertwined with the myth of Los Angeles. Has LA played a prominent role in shaping your style?

No more than New York has. There's a lot of New York mythology in the songs too. I was living in New York when I made my first albums and that environment inspired many of the songs – 'Chelsea Morning', 'Marcie'. I hadn't quite gotten hold of that city's wavelength at that point and it was a period of disenchantment for me. Plus, New York's self-esteem as a city was at a low ebb then.

Do you think there's any truth to the clichés about Los Angeles?

It's definitely true that the city suffers from a lack of community, but the geography here doesn't allow for that. And, yes, it is a rather indulged, spoiled place, but there are good people here too.

What do you see as the recurring themes in your music?

Well, there's ecology, although I did throw cigarette butts out the window the other day so I have no right to talk [laughing]. Of course, the anatomy of the love crime is my favourite subject. There are many kinds of love and there doesn't have to be a victim for it to be love, but the big hurt and the big pay-off seem to be the most popular form of love. I think that's just a bad habit this culture has, because there are cultures where love doesn't work that way.

Your music is sometimes described as being introspective to the point of moroseness. Is that a fair assessment?

Most of my writing has dealt with the inner landscape, and we're living in a time when a lot of people have become numbed-out adrenaline addicts. I write about personal, inner intricacies and people who prefer not to deal with those things probably do see my music as depressing. I think depression is generally misunderstood, though. I hate to get poetic on you, but it's sort of like winter and is necessary for further blooming.

Do you have to be in a winter state of mind to write?

It helps, because if you're rolling along having a real good time you're less likely to put yourself in the isolation that writing demands. I admit that I am an overly sensitive person. I have a kind of loud antenna and sometimes I pick up too much, to the point that it becomes chaotic, but I don't see myself as a melancholy person. My wonder is still intact and I laugh a lot. There's certainly plenty in life to make us sad and pensive, though. This is kind of a weird anti-climax to the industrial revolution we're living in!

What aspect of your career have you found most difficult?

I love the behind-the-scenes processes and go willingly to a canvas or recording studio, but it is hard for me to work up enthusiasm for touring and doing interviews. So I guess I find the more public aspects hard.

Has fame forced you to lead an insulated life?

No, on the contrary. But then, that's kind of a hasty thing to say. Fame does cause you to get very unnatural responses from people. Somebody will call you an asshole in a public place, then someone tells that person who you are and they light up like a Christmas tree. I receive an inordinate amount of affection, which is a lovely thing, but sometimes, depending on your own undulating patterns of self-esteem, it can be terrifying. If your self-esteem is at a low ebb and you're being showered with affection, it seems out of whack. It's like someone you feel nothing for telling you they love you. It's a weird feeling.

I was very maladjusted to fame in the beginning and it's taken me ten years to learn to deal with it. It was easily the biggest upheaval in my life and when it first hit, it was so extreme that when people looked at me I wanted to shrivel up. I just couldn't get used to people sucking in their breath when I walked by. But I insist on my right to move about the world, and I go a lot of places by myself – as a writer you have to.

Every few years I take off on a long car trip by myself and I encounter people in little restaurants in the boonies who know me, and I'm as capable of being comfortable with that as they are. My relationships really sort of depend on how comfortable the other person is with my career. If they're too impressed by me, what usually happens is [that] the first time I show any signs of being human they're disappointed and they attack! [Laughing]

You know, one of the things that attracted me to the jazz world was the fact that a lot of jazz people didn't know who I was and there was no phenomenon surrounding me there – I found that delicious. I also like the fact that the jazz world allows you to grow old gracefully, whereas pop music is completely aligned with youth.

In reading past interviews you've done, I got the impression that you considered jazz to be the superior form compared with pop.

I have to admit that *Nefertiti* and some of Miles Davis' romantic music is something I've always revered and looked to as 'the real shit'. To me it had incredible contours, depth, whimsy – it had everything. Miles had the full musical talent: a gift of composition, shading, emotion, everything was there.

At the time when that music came into my life, pop was in a formularised, simplistic phase. It had fallen into the hands of producers and been packaged for commerce and a lot of it was very sterile. Of course, that happens to every musical form at one time or another, and then a temporary messiah comes along and revitalises it. The Beatles brought new blood to rock'n'roll after a very bland period, and punk brought some new textures in as well. Punk interested me as an act of revolution, but its strength was in social rather than musical ideas. I keep hoping that something musical will flower out of it.

You once commented that Lambert, Hendricks, and Ross' The Hottest New Sound in Jazz *was your* Meet The Beatles – *the first music that completely thrilled you. What was it about that music you found so appealing?*

It just had a sassiness and dexterity that I loved. People talk about punk having an attitude but that music *really* had attitude! It was sophisticated, wry and it just really swung. The harmonies were so far out I'd sit there thinking, 'Wow! How can they do that?'

Did you grow up in a liberal bohemian atmosphere?

Not really. I recently went home to this sort of class reunion and met a man I didn't remember as a child but who lived across the street from my best friend Frankie. Frankie was a piano prodigy who could play the church organ when he was seven years old and I thought he was just splendid. He and I were the only artists in what was basically a real jock community.

This man I met never liked Frankie and wouldn't play with him when they were kids, and at this reunion he said to me, 'You know, you and Frankie were the only creative people in a town where everyone threw balls and stones.' So, liberal? No.

Have there been pivotal episodes in your life that shaped you as an artist?

Yes. I was an only child, I had a lot of childhood illnesses and we moved a lot. You can see in early pictures of me that I started out as an extroverted, hammy kid. But a number of moves, then polio, scarlet fever, chicken pox bordering on smallpox, nearly dying with measles – all that isolated me a lot. Every summer all the kids that threw balls and stones would hang out at the lake, but my family would pile into the car and drive someplace like Minnesota.

Do you see your new record as a step back in the direction of pop?

I don't see it as a step *back*, but rather as a synthesis of a lot of things I've done. There is a return to rock-steady rhythms which I'd abandoned for a while simply because I was sick of the backbeat, but I think the music is quite progressive. And there is still a lot of jazz in the vocal phrasing.

What sort of rules and boundaries do you set for yourself when you work?

During the making of an album I become sort of musically narrow-minded, yet open at the same time. I'm kind of hard to please because I'm looking for something fresh that I haven't heard before, but I can't ask for it because I don't know what it is – yet.

I like to hear every musician play with a ripe, blooming personality rather than lock them into a military drill. The records are very much a collaboration between myself and the musicians I work with. A musical talent is a complex thing and there aren't many people who have all of its facets. There are players who have power, dexterity and technique but perhaps aren't aware of subtleties in structure. Or maybe they don't listen to the lyrics and play licks instead of moods, and I'll have to lead them to shade the song in a particular way. Generally I'm very pleased with the new record because I think the musicians did play more than just notes.

What sort of things do you keep in mind in laying down a vocal track?

Unless a song means something to you, you're not gonna get any magic, and that's all there is to it. I have an acute sensitivity to false sexuality or false emotion in a voice. Moans and groans are okay if they're stylised to the point of parody but if it's trying to pass itself off as real heart it usually just seems like bad acting.

Do you think most people have a finely tuned enough ear that they're able to detect that kind of falsity?

Yes, I think people hear music more comprehensively than they know but it varies how much a person will connect what he senses intuitively to his intellect. For example, on *Shadows and Light* there's a spot where twenty-six voices are overdubbed and they're all tangled up together. One of the voices was really out of tune but the way we'd worked up the piece made it impossible for us to correct it. David Geffen came to hear the song at a playback and when it hit that note he noticeably started as if a doctor had hit his knee to check his reflexes. After the thing was over I asked him if he'd heard a sharp note and he said, 'No'. I told him your *mind* may not have heard it but your body did!

You've always managed to get by producing your own albums. Is producing an overrated skill?

I once tried working with a producer on a song for my second album and it nearly broke my heart. He was so fussy about his sound that if I closed my eyes and swayed off the microphone he had a fit. The guy was constantly hitting the button and he made me a nervous wreck. David Crosby did produce my first album but he did it with the idea that he'd keep producers off me. For the most part, producers are spirit-bruisers. They're formula people who usually only know what's been before. They hire a player for what he's played before, and I don't want a musician who recycles old licks. It's not going to thrill me unless he comes up with something that surprises him too.

What step in the music-making process is most likely to prove the undoing of a record?

Cocaine. There are entire albums that would probably be different if that drug didn't exist. Cocaine seals off the heart and creates a very intellectual mood. It takes all your energy out of your spine and sends it right up to your brain.

Your records are sometimes described as being cinematic. Do you think that's an accurate description?

Yes, I think they do have that quality. I should preface this by saying that I think of the album as a modern form comparable to a symphony or sonata. Most of today's serious musicians aren't going into classical music, they're getting into the popular recording industry, so I think it has to be taken seriously.

As far as the cinematic qualities in my music, there's one technique in particular that I use that's sort of like sticking clips of old newsreels in a film. For instance, in 'Harry's House', a song on *The Hissing of Summer Lawns*, I inserted a passage of 'Centerpiece', which is an old Lambert, Hendricks and Ross song. On the new album there's a song called 'Chinese Café', that includes bits of 'Unchained Melody' and 'Will You Love Me Tomorrow'.

Does the idea of having hit singles still interest you?

As we were making this album we found ourselves saying, 'Gee, that sounds like a single.' But I really don't know what a single in 1982 is. I'm interested in musical trends, so I listen to the radio a lot and most of what they play reminds of that banal spell in the early '60s when music went through a very anti-intellectual phase. I really think that Bobby Dylan and that movement, we did our part in growing up the American pop song but I don't find much deep thought in the music on the radio right now. And by deep I don't mean it has to be down – there isn't even much wit in current popular music.

I know you're presently very involved in your work as a visual artist. If your career as a painter took off, would you be content to leave music in the past?

I'm there already. I've always considered myself a painter first and a musician second. My main drive is to paint, and since I turned this record in I've had no desire to pick up an instrument. When I made this album I wanted it to be my swan song, because in a way it summarises everything I've got to say about love. It was to be my last record for Elektra but as it turns out, it's the first of five records I'll do for Geffen Records – and there are days when I regret making that commitment.

David's pretty good with me, though. We're friends – we lived together for a few years. He knows I wanted to quit so I don't think he'll pressure me. But I'm sort of like a good girl in that when I make a commitment I pressure myself and I told him, 'Look, if I sign up for five years I'll be back under the harness and I'll make myself do it.'

Why did you make that commitment if your heart is in painting?

Out of some kind of obedience, I guess. There is some logic to the decision, though. The new album is good and has the potential of reaching a lot of people and I haven't made an album too many people could relate to in a long time. So the idea is to get a lot of mileage out of it and then I can afford to drop back.

Does it frustrate you that you're known as a musician rather than as a painter?

No, because I haven't come into my talent as a painter yet. I've been painting all my life but I haven't reached my stride and the work is really just beginning to ripen.

Will your career in pop work for or against you in trying to break into the fine arts world?

Basically, I've got two strikes against me. First, a woman has to be twice as good as a man to make it in the art world. Second, coming into the fine art world from the pop field, you've got dilettante written all over you. My friends in New York have told me that if I show my paintings in Los Angeles first, I'll be categorised as a movie star painter like Henry Fonda or Red Skelton, who paints clowns.

Are you looking forward to touring again?

I'm look forward to touring but I'm dreading the rehearsal. I don't remember anything! I don't even remember the titles of some of the songs on the new album. The past is the past. My manager Elliot Roberts gave me a pep talk the other day: 'Run, Joan! Swim, Joan!'

He says that when you're pushing forty you have to run back and forth like Mick Jagger. I told him to just push me out in a wheelchair and I'd do the whole set sitting down.

Who is your audience now? What sorts of people do you expect will come to the shows?

Elliot tells me that most of my audience is dead already! [Laughing] I expect that kids who are unfamiliar with my music will make up the bulk of the audience for these concerts, because there seem to be large numbers of kids turning out right now to see the old guard perform before they croak!

What sort of show do you plan?

I don't know – maybe I'll just go out there and throw paint at a canvas and hum.

You seem to be in a pretty good frame of mind about the tour and things in general.

Yeah, I think I'm learning to accept life. You just get up every day and try to make the most of it. Hopefully you'll see or feel something in the course of that day that makes it worthwhile. There have been times when I feared I might be done in by the conflict around me but I think that the major crises of my life are behind me now. And every time I flirt with one of them again, I get the dreaded feeling it's going to latch on and stick to me but it never does. This isn't to imply that I've solved anything, because nothing is ever dealt with and done with and human beings are always in conflict. And for an artist, to run away from conflict is the kiss of death.

Review of Show at Jones Beach Theatre, New York City

Wayne Robins, *Newsday*, 26 July 1983

During the course of her unpredictable but resilient career, Joni Mitchell has been the dewy-eyed sophomore, the slit-eyed hipster, the clear-eyed visionary. Her songs of innocence and experience have taken her from strum-along 1960s coffee houses to collaborations with the late Charles Mingus, one of this century's most indomitable jazz composers and bandleaders.

Each incarnation seems effortless, and that was the case Sunday night at Jones Beach when Mitchell and a four-piece band played straightforward rock with a direct and seamless roll. Of course, when Joni Mitchell plays rock'n'roll, it's not always of the conventional, kick-'em-in-the-solar-plexus variety. On the opening song, 'Coyote', the playing was fluidly graceful. Each line ended with stinging little burrs of sound, enhancing the long-breathed melodies that clung to the shaggy-dog logic of her lyrics.

Both her 1973 standard, 'Free Man in Paris', and 'Cotton Avenue', from the aptly-titled 1977 album *Don Juan's Reckless Daughter*, did have an uncharacteristically blunt-edged hard rock approach. For a moment, one thought that Mitchell's band – bassist Larry Klein, drummer Vinnie Colaiuta, guitarist Mike Landau and keyboard player Russell Ferrante – had been woodshedding with Def Leppard.

The jazz attitude and phrasing that has given Mitchell's rock its Tiffany touch returned quickly. 'You Dream Flat Tires' was vigorously up-tempo, but Mitchell retained the sly, impressionistic delivery that made the song such a standout on her recent *Wild Things Run Fast* album.

The bridge to what might be more precisely defined as jazz was easy to cross from that point. 'God Must Be a Boogie Man', composed by Mitchell in her 1979 tribute to – and partial collaboration with – Mingus, showed traces of some of the master's kinetic swing. Klein took the spotlight, playing bass as if it were lead guitar and delivering the most perceptive and propulsive individual instrumental performance of the night.

Mitchell's band wasn't always as delicate, and the most memorable parts of the show were those performed by Mitchell alone or with the band in a more passive frame. She performed 'Big Yellow Taxi', still the most lucid and flinty song anyone has ever written about ecology ('they paved paradise and they put up a parking lot') accompanying herself on electric guitar. Her tough chordings evoked a latter-day Eddie Cochran.

A second set after intermission rocked just as surely. Mitchell oldies such as 'Help Me' and 'Raised on Robbery' were balanced by rock standards such as Leiber and Stoller's '(You're So Square) Baby I Don't Care', initially recorded in 1957 by Elvis Presley, and a churning encore of 'I Heard It Through the Grapevine'. Mitchell may be conscious of growing older – her reading of the poignant 'Chinese Café/Unchained Melody' was both brittle and bittersweet – but her passionate artistry shows no sign of abating.

Review of *Dog Eat Dog*

Helen Fitzgerald, *Melody Maker*,

23 November 1985

S o Joni's discovered the beguiling (and it seems inevitable) attractions of the Fairlight computer now, has she? But don't worry, all
you purists, she hasn't gone electrobop all of a sudden: the synths
merely add a precision and some background shading to that distinctive style of poetic confessional/analytical narrative that warms
the cockles of a romantic nature.

Thomas Dolby (who seems to be spreading his considerable talents around a diverse catalogue of artists) co-produces and plays on
this, on which Don Henley, James Taylor and Rod Steiger (as a mad
Evangelist) also guest. Sentimental she's always been – emotional
and instinctive responses are her inspiration – but *Dog Eat Dog* is
less of an introspective journey and more of a disenchanted vision
of the '80s by a saddened '60s idealist.

She's ditched the recent jazz preoccupation for more classic
Mitchell, meandering and full of warm inflections with a
contemporary instrumentation. 'Fiction' casts a sad eye over
media-influenced imagery ('elusive dreams and vague desires
fanned to fiery needs by sexy boys in flaming TV fires'), 'The Three
Great Stimulants' decries the pressures of fast-lane society, while

'Tax Free' is rich with sarcasm for those Moral Majority evangelical preachers, censors of free expression who line their own pockets in the name of Christianity.

A Song Near the
End of the World

Adam Sweeting, *Guardian*,
14 December 1985

'**I**'m a lucky girl,' sings Joni Mitchell in a song from her four-teenth and latest album, *Dog Eat Dog*. She has staying power too. In 1970 Graham Nash wrote 'Our House' about his life with her, while her own song 'Woodstock' celebrated the high tide of hippiedom. Nash still sends her flowers on her birthday and attended her wedding to co-producer and musician Larry Klein in 1982.

Maybe it's something about Canada, but Mitchell, born in Alberta and raised in Saskatchewan, shares a capacity for survival and change with her Canadian contemporary Neil Young. Lately, Young has headed back to the country and developed an inexplicable fondness for Ronald Reagan. Joni Mitchell had headed the opposite way. Her new songs are sophisticated but accessible, and are the first she's released since her LP *Wild Things Run Fast* three years ago. They reflect varied cultural, social and political concerns.

'Neil and I were similarly affected by things and yet had opposite reactions,' she reminisced, in London to promote the album. She was dressed in a long red cardigan, dark trousers and a beret, appropriate clothes for a woman committed almost as much to painting these days as she is to music.

'We have so much in common – we both come from the Canadian prairies, we both had polio in our right leg and our back in the same epidemic in 1953. We made our exodus from the prairie to Toronto, which was the music city at the time, at approximately the same age – he's a little younger than I am. We both ended up in California, where I introduced him to Elliot Roberts, who was my manager and who became *his* manager.'

Mitchell is far from being the breathless, giggly folk singer who made her recording debut in 1968. For ten years or more her music has owed as much to jazz as to rock. Most of all, it hinges around her singular and personal conception of melody and harmony.

'I made a shift into jazz out of necessity,' she explained. 'I had two choices, either to continue to play by myself or to play with jazz musicians, because rock'n'roll musicians could not hear the voicings that I used. To them, they were weird chords, they couldn't understand them, and what they would play against them would kill off the internal harmony. Finally someone said to me, "Joan, it's apparent that you're gonna have to play with jazz musicians," so I started searching around in the clubs. Even they found the music quirky.'

She describes her musical evolution as 'an intuitive process – idiot savant,' phrases typical of her oblique imagination and slightly ornamental vocabulary. When she talks, it's as though her mind is shuffling several possible answers and sifting out the most appropriate choice, which is not always easy.

Pressed on the subject of her new song 'Tax Free', an alarming investigation of America's right-wing evangelists with a spoken narration by Rod Steiger, Mitchell's descriptive powers are taxed to the utmost.

'Reagan feels that Armageddon is inevitable and it's dangerous when you have a president who thinks that way since he's the one who can call for the pushing of the button. He sees himself in his personal drama, I think, increasingly as a religious leader and he has public lunches with some of these very powerful evangelists, Pat Robertson and *The 700 Club*, for instance. In other words, you have the Church stroking Reagan and saying, "Yes, yes, aren't they saying nasty things about you, they must be communists. Therefore they threaten both you and me. Don't you think we should silence these communists from speaking?"' She laughed, high and nervously. 'This is my vision. I get like a zealot. It's scary to me because it threatens freedoms of mine.'

She's convinced that rock music can, indeed must, make a stand against a moral majority keen to impose restrictions on it. 'There's one preacher in particular who beat into his congregation that rock'n'roll was the devil. Why are they making it an enemy? Because it still has a voice. Well, then, let it be a worthy foe. Suddenly I felt a responsibility – use it or lose it. There's a definite battle going on here, and people's rights are at stake and the diversity that America always promised is being threatened.'

Her attitude to rock's great crusades of the last year, against famine in Ethiopia and apartheid in South Africa, is less impassioned and more equivocal. Her song 'Ethiopia' questions the way the West treats that country as a problem 'over there', rather than as part of a growing ecological crisis which threatens to engulf the entire planet.

'This, to me, is the issue of unification. It concerns everybody, so further isolation by drawing religious barriers at a time like this and creating more friction when we're all in the same ecological mess seems to me a very short-sighted obsession.'

Mitchell was invited to contribute to Little Steven's all-star 'Sun City' recording but declined when she discovered that the original 'Sun City' lyric singled out her friend Linda Ronstadt for having performed in South Africa.

'I know Linda played there in all innocence, being an apolitical creature who felt that art should cross any border. I'm not opposed to that point of view. I don't see her as having committed any great crime, and yet they would have crucified her in this verse, which tastefully they left out in the end. Y'know, when we start with hunting among our own peer groups . . . '

Stars, of course, have the luxury of choice in these matters. Joni Mitchell may go on tour in 1986, or she may stay at home and try her hand at writing short stories. 'Right now, I'm at an epic part of my life where I'm remembering things from way back that I may not remember again, and I wonder if ten years down the line this kind of thinking will occur again. Perhaps it's the time to capture them.'

Review of
Chalk Mark in a Rain Storm

J. D. Considine, *Rolling Stone*, 21 April 1988

Back when Joni Mitchell first began to make a name for herself as a singer and songwriter, what appeared to matter most about her music was the words. Sure, the melodies were important – she was a songwriter, after all, not a poet – but they always seemed secondary, merely a framework for her energies and the ideas of her lyrics.

As Mitchell has grown older, however, the assured priority of words over music has slowly reversed itself; what is being said in her songs has become less important than *how* it is being said. This shift in emphasis can partially be chalked up to her flirtations with jazz – it's kind of difficult to keep the focus on Joni Mitchell when the title proclaims *Mingus* – but for the most part, her shift in focus has less to do with musical style than with an attention to form, as she wrestles with music itself in an attempt to make the form of her songs as telling as their content.

Ambitious? You bet, and as *Chalk Mark in a Rain Storm* makes clear, it does have its merits. It isn't simply that her wordplay is unusually clean and concise; she's finally found a credible means by which to merge literary devices with musical ones. 'My Secret Place', for instance, uses its duet format and the similarities between her voice and Peter Gabriel's to illustrate the shifting confidences of shared intimacy, swapping lines or pulling back into separate verses as the balance within the relationship wobbles and shifts. 'Lakota' goes even further, building its cadences off the rhythms of a native-American chant to lend Mitchell's lyrics an almost folkloric cast.

Still, those aren't the sort of qualities anyone is likely to notice without concentrating some, and that's indicative of the album's Achilles' heel. *Chalk Mark* may have its strengths as a piece of songwriting, but melodic accessibility isn't one of them. Mitchell has no trouble setting up a hypnotic catchphrase strong enough to hold a song together, but she doesn't seem quite up to matching that construction with an equally strong melody line. As a result, the verses to 'Number One' and 'The Tea Leaf Prophecy' come across almost as afterthoughts, as if they'd been sketched in over the painstaking rhythm bed.

Unsurprisingly, the album is at its most confident when Mitchell reworks existing melodies, as in her eerie resetting of 'Corrina, Corrina' within 'A Bird That Whistles' or her subtly stunning remake of the cowboy classic 'Cool Water'.

To her credit, the sound of *Chalk Mark* is slick and enticing, with Mitchell making the most of her wide-ranging musical guests (the most unlikely and effective being Billy Idol, who growls engagingly through 'Dancin' Clown'). Alluring as its surface is, this album doesn't invite repeated listenings; in that sense, *Chalk Mark in a Rain Storm* is all too aptly named, for its pleasures simply wash away with time.

Joni Rocks Again

Ben Fong-Torres, *Chatelaine*, June 1988

Joni Mitchell was a folk star in the '70s, ignored in the '80s when she turned to jazz. Her new album, which tackles everything from Yuppie materialism to environmental destruction, has a slick rock gloss that is putting her back on the airwaves.

Joni Mitchell sits behind the wheel of a brand new, black Mercedes-Benz 560 convertible, and she is not happy. She's in this car, a rental, because her own car has just been stolen.

Mitchell feels as if she's lost a pet or a best friend. The car was a Mercedes-Benz she called Bluebird. She bought it brand-new in 1969, with her first royalty check from Warner Bros. Records. It was beautiful, powerful, a survivor.

Now she's got to contend with this new car her management company has leased for her and which feels . . . not quite right. On our way to a photo shoot for *Chatelaine*, she's jerking along the street until she discovers the brakes are on. We consult the manual to find the brake release.

We do, and Mitchell gets rolling – for about three hundred metres. She pulls over. Both the left- and right-turn signals are flashing. A parking attendant from a nearby restaurant pops up at her side. 'Oh, sorry, we're not going here,' a flustered Mitchell tells him. 'We're having car trouble.' She locates the signal switch. 'We're back in the flow,' she says, as she pulls out. 'We're back in the flow.'

She could be speaking about her career. In the last decade, it's been a series of stops and starts. Now, she hopes, with her new album, *Chalk Mark in a Rain Storm*, she is back in the flow again.

An hour before our joyride, she had been in the Hollywood offices of her managers, Peter Asher and Barry Krost, chain-smoking Camels and doing press interviews. Dressed in a simple black suit by Comme des Garçons, her blond hair defrizzed and once again draping her shoulders, the 44-year-old Mitchell didn't look so different from when I had seen her last, in 1969. She had one album out then and she had just settled in Laurel Canyon, folk-rock's answer to Beverly Hills.

Her early albums – *Ladies of the Canyon*, *Blue* and *For The Roses* among them – are still remembered by millions for their witty, whimsical, literate and true-confessional songs. After a string of snappy hit singles that gave her pop-star status in the early '70s, she embraced jazz and released the exotic and challenging *The Hissing of Summer Lawns*. Her last jazz album, in 1979, an immersion in the music of avant-garde jazz bassist Charlie Mingus, was a commercial and critical flop. Around that time, she visited Georgia O'Keeffe in New Mexico and her painting blossomed. (Mitchell has since exhibited her work twice in New York and plans a show in Tokyo this year.)

In 1982, she was back to pop and rock with *Wild Things Run Fast*. Having married Larry Klein, a bass player thirteen years her junior, Mitchell waxed romantic. But radio wasn't listening to Joni any more. *Dog Eat Dog*, in 1985, reflected her disenchantment with the American government – but the timing was all wrong. 'It was released in a rah-rah America-is-wonderful time,' she says.

For Mitchell, making albums in recent years has not equated with making money. Which explains why she hasn't gone on costly tours to push her new one and why she's spending days on end, here and on the road, meeting the press.

'The first feedback you get is with reviews,' she says, 'and my reviews for years now have been incredibly disappointing. I've done good work. Any worker in any field needs the encouragement that her work is good. Otherwise she gets another job. So, if I don't get some enthusiasm somewhere soon, I'm done in this business. It's as simple as that.'

'That sounds like something she says just prior to the release of a record, because she's expecting another barrage of criticism,' says Larry Klein. Mitchell, he says, is always coming up with new songs, and then she has to record them.

Chalk Mark has a chance, if radio's response to the track 'Snakes and Ladders', about a love affair fuelled by materialistic aspiration, is any indication. It got heavy airplay as a pre-album single release. Ed Rosenblatt, president of Geffen Records, Mitchell's label, says: 'I think we're at a time when radio's perception of Joni is that she's hip. Perhaps it's based on the older artists selling.' Last year was a great one for George Harrison.

On *Chalk Mark* Mitchell writes and sings about her parents' courtship in Regina during World War II, about war between nations; and, as a devoted environmentalist, she writes movingly in defence of the land. But the album's not all gloom and doom. It has a clean rock'n'roll sheen to it, with guest musicians like Peter Gabriel and Tom Petty, and includes an unlikely but raucous duet with Billy Idol.

The rapport she felt with Idol was the same feeling she got when rock'n'roll was born and she was Roberta Joan Anderson, an itchy kid, full of art and energy, in Saskatoon. (Mitchell, an only child, was born an air force brat in Fort Macleod, Alberta.) 'Rock'n'roll,' she says, 'was the call of the wild. It was the thing that split a generation.' She lived for weekend dances. She also got a ukelele and a Pete Seeger instruction record and, during her one year at the Alberta college of art, in 1963, sang for free in the local coffee house.

Her songwriting began in the mid-'60s, after she had migrated to the Yorkville folk scene in Toronto and formed an act with folksinger Chuck Mitchell. They married and lived in Detroit but divorced after a year as her star rose and such artists as Judy Collins and Tom Rush began recording her material. Mitchell moved to New York in 1967 and connected with Warner Bros. Records. To sign her contract, she went to California and never looked back.

In Laurel Canyon, just above Sunset Boulevard, Mitchell lived with musician Graham Nash and was, indeed, the lady of the canyon. When she became involved with James Taylor and, later, other musicians, she fuelled her notoriety, alluding to various friends and lovers in her songs. 'I'm not a kiss-and-teller,' she says. 'I never named names.' In the early '70s, *Rolling Stone* magazine published a diagram of rock stars and their various amours. Mitchell was connected to a long list of musicians, managers and media stars. She swears the list was 'padded . . . with men I barely knew – and never dated.'

Larry Klein, she says, entered her life in 1981, at just the right time. Dating had become 'nerve-wracking . . . I read a magazine article called "The End of Sex", and the thing the writer said that sticks in my mind is: if you want repetition in a relationship, see other people. If you want infinite variety, stay with one person.'

Since getting married six years ago, Mitchell and Klein have been homebodies at Mitchell's house in the Bel Air section of Los

Angeles. Says Klein, 'We're both compulsive creative types. We'll stay home and Joni will be at one side of the house painting and I'll be working on a song. Maybe later we'll go to a movie.'

Mitchell regularly sees two close women friends – neither of them musicians. 'They're women you can entrust your intimacies to without fear of betrayal,' she says. 'We meet once a week for what we call "ladies' night out" and now it attracts other women.' She laughs, thinking back to childhood friends. 'I had that kind of sorority with women when I was a preteen, just before the race for men occurred or whatever that thing is that happens between women.'

We're zipping down Melrose Avenue in the rented Mercedes, whizzing by the latest shops (Wacko) and hangouts (Johnny Rocket's). I ask Mitchell if she's ageing gracefully. 'I could do better,' she says and breaks out in laughter. Then she asks, 'Think I should get nipped and tucked?' I, of course, say no. But is she seriously considering it? 'We all thought about it after we saw Cher,' says Mitchell. 'Usually it looks grotesque and shiny and weird, but Cher's plastic surgery has *inflamed* the Hollywood community!' Mitchell laughs again, enjoying her dip into showbiz gossip.

She has no regrets about not having had children. 'The children of artists are nearly always a terrible mess. They end up being emotionally deprived.' Besides, she adds, 'The creative drive is a family in itself.'

Arriving at the photographer's studio, Mitchell apologises for wearing black. 'I'm in mourning for my car,' she says. But she's brought a bright chief's blanket that she can toss over her shoulders and cinch with silver belts, and a neck-load of Tibetan beads.

In her dressing room she discovers that the makeup artist and a woman from her management company are from Canada and the three dive happily into home-country talk, about the weather, restaurants, Mounties and dialects. 'There's that old-country accent,' says Mitchell. 'It's like,' she drops into a drawl, 'Don't forget to throw the cow over the fence some hay, eh?'

Mitchell moves into the studio, and the photographer's first few rolls capture a lacklustre woman near the end of a long day of explaining herself. But a break and quick costume adjustment later, she's a different woman. With the chief's blanket on, she brightens. Peter Gabriel's on the CD player and, long day to the wind, the stops-and-starts woman begins shuffling and swaying, smiling blissfully, as if it's a weekend night in Saskatoon many songs ago.

Part Five

Doomsday Joan (1991–1998)

Review of
Night Ride Home

Betty Page, *Vox*, March 1991

It's hard not to be daunted by the sheer quality of Joni Mitchell's back catalogue. Her recorded output stands behind her like a set of carved stone tablets, reflecting one acutely sensitive singer/songwriter's worldview over three decades. But she never appears weighed down by past achievements or worries about surpassing her own superlative standards. She just gets on and sings.

This is her sixteenth LP, the first since *Chalk Mark in a Rain Storm* three years ago, and it's a joy to hear the master craftswoman at work. *Night Ride Home*, which stylistically picks up where she left off with *Chalk Mark*, has a soothing quality which improves your inner glow with every listen. It's an intimate, one-to-one kind of listening experience in which Joni gently reaches out and hooks you in with her exquisite melody lines and that wonderful birdsong of a voice.

Much has been made of her wordplay, but don't strain too hard to catch the clever couplets; it's just as rewarding if you merely pick out the odd word, phrase or intonation. It's clear that greed comes in for a good battering on 'The Windfall' ('In this land of litigation, the courts are like game shows') and that she continues to bemoan the folly of man, using religious symbolism in the delicate but barbed 'Passion Play' ('Who're you gonna get to do the dirty work when all the slaves are free?'). The central piece, 'Slouching Towards Bethlehem', is a pessimistic view of the second coming, adapted from W. B. Yeats' poem of that name. On side two she returns to a self-analytical mood for 'Come In From The Cold' ('I am howling in the dark') but lightens up for 'Ray's Dad's Cadillac'.

Apart from her departures into jazz, Joni Mitchell has rarely altered her style: it's pure, it's clear, it's honest and sincere: just her voice, her acoustic guitar and a minimal but always effective backing. She is what she is and does what she does with consummate style and a perception that remains pin-sharp. And the bottom line is that her songs still say it all.

Lookin' Good, Sister

Mick Brown, *Daily Telegraph*, 23 February 1991

The hair still tumbles to the shoulders, sunshine-blonde; the smile is as winsome as ever; the perfect bone structure remains, well, perfect.

The hippie threads, of course, have long since gone. At forty-seven, Joni Mitchell dresses expensively, all in black, her dress studded with exquisite silver jewellery. Even the cigarettes she smokes are particular. They are called American Spirit and come in a sky blue pack and they say a lot about Joni Mitchell. For these are truly designer cigarettes, free of artificial additives: expensive. Mitchell volunteers the long and detailed explanation of the true smoking aficionado: ordinary cigarettes contain saltpetre, which makes them burn down quicker; these cigarettes last longer, but you still have all that addiction-quenching nicotine.

Joni Mitchell smokes incessantly; even as the last plume of blue smoke from one cigarette is melting in the air, she is relighting another. One sees in this a small but telling gesture of defiance. In California, smoking is regarded with the puritanical disdain of a social disease; Joni Mitchell – for many, the very personification of a certain Californian way of life (although she is actually Canadian) – doesn't care.

This lends her a go-to-hell rakishness. Mitchell's early songs depicted her as a restless free spirit; men loved her for it and women envied or identified with her. She was the neophyte spirit of the age; the author of 'Woodstock', the song of the event; the girl who was muse to rock stars, and to whom they in turn played muse themselves. How Joni Mitchell has aged is therefore of more critical concern than might usually be the case. The news, in short, is well.

The romantic tribulations charted with unabashed candour through her early albums have been stilled. The long line of suitors finally stopped at Larry Klein, a musician thirteen years her junior, whom she married eight years ago. Mitchell refers to him often, not as Larry but rather as 'my husband', with a proprietorial formality which is surprising. It is a happy marriage, a happy life. She has developed a second career as a painter and is wealthy enough to maintain four homes: one in New York, a retreat in British Columbia, a beach house at Malibu and a Spanish-style property in Bel Air. Some of her songs have become American institutions. 'Big Yellow Taxi' is sung in primary schools to teach children about ecology; 'The Circle Game' is sung at high school graduation ceremonies, and 'Both Sides Now' has been recorded by Frank Sinatra and Bing Crosby.

For someone so revealing in her songs, Mitchell guards her privacy. We met at the photographer's studio in Hollywood. Her new record, *Night Ride Home*, percolated gently, recurringly, over the hi-fi. 'Fabulous,' breathed the make-up artist. The photo session was interminable but Mitchell bore it with a stoical patience – turned it, indeed, into a team endeavour, talking knowledgeably about angles, planes of light, moods – striking poses and smoking all the while. Photography turns out to be a passion. When she is not writing or recording, she paints; when she is not painting, she takes photographs; she describes this process as 'crop rotation'.

'When I first started taking pictures,' she said, 'I liked Cartier-Bresson – that idea of pick your location and lay there and wait for the one shot. And that's made for some beautiful days; just get in the car and drive off to some spot and wait there for the action to occur, and suddenly two other bits of action you hadn't anticipated happen also. To me the thrill of life is when things turn out better than you thought. The mystery of surprise is probably my favourite . . .' – she savoured the word – 'my favourite kick.'

As an only child, growing up in the prairie lands of Saskatoon, Saskatchewan, where her father ran a grocery store, she was prone to illness and solitary by nature. She developed 'a strong inner life'. 'I spent a lot of my childhood just sitting out in the bush all by myself, watching the light come through the leaves. I always was thrilled by colour and landscape.'

After high school she attended art college in Calgary. But she left after a year, disenchanted. 'I wanted to sharpen my eye for a more realistic kind of painting, but it mistimed. When I was there, all the professors were infatuated with abstract expressionism.'

She had had a passion for language, written poetry, ever since being taken under the wing of her English teacher at the age of twelve. 'He saw me pinning up my paintings for a parent-teacher day and said to me, "If you can paint with a brush you can paint with words." But that teacher, Mr Kratzman, boy, was he hard on me. I remember an epic poem I wrote about a mustang being chased and tamed; it was very ambitious because I loved him and I really wanted him to think it was great. He said, "How many times did you see *Black Beauty*? You tell me more interesting things about yourself every week; write in your own blood."'

With Mr Kratzman's words ringing in her ears and inspired by the example of the young Bob Dylan, she took up the guitar and started writing songs and performing in local folk clubs. At this point her life took a messy turn. At twenty she gave birth to an illegitimate daughter, whom she named Kelly. Broke, struggling in her career, she put the child up for adoption. It is a subject seldom mentioned. She also made an unhappy marriage, to a folk singer named Chuck Mitchell, whom she wed after a thirty-six-hour romance. The marriage took her from Canada to Detroit, where they worked together as a duo, Chuck and Joni; it lasted barely two years.

By then Mitchell was already outstripping her husband, making a reputation for herself as a songwriter. Her work was championed by other singers, and by the time she arrived in California and recorded her first album in 1968 (dedicated to 'Mr Kratzman, who taught me to love words'), her reputation was already made.

Mitchell settled in Laurel Canyon, an enclave of artists and singers in the hills above Los Angeles. Time has imbued this period with a certain mystique; bearded troubadours, spirited womenfolk, endless sunshine – popular music's last true idyll before the rude intrusion of reality. With her flaxen hair, toothy smile and cornflower blue eyes, there was no more fragrant flower child than Joni. Nor, in an era of confessional singer-songwriters, was there one more candid, more revealing of emotional frailties. Mitchell raised candour to a high and sometimes dangerous art. *Rolling Stone* magazine once published a family tree of her most famous liaisons: James Taylor, Warren Beatty, the singers Stephen Stills and Graham Nash and record company entrepreneur David Geffen.

Mitchell betrays a certain weariness when all this arises. She has long since tired of justifying her candour. 'It was a nasty job,' she says, slipping into a tough-guy parody, 'but somebody had to do it. The songs wouldn't have had any life otherwise. If you're sitting in a bar, going into an introspective period brought on by a broken heart, then it's good to have a song to listen to. It's a comfort to people who see themselves in those songs. The only thing I find embarrassing – and this is the plight of the pop artist, really – is that it always gets thrown back at you. There's always more focus on the artist in this business than on the art.'

It must be said that the public absorption in her life has waned somewhat. The days of platinum-selling records are long gone. Like Bob Dylan and Van Morrison, her career has transcended the short-lived incendiary flash and settled into a more stately – if sometimes fitful – progress.

On reflection, the turning point came in 1979 with her album *Mingus*, a collaboration with, and tribute to, the jazz musician Charles Mingus, recorded in the last months of his life. The record was a brave venture artistically, eschewing the easy melodies of old and indulging her interest in jazz; it was also her worst-selling record ever. 'At least,' she says wryly, 'it gave me a taste of jazz obscurity.'

And yet her music has remained no less absorbing, for above all else Mitchell has remained true to herself, a trick that few of her contemporaries managed to pull off. Her music became steadily more ambitious, more demanding and, in the process, more timeless. The songs about being young and innocent gave way to songs about being middle-class, middle-aged, and the compromises, disenchantments and joys it may bring. Notably, her new record (her sixteenth [fourteen studio albums excluding *Miles of Aisles* and *Shadows and Light*]) includes one song about alimony payments ('You'd eat your young alive/For a Jaguar in the drive') and another about nostalgia. Mitchell makes no bones about writing for an audience old enough fondly to remember being young.

Perhaps the most fatuous thing ever written about her was that she was 'a flailing liberal unwilling to jump what was left of the good ship Woodstock', as if idealism were something that should be given up. Still, the accusation stings. Although she wrote 'Woodstock', the song that would, for a short while, become the anthem for the moment, a traffic jam prevented her from attending the event herself (a misfortune that turned out to be a prophetic metaphor for the whole shooting match).

The centrepiece on her new record, 'Slouching Towards Bethlehem', is a measure of the distance between those times and these, a mordant invocation of apocalypse adapted from W. B. Yeats' poem 'The Second Coming' – 'And what rough beast, its hour come round at last/Slouches towards Bethlehem to be born?' When I mentioned the song, she launched into a detailed and accurate account of the Book of Revelation (I checked later, in the Gideon Bible tucked in the top drawer of the dresser in my hotel) and its pertinence to the Gulf War as the final judgment made manifest.

'Believe me,' she said, all intensity, 'I don't want to be Doomsday Joan or anything, but all the images kind of hook up . . . ' The conversation took a distinctly pessimistic turn at this point; war, famine, the polluted planet. 'I've been struggling to warn everybody my whole career, and now it's here,' said Mitchell, earnestly – then laughed. 'My songs are just full of ecological catastrophe and romantic collapse.'

Actually, her career can be seen in another way, as a sustained attempt at reconciliation: between the desire to be a free spirit and the desire for emotional security; between a naturally cheery disposition and the vagaries of the real world; between bourgeois comfort and bohemian aspirations.

'How do you retain spirituality,' she laughs, 'and still have a nice living room? . . . I haven't solved that one but it doesn't pinch like it used to. I think you have to be balanced.' Thus, she considers herself 'a curator' of the large collection of American-Indian art she owns, 'because they're only in my possession for a while, and I have a responsibility for them'. And royalties from the songs 'Lakota' (about the plight of the Indians) and 'Ethiopia' (about famine) go to a special fund for charitable use.

One reason, perhaps, that some men warmed to her records was because they depicted a woman in thrall to the security and excitement a man could provide. Some women distrusted her songs for exactly the same reason. 'I've never been a feminist, I kind of think women should be kept in their place,' she said, though I think she was putting me on. 'But no one can keep me in my place; it's too late for me.'

Mitchell is a beguiling conversationalist, one minute displaying the earnestness of the studious child, the next a playful disingenuousness. At times she has that air of spit-in-the-palm-and-slap-the-pants enthusiasm and free-spiritedness which is one of the most endearing qualities of the American character.

She told me a story which was very revealing about how she had been walking down Hollywood Boulevard one day, looking for a costume to wear to a Halloween party, 'when all of a sudden this black kid goes by with a New York walk – you know, the diddy bop, with one leg shorter than the other and the hand curled back – and as he passed by he turned and gave me this most radiant grin and said, "Lookin' good, sister, lookin' good"' – the mimicry is perfect – 'And he gave me a grin and it was such a genuine, sweet smile; it woke up the spirit in me.

'I began walking behind him, imitating his walk; he just took me into this very fun-loving mood. And he caught me at it and laughed. So I thought, "I know... I'm going to this party not as him but as his spirit."' Outfitted with a blue polyester suit, a phallus-shaped cocaine-spoon, an Afro-wig and copious amounts of Lena Horne pancake, Joni Mitchell thus embarked on a short, but apparently riotously eventful career at parties and social functions as a black man.

I liked this story. It suggested an innocent's pleasure in the moment and a spirit of untrammelled anarchy in equal measure.

It is easy to believe that, in many ways, Joni Mitchell has attained the perfect life. She makes records at her leisure. She is as successful as a painter as she is a musician: an exhibition of her work over the past ten years was recently seen in London and Scotland, and her paintings command prices most other living artists would envy. She is at peace with herself.

'I know myself pretty well. My husband and I have been together nine years, and I like him and love him. It just gets better. As for myself . . . you know the old thing; you work out what you can change, and hopefully lighten up and laugh at what you can't.'

It was a pat response. But she said it earnestly. Then giggled, and reached for another cigarette.

Review of
Turbulent Indigo

John Milward, *Rolling Stone*, 15 December 1994

'Let me speak,' sings Joni Mitchell on 'The Sire of Sorrow (Job's Sad Song)'; 'let me spit out my bitterness.' Few songwriters could write, let alone convincingly convey, such blunt, honest language. Mitchell's words are honed by a life dedicated to the notion that songs, like all great art, can illuminate deeper truths. Plenty has been written about the rockers of the '60s hitting their fifties, but Mitchell is virtually the only female pop star to pass that mark with her artistry undiminished. *Turbulent Indigo* is Mitchell's best album since the mid-'70s and a work that is highly musical, poetic and very, very sad.

The stark, precise language of *Turbulent Indigo* will draw comparisons to *Blue* (1971), but the songs and arrangements also recall the pop-rock of *Court and Spark* (1974) and, to a lesser degree, the meditative, jazzy style of *Hejira* (1976). The sound is spare, with songs anchored by the singer's piano ('Not to Blame') or guitar ('Borderline'). It's on guitar, however, that Mitchell's a true stylist, with a technique characterised by unorthodox tunings and a strum peppered with percussive fills.

The words make the poignant melody of 'Not to Blame' sing – and sting. Consider the opening: 'The story hit the news from coast to coast/They say you beat the girl you loved the most.' It's chilling but ultimately irrelevant that Mitchell wrote this song of domestic violence before somebody slit the throat of Nicole Brown Simpson. 'Six hundred thousand doctors are putting on rubber gloves,' sings Mitchell. 'And they're poking at the miseries made of love.'

The spine-tingling 'Sex Kills' profits from Mitchell's recent work with synthesised textures. The lyrics to Mitchell's most famous songs evoke a confessional voice but here she rips horror from the headlines, blending individual crimes ('All these jack-offs at the office, the rapist in the pool') with more universal fears of AIDS and a deteriorating environment. 'And the gas leaks, and the oil spills,' she concludes, 'And sex sells everything, and sex kills.'

Turbulent Indigo was produced by Mitchell and Larry Klein, who also plays bass. The soprano sax of Wayne Shorter, a long-time collaborator, provides an emotional counterpoint to Mitchell's voice on five tracks, including the beguiling 'Yvette in English', written with David Crosby. Seal sings with Mitchell on 'How Do You Stop', a surprisingly compatible cover of a song originally cut by James Brown.

The words are brutally confidential on the closing 'The Sire of Sorrow (Job's Sad Song)'. Mitchell's background vocals underscore her lead voice – 'Man is the sire of sorrow' – like a chorus recruited from 'The Magdalene Laundries', her song about an Irish work convent for fallen women. 'The Sire of Sorrow' ends with Mitchell drawing blood with three repeats of a line that cuts to the emotional bone – 'You make everything I dread and everything I fear come true.' Mitchell knows that love hurts – her own marriage to Klein fell apart around the time she was working on *Turbulent Indigo* – and is living proof that art endures.

Conversation

Barney Hoskyns, previously unpublished,
14 September 1994

Barney: *I really like* Turbulent Indigo.
Joni: Thank you very much.

And that's not just a diplomatic way to start an interview. I think it's really great and I want to start with the last song, which must be one of the most harrowing things you've ever written.

Well, I collaborated with God, you know. [Laughs]

Tell me what else went into making it as powerful as it is.

Well, I'll tell you the catalyst for it was – I'm separated from my husband now but we're very good friends –

Is he on the album?

Oh, yes. We separated and then we began the album the next day, if you can imagine. It was tense for a few weeks. We bought kittens to put in the studio to lighten it up, and even under what should have been extremely difficult conditions we worked very well together. There was a certain amount of, I would say, normal separation perversity, like withholding of understanding – 'I don't know what you mean by that.' 'Well, you do so!' You know, that kind of silly stuff. But for the most part it was a wonderful growth experience, I think, for both of us. Klein would say the friction created a pearl. It made me lay down tighter boundaries on his playing: 'Oh, don't play like that, you played like that last time.' [Laughs] And my guitar playing had become more percussive, more orchestral.

So Klein had to play very stretched-out, minimal, and with the tinge of depression that accompanies a separation, the loss of a long-term friend – he'd spent a third of his life with me. I spent a quarter of mine with him, you know, so it shouldn't have been the most inspiring of times. I played some of the percussion myself, Indian shaman rattles and things, but still, all in all, it's fairly sparse. It's basically three guests: Wayne Shorter, Greg Leisz and Bill Dillon, who played the guitorgan, that organish sounding thing on 'Yvette in English'. And then some of the keyboards behind that are samples of Bill, what we call the 'Billatron'. The Billatron is a collaboration between Bill Dillon, Larry Klein and myself. Bill Dillon played it, Klein synthesised it, changed it sonically considerably, and then I accessed the construction or the architecture by a keyboard.

When you say that you and Klein split up the day before you went in the studio, do you literally mean that?

Moved into two houses.

Really?

Yeah. Strange way to start a project. But getting back to 'Job', Klein had gone to visit his grandmother. She had become a Christian at a certain point in her life and she was reading the Psalms. He came back and said Grandma Mary was all in a reverie about how beautiful the Psalms were and I thought, you know, 'I'm an old Bible reader from many years on the road – the Gideons in hotel rooms, you know? It makes a scholar out of you after a while.' So I thought, Gee, the Psalms, I only know the twenty-third Psalm, which is a beautiful poem. It's a strength-giving poem, doesn't matter what your religious background is: 'The Lord is my shepherd, I shall not want . . . ' You know, it's a poem I've found myself reciting when walking down dark alleys [laughs]. So I read the Psalms or I intended to, but they're right next to the Book of Job. So I took a scouring glance at the Book of Job, and then I got the St James' and the New Jerusalem and the Gideons, all three translations. It's quite a massive poem and has a lot of redundancy in it – there are a lot of lines that say the same thing slightly differently – so you take your favourite way of stating that thought from the many that are chosen in each translation.

Then I searched among them for rhymes, so I had to rearrange much of the thinking sequentially, but I don't think I disturbed the general idea or condition of this man being tried for his soul. And I think everyone in a lifetime, at one time or another, sinks to the pits – or as God says in his speech, 'sees the janitors of Shadowland'. I think it's a good life that sinks that low, because without that you don't really have powers of empathy. You may be sympathetic, which is a little shallower, but empathy, having been to the bottom, gives you the opportunity to be a more compassionate person.

I was mad – I'd had a lot of trouble, as women do with doctors, you know, and so the physician aspect, these friends of Job's who come first as mourners and then as antagonists –

'Pompous physicians', you call them –

Yeah. 'What carelessness', I think I added that. I added a little bit of personal thought sometimes, and sometimes I had to paraphrase to get a rhyme. But for the most part it's from the Book of Job, three translations, restructured.

The obvious question is how much personal experience and feeling is being vented through the adaptation.

Oh, I identify with Job completely. I played the track for an ex-LA city cop who'd had his family killed, a good cop who found something rotten within the force and wanted to cure it. Of course I identified with it. I identify with everything I write. 'I am Lakota.' I'm not a Lakota Indian, but I'm a Sami. I don't think I could write anything or sing it without understanding it to a certain degree. And I have had a difficult life, as most people have, but it has been peculiarly difficult: a life of very good luck, very bad luck, a lot of health problems, therefore a lot of contact with medical carelessness and so on. So on that level I identify. I don't think I've ever become faithless. I've never been an atheist. I can't say what orthodoxy I belong to. I'm kind of a student of religion, comparatively speaking, and I like bits and pieces of all of them.

Early in the song you talk about spitting out your bitterness. It made me think of things you've said about perceiving hate in your heart. I wondered to what extent you still feel you have bitterness in you that you want to spit out.

Oh, yeah, you've got to cleanse yourself. I mean, here's the thing: I want to be happy. Therefore I want to be affectionate and receive affection. Krishnamurti said something interesting: 'The man who hates his boss hates his wife.' And I believe that's true. If you're holding resentment or dark feelings for anyone, it carries over into your relationship, you burden them with your bitterness and so on.

The '80s were really difficult for me physically and emotionally – a lot of betrayals for money and simultaneously bad health and bad medicine. Without going into detail, the '80s were really like being a prisoner of war.

Have the '90s been better so far?

Oh, yeah. Much of it came to an end in the '80s. I think even the Yuppies noticed that goodies only make you so happy, you know. The toys aren't the answer, you know. And, you know, all of the human relationships are so malformed at this point. The heterosexual relationship is extremely malformed. We come up on it in 'Not to Blame'. Every other woman is raped in her lifetime. Generally, if she's raped once she's raped many times, because rape occurs by a brother or a father or a priest and they have access repeatedly. That's every other woman. If she's raped as a child, she will not be a well-formed adult woman.

So, you know, you have to wonder why it is that men are so frustrated that they're beating on women, why they feel they have the licence. Contemporary music is very, very full of woman-hatred. You know, I've never been a feminist. I like men's company. I never go 'Oh, men!' I might say, 'That man's an asshole,' but I don't – it's never gotten to the general with me, nor do I like the traditional directions of feminism because it's too apartheid; it's them and us, whereas my thing has always been the relationship, you know: 'Why are we doing this? I like this about your action but not *this*.' I believe in the beauty of closeness across the barrier of difference, be it man-woman or across the barrier of race.

I was very struck by 'Not to Blame'. Apart from anything else, it seemed to empathise with the lot of womankind in a way that I can't recall any of your earlier songs quite doing.

No, because I'm more of a companion to men; I'm a tomboy. So, you know, as I get older I have more women friends. And also the thing between the man and the woman has gotten so out of line, especially in pop music, between the maltreatment of doctors, most of whom as a group seem to be woman-haters, and the popularity of rap, which came out of the pimp's tradition of 'My bitch is badder than yours'. I mean, in America wife-battering is a national pastime: the day the hospitals are spilling over with bleeding women is the Rose Bowl game. So violent sports and wife-battering are synonymous.

There's a huskiness about your voice now – and a sense of vulnerability that's very moving on this record. How do you feel about your singing at the moment?

I'm finally developing enough character in my voice, I think, to play the roles that I write for myself. Like, 'Cold Blue Steel and Sweet Fire' I could probably sing better now because it's about the seduction of heroin. I never did heroin but I was around people who were doing it. There are some songs that I think that I was miscast in, in that I performed them as an ingénue. Even 'Both Sides Now', which was one of my first songs I wrote when I was twenty-one, I think it's better sung by someone in their fifties or sixties reflecting back on their life.

Sinatra did it, didn't he?

Oh, but poor Frank, though. They gave him this terrible arrangement that was all wrong for him. And on the album cover he has his hand over his face and he's sitting on the curb. I felt for him. I wish he'd sung it like 'It Was a Very Good Year' – in his own genre rather than trying to make a folk-rocker out of him. [Laughs]

You sang 'Woodstock' at the Edmonton Festival. What have your thoughts been about the anniversary hype this year?

Oh, it's silly.

Yeah?

Yeah. [Laughs]

Before Edmonton you told an interviewer you hoped people wouldn't use you as a 'sentimental journey'.

Well, I understand how that is. Usually people get intensely involved during their courtship years, which generally speaking for people is in their youth. And all their best years are wrapped up against that music and those times. And they tend to listen to music less and less as they get older, right? But I'm a maker of music and I have a painter's spirit, really, more than a musician's spirit and I like pioneering. I like to keep moving forward rather than getting stuck in a regurgitating situation, you know, where I'm painting the same thing over and over. I don't want to become a duty player, as Miles Davis would say.

Is there any kind of justification for the Stones or the Eagles heading out on the road yet again?

I don't know. People think we make a lot of money out there. I was out for nine months the last time I toured. I made $60,000, less than my roadie. The artist is the last to get paid when you take a big show. I heard the Eagles made a lot of money, but the gross and the net is an entirely different animal. I want to make money this time out. I've never been money-motivated but I never understood my finances. Unfortunately, I'm no longer ignorant and I've been burned a lot, so this time I'm going to try and make some money. Looking at it on paper, it's very difficult. By the time you pay your lawyers and all the people that have a piece of you and your overhead, there's not that much left. Unless you get a sponsor. And who's going to sponsor me – tobacco companies?

How do you look back now on the folkie years? John Martyn said that, for him, the problem with folk was that it didn't swing. Do you agree with that?

Well, I don't know. I swing, but then I'm not really folk.

Yeah, but when you look back on the first two albums, there wasn't a lot of swing there, was there?

But see, I was born in a swing era and I was a rock'n'roll dancer before I became a musician. Well, first of all I studied classical when I was a child. My playmates were classical child prodigies, 'cause they were the only creative kids where I came from, right? So my first musical love was classical music, and then rock'n'roll was born. And I had polio. I was paralysed, I had to learn to walk again. As Neil Young did.

Right, there was a big outbreak, wasn't there, in Canada?

Right. I had my legs taken away and then when I got 'em back, by God I danced my way through my teens. And I think that gave me a sense of rhythm. But the first albums I made, as I began to write my first songs, were quite intricate and quite classical. My friends who only knew me as a party doll and dancer thought, What is this and where is this coming from? As I began to write, it got more Celtic, really. And even like German lieder when I added the piano back into it. And then it began to swing. Well, you know, like I say, I was born in the swing era, so I was steeped in it. Sometimes it takes a long time for your influences to show up and become your own. It's all pretty pure stuff and it just kind of bubbles up and you say, 'Oh, my God, listen to that note, that's a Tony Bennett note.' Or, you know, even people that you never really admired that much: occasionally the note will creep out and you'll say, 'Oh, my God, I've assimilated that too!' [Laughs]

Do you ever look back on famous songs such as 'Both Sides Now' or 'The Circle Game' and think how far away that girl seems now? There's something so kind of virginal and maidenly about that voice – the purity of the phrasing and the whole style.

Yeah, well, I sang 'Circle Game' as an encore in Edmonton, but I kind of avoid it because I think of it as ingénue. A lot of children learned 'Circle Game' in school. I got a letter from a boy who was twenty-one and he said, you know, 'I sang that song, "Circle Game", in summer camp year after year after year. I had to.' He said, 'I never understood it. I just turned twenty-one.' You know. It was a nice letter to receive. So that and 'Big Yellow Taxi' have become culture. It's taught to grade three-ers as a kind of a nursery rhyme. I'm very pleased. I didn't write it as a child's song but I'm very pleased to see it go into the culture at that age.

I'm more tempted to run by some of the songs that I felt maybe I never received a compliment on. 'Moon at the Window' is one, for instance, I did in Edmonton, and it was very well received. And no one ever really noticed it on *Wild Things*.

There was a review of that show by an Edmontonian who wrote about how much it meant to everybody that you went back there.

It was a sweet experience. There was a neighbourhood very close to the hotel and there were bike trails. My boyfriend, who's also a prairie boy, rented bikes and we went down to this poor neighbourhood with wooden sidewalks, beautiful little clapboard grocery stores and everything. It was still fields with wild weeds that I remember from my childhood. It's very well kept and neat, and tiny little houses, you know? We went cycling almost every day when we were there. We had popsicles at the little corner store. It was like, you know, reliving our childhoods.

The conflict between a fear of the crowd on the one hand and the temptations of fame on the other seems to be a preoccupation of some of the songs in the '70s and maybe even the '80s too . . .

Can you give me an example?

Well, I'm thinking of your being lured back to Los Angeles and –

Oh, 'I couldn't let go of LA'?

Yeah . . . and 'it sounded like applause', the sound of fame coming through the airwaves –

Well, I withdrew from society. The original cover of *For the Roses* was a horse's ass. They made a billboard of it on Sunset, a cartoon of a horse's ass with a wreath around his neck and a big balloon and a big horse grin and a balloon coming out of his mouth that said 'For the roses'. Geffen wouldn't let me use it for the album cover, but he did let me put it up as a billboard on Sunset. I was really mad at show business at that time.

I liked small clubs. I am a ham and I am an enjoyer, you know? I enjoy partying, so a club is kind of a party, it's fairly loose. But on the big stage, you know, timing is of the essence. I work in fifty different tunings, you know, so there's this interminable thing to get it right – and if I don't get it tuned right in tight, I don't enjoy myself. On the big stage your sound gives you sonic distortion. It's very hard to tune when the thing has the juice running through it. I can tune real quickly in an acoustic environment in a small room. But on the big stage you get all these overtones – it's like you're getting an inaccurate feedback. You know, standard tuning would have been easier but then of course I wouldn't have had all of that original chordal movement and, um . . . the tunings coughed up wonderful compositions.

So it's a trade-off. At a certain point, yes, I became too contemptuous of the audience. Critics seemed to praise me when I felt I was poor and slam me when I felt that I was at my peak. So that also fed my bad attitude towards the business – and especially the performance aspect. I've always loved making the albums and the writing. That's more like the painting process anyway. You know, painting and exhibiting. But the self-promotion used to be distasteful. Now it's just kind of funny to me. It's one of the beauties of getting older, you know: you have less energy to worry, you know? [Laughs]

You've said at various points in your career that you regard yourself as a painter first and foremost. Is that still true?

Oh, yeah.

What tipped you over the line towards becoming a performer?

Art school. You know, I drew and I wrote poems. I wrote poetry secretly and I drew all through my notebooks. Basically I was a poor scholar: like most poets I was a bad learner. I was always very involved in music but not in any kind of career direction. Like I say, as a dancer, mostly as a spirit-lifter. So the irony that I would become a confessional poet and a serious musician to people who knew me in my teens was kind of out of context.

Just before I went to art school, I picked up a ukulele with the intention of accompanying dirty drinking songs at wiener roasts, no more ambition than that – just for having a good time. When I got to art college there was a coffee house there and I went down to see if I could pick up some pin money because I was on a student's budget. And they were willing to pay me, like, $15 a night or a weekend or whatever it was, and that had some buying power in those days. So I spent my weekends performing and the art education was extremely disappointing to me because all the profs were fans of De Kooning and Barnett Newman and the abstractionists and I wanted classical knowledge, you know? It was not given at that time. So I was in conflict with my profs, I wasn't learning what I wanted to learn. I was making money with the music, and then I went east to hear the Mariposa folk festival and Buffy Sainte-Marie was the headliner. And in Toronto at that time there were seventeen coffee houses functioning but I didn't have the money to get into the Musicians' Union. So they wouldn't hire me.

I went to work in women's wear and I played occasionally here and there, like little hoots and things around, but Canada has a tendency to eat its young alive and they would hire mediocre Americans instead. That's the unfortunate mental sickness of my people. Once I crossed the border I began to write and my voice even changed. I no longer was imitative of the folk style, really. My voice was then my real voice and with a slight folk influence but from the first album it was no longer folk music. It was just a girl with a guitar that made it look that way. And no section could play it, it was too intricate harmonically and rhythmically. I tried for four projects to find a band and I tried things with players but it always squashed it. Finally it was recommended to me by the players I was trying to work with that I look for jazz musicians. And I found the L.A. Express and that worked well on *Court and Spark*.

If the professors at Calgary had given you the classical knowledge you wanted, you might not have ended up performing.

I would have devoted myself to painting. But then if I had not had polio I would probably be an athlete and not an artist at all [laughs]. Also, the life of a painter is very isolated and there is not much feedback. You can do a masterpiece and everyone will stand there and go, 'Mm-hmm,' and rub their chin, whereas a good song will knock somebody off the back of their chair. With my early songs, I wasn't sure what a song *was*. I used to get songbooks with 'Tutti Frutti' and all the words to the rock songs in it, and I never thought poetry and songwriting had anything to do with each other – except for Chuck Berry, who really was a kind of a folk-poet. And I loved 'Will You Love Me Tomorrow', which was Goffin and King, you know. But still that was great songwriting, not poetry.

It wasn't until 'Positively 4th Street' that a lightbulb went off in my head. Up until then, Dylan seemed to me like a Woody Guthrie clone and I was a detractor. You know, I was always in debate in the coffee houses, 'Oh, what's the fuss over?' you know; 'he's just second-generation Woody and it's kind of silly, he's a middle-class kid, you know, he's not riding the boxcars.' But then his stuff started to really come from his own blood, you know? And when he wrote that song I thought, 'Oh, my God, we can write about *anything* now.' It was just, 'You got a lotta nerve/To say you are my friend . . .' Just that one line, 'Whoa, what an opener!' So that changed my direction, and after that my songs got real, 'He said/she said', kind of like playlets and soliloquies.

You've claimed that David Geffen said that you were the only star he knew who wanted to be ordinary. Does that now seem a little disingenuous?

When I was a kid I started fads. If I did something, kids would follow suit. If I pasted stars all over my blue suede shoes, the other kids would all do it too. And in high school they gave me a column in the school paper called 'Fads and Fashions', so I played around with those games in my teens. What was the question? Focus me again.

Well, the idea that you wanted to be ordinary. Because you'd always been the opposite. I mean 'the search for higher achievement' and all that. Perhaps by a relatively young age you'd had enough of being the high achiever.

In New York, strangers on the street holler at me across the street like someone at school – you know, 'Hey! Joni! When you gonna do a concert here?' That is extraordinary but it's ordinary. They don't suck in their breath. When you were playing in the clubs, you could go down and have a drink with people and maybe even go over to their house and listen to music, you know. That's what I mean: you're not quite ordinary but you haven't lost your access to life. Right?

I guess what Geffen meant was that in some areas I need exceptional treatment, you know; it's a courtesy to offer me exceptional treatment, it's practical to offer me exceptional treatment. But in other cases it's stupid to offer me exceptional treatment – and lonely-making.

Tell me about moving back to Reprise after twenty-odd years.

I had my choice. You know, I could have given this record to Geffen and call it *Swan Song*, which I was tempted to do. But the feedback I got from everyone around me was that that would be a shame, you know? And Mo [Ostin] at Warners was very enthusiastic to have me back. There hasn't been a lot of excitement for my albums coming out but there is for this one. People are ready to listen, you know; they're ready to take something a little more to heart and mind than they have in the past. I've always been a couple of years ahead of people in my personal changes. When my records come out, people kind of dump on 'em, and then two years later they go through the changes and something becomes their favourite. But by then it's too late. The child's been bloodied on the playground, so to speak. A lot of them have been out of sync that way.

So I had to weigh a lot of things up. I really was tempted to get out, you know, and head up into the Canadian back bush and to garden and paint and get on with my life. On the other hand, I don't feel like many of my peers. I haven't hit a writer's block. If I hit a writer's block, I paint. That's an old farmer's trick – I just crop-rotate so that you never notice.

I'm over the middle-age hump, you know, with becoming an elder, but I wondered whether a woman could continue in this youth-oriented genre. As a painter you're just beginning to ripen at fifty. As a musician there's a lot of scrutiny on how you look, da-da-da-da, and it's such a shallow, fickle business. Not that the art world is any bowl of cherries – it isn't. It seemed almost economically sensible to reduce my holdings: like, you know, I have a house here and I have a house in Canada, taxes are going up, things are going up, and in this business everybody has their hand out, you know. It almost seemed wise to get out of the business, but on the other hand I did have a public voice, a somewhat rare public voice, and perhaps I was needed [laughs].

There's a kind of full circle in the fact that you're back on the label where you started, and also that David Crosby co-wrote 'Yvette in English'.

That was the first song of this collection born. David called up; he wanted me to produce him. I didn't feel I could so then he called up and asked if I had any songs. I didn't have any, so he asked if I would look at something he'd written. I paraphrased some of it, kept some lines, restructured it, set it to music, and sent it back. He recorded it first.

What were your first impressions of Los Angeles at the time that Crosby produced your first album? We're going back to the era of Mama Cass and B. Mitchel Reed.

I remember driving around up in the canyons in Crosby's car with *Magical Mystery Tour* on a good stereo. There were no sidewalks, no regimented lines like the way I was used to cities being laid out. Having lived in New York and then coming here and having trees in the yard and ducks in my neighbour's pond, the ruralness and friendliness of it was extraordinary. Two strange girls in the '60s showed up at my door and asked for sanctuary. I gave them the keys to my house, told them to feed my cats and said I'd be back in two weeks. You did things like that.

You're going to tell me they turned out to be two of the Manson girls –

No, no! But I did have some of the Manson clan in my garden, you know? There was one guy, I forget his name, but he had a parrot called Captain Blood and he was always scribbling things on the inside walls of my house – Neil Young's, too. Real cryptic things. There were a lot of weird people around.

Are the accounts of Crosby sort of showing you off to his superstar pals accurate? There's that famous Henry Diltz picture of Eric Clapton sitting there, watching you play.

I met David in Florida in a club and he came in and he loved the music. He was twinkly about it, very enthused, and his instincts were, 'I'm going to pretend to produce you but I'm not actually going to do anything.' Because at that time he was in the Byrds, he was the new wave – folk-rock was happening. So basically he was going to protect the music, because he liked it the way it was, you know? We just went in and went for the performance and I did a little bit of sweetening on it. I think perhaps without David's protection they might have forced some kind of producer on me who would try to make an apple out of an orange.

I don't think I would have survived it, because that's what happened on the second record and it was such hell. I said, 'This will kill my love for music – I'll never want to record again if I have to go through this process.' The producer, who was a hotshot, went away for two weeks and I said to Henry [Lewy, the engineer], 'Could we get it done in two weeks before he gets back?' That was the beginning of a relationship. Henry and I made thirteen albums without a producer, you know. I didn't need a babysitter, I didn't need an idea man. I worked in a focused way in the studio, so I didn't need somebody reeling me in because I was wasting time.

Review of Show at the Gene Autry Western Heritage Museum, Los Angeles

Todd Everett, *Variety*, 30 January 1995

Joni Mitchell missed a great opportunity Thursday night when she failed to alter the lyrics of one of her best-known songs to 'they paved paradise and put up a Western Heritage museum.' In fact, hits weren't the order of the day at an informal show in the Griffith Park facility's Wells Fargo theatre, broadcast throughout the nation as a promotional tool for her most recent album. The show was initiated and promoted by local triple-A station KCSA-FM (101.9), with syndication to approximately a hundred triple-A, AOR and public radio stations coordinated by Warner Bros. in-house. ('Triple-A' doesn't signify a farm team, exactly; the term stands for the Adult Album Alternative programming format).

Turbulent Indigo is the revered singer-songwriter's first album in three years and the first for Warner Bros.' Reprise label since 1971. There's a bit of a Mitchell revival afoot, with current versions of her 'Big Yellow Taxi' in release by Amy Grant and Clannad's Máire Brennan, and of 'Woodstock' by Tuck & Patti.

Mitchell didn't perform either of those or any other of her better-known early songs. Instead she concentrated on her more subtle work, with meandering melodies, literary lyrics and no perceptible hooks.

The theatre's proscenium stage was dressed to resemble an artist's workroom, the walls decorated with paintings and a stand-up cutout of Roy Rogers peeping through the window. Mitchell played acoustic guitar, sitting or standing, and proved herself a capable and charming – if nervous – host.

She chatted about her songs, the environ, and her own history as a cowboy-in-training. (Another set decoration was a stand-up cutout of herself, at age eight, dressed in Rogers' gear. Evidently Gene Autry wasn't as big in Saskatoon.)

The programme featured songs from the current album, including 'Sex Kills', 'Yvette in English', 'The Magdalene Laundries' and 'Sunny Sunday', plus earlier numbers including 'Cherokee Louise', the title track from 1976's *Hejira*, and a song called 'Happiness is the Best Facelift'. A slinky version of 'Moon at the Window' (from 1982's *Wild Things Run Fast*) was a highlight.

The use, by Mitchell the composer, of odd and different tunings for almost every number, forced Mitchell the performer to retune frequently throughout. More conventional tunings or delegating the task might have resulted in a few more songs.

Review of
Hits and *Misses*

Susan Whitall, *Houston Press,*
26 December 1996

In a pop world where female musicians are designed, micromanaged, and as carefully positioned in the marketplace as a new brand of air freshener, how wonderfully earthy and real is the art of Joni Mitchell. It's jolting to put on Mitchell's new pair of collections, *Hits* and *Misses,* and be reminded that music made by women wasn't always a thing controlled and 'spun' by male music-business professionals. It's almost painfully funny to imagine a young Mitchell collaborating with an older man on a song about a young woman shrieking at her ex-lover about oral sex. Or singing with no irony or humour whatsoever a song about God riding on public transport.

The concept is as outlandish as the possibility of finding Mitchell's work on any of the zillion radio stations that play her putative acolytes, the Alanis Morissettes and Joan Osbornes and Sheryl Crows, those lightweights who took Mitchell's feminine adventurousness and co-opted it into prefab, potty-mouth music for angry grade-schoolers.

Mitchell is our most fearless, fully realised female pop artist. And she has the quality absolutely vital in an artist – she isn't afraid of not being 'nice'. Equally important in today's pop world, she doesn't fear appearing vulnerable, isn't reluctant to strip away all emotional protections and create an album from total pain, as she did with 1971's *Blue*.

Listeners are probably most familiar, though, with the ironic, detached, chain-smoking, ticked-off Mitchell, the woman who, while known as the girlfriend of famous musicians, doesn't hesitate to eviscerate those same lovers in song. Called on this, she'll even tell you she could have – even should have – been nastier. For example, it seems that 'Carey', that mean old daddy she invites down to the Mermaid Café for a bottle of wine, was a jerk who deserved to be trashed even more. But Mitchell decided that documenting him as an irascible ex-boyfriend, a funny 'character', was more interesting.

Hits touches on all the commercial high points of Mitchell's career, from 'Chelsea Morning' to 'Big Yellow Taxi' to 'Turn Me on, I'm a Radio'. *Misses* draws more heavily on her later, jazzier meanderings, all of which were panned by the mainstream pop press, although it also includes last year's 'Sex Kills', which was as close to a hit as Mitchell's been in some time. And *Misses* also includes songs such as 'River' and 'A Case of You' from *Blue*, the album that helped several generations get over tainted love affairs. So that *Misses* name is a bit misleading.

Still, it's hard not to be drawn more intensely to *Hits*, as it captures that irresistible moment when the planets converged, the sun broke through the clouds, art and commercialism somehow coalesced, and a song from a Joni Mitchell album could crack the Top 10 (1974, when 'Help Me' from *Court and Spark* was a hit).

In the earlier years chronicled on *Hits*, Mitchell is the still-childish prodigy, sketching interesting characters, pulling literary allusions out of the air and taking one's breath away with alluring melodies and chord changes. She could always call up characters made immediately recognisable with just a line: 'Look at those losers, glued to that hockey game', as she sings in 'Raised on Robbery'. In the middle years – the *Blue, For the Roses, Court and Spark* era – things took a more personal turn. Mitchell's exquisite turns of phrase could provoke tears or sighs of recognition as she sang about being 'tethered to a telephone' and 'listening for your car climbing the hill'. They're visceral images that anyone who's ever longed for a lover can understand in their bones. And who could more eloquently snort at a lover's compliment – 'You're as constant as the Northern Star' – by coming back at him with this line from 'A Case of You': 'Constantly in the darkness? Where's that at? If you want me, I'll be in the bar'.

If there's always been a strong undercurrent of self-deprecation and toughness in Mitchell's work, it's probably the protective impulse of the wary Canadian. Much of Mitchell's bitterness may also have come from seeing her male counterparts – many with far less talent – surpass her in fame and fortune. If this were a fair world, she would be on the same level professionally as Neil Young, an artist who's also been ridiculed for some musical odd turns but whose reputation as a potent artistic force endures. While a few Young albums have been panned, he's never been as viciously attacked as Mitchell was by *Rolling Stone* when she released *The Hissing of Summer Lawns* in 1975. 'Worst Album of the Year' in a year that saw the release of two by Kansas? I think not.

Mitchell, 'as humble as Mussolini', as her friend David Crosby likes to say, often compares herself to Bob Dylan and, given how diminished Dylan has been in recent concerts, she'll get no argument from this corner. Both Young and Dylan have kept the lifeblood of their careers bubbling through constant touring. Mitchell won't do that. She rarely performs live, and this lack of generosity toward her audience diminishes her reputation. Even when she does tour, if all the celestial aspects and audience vibes aren't right, you'll see a bad Joni Mitchell show.

The artist was brought partially back into the fold this year when she won two Grammys for *Turbulent Indigo*. It's as if, with the Grammy, the music business was saying, 'Sorry, Joni, for revering Sting for using polyphonic harmonies when you were rejected for the same thing just a few years earlier. Sorry, sorry, sorry . . . '

She may have accepted the Grammy and its accompanying warm beam of inclusion with smiling grace, but if she's still the Joni Mitchell we know and love, she'll be back with a sucker punch for the music-biz weasels fairly soon, cigarette dangling from her mouth, laughing in that bitchy, sardonic way.

You go, girl.

Review of
Taming the Tiger

Stuart Maconie Q, October 1998

J oni Mitchell, let's see: born 1943, christened Roberta Joan Anderson, equine *grande dame* of American song, always enjoyed a glowing establishment consensus and so forth. Well, actually, not so. In 1975, *Rolling Stone*, in a fit of blather that makes Richard Littlejohn seem shrewd, denounced *The Hissing of Summer Lawns* – now routinely rated a classic – as the worst record of the year. In a music scene dominated by Lester Bangs, Lou Reed's *Rock'n'Roll Animal* and the Tubes, only the bravest gave their vote to the angular bohemian hi-tech jazz balladry that's dominated her oeuvre ever since.

The wing-collared shirts were out in force, though, to shower Grammys on her last album, *Turbulent Indigo*. *Taming The Tiger* finds her in better form. Jazz still exerts a shaping influence but there are other, less easily categorised forces at work. Witness the introduction to 'Harlem in Havana', where a reassuringly elegant tune emerges from dislocated noises.

Lyrically she's as skilled as ever, although even Mitchell can make too many allusions to cafés, saxophones and raincoats. 'Lead

Balloon's choicest couplet, 'An angry man is just an angry man/But an angry woman/Bitch!', is just the rueful side of hectoring. Moans about the music biz from insiders are rarely essential, but the title track is better than similar efforts as it correctly identifies the 'whining white kids' of modern American music. 'Face Lift', smouldering with righteous anger and sadness, finds a daughter telling a parent that 'happiness is the best facelift'.

Top-flight chums abound – Wayne Shorter, ex-boyfriend Larry Klein etc. – but the sound has a pleasing unity, its most notable feature being attractive guitar washes *à la* Daniel Lanois and Vini Reilly framed in Mitchell's unfathomable tunings as showcased in the pointlessly hidden instrumental 'Tiger Bones'. She's never sung better, either, the clear and precise enunciations now gone nicely husky so she sounds like Elvis Costello's worldly older sister.

Mitchell continues to grow old without growing soft. This is tasteful and distinctive stuff, but clearly a bespoke product for grown-ups. A fifteen-year-old is as likely to possess it as they are a camelhair overcoat. Marketing men have to worry about that stuff. Joni Mitchell doesn't.

The Unfiltered
Joni Mitchell

Dave DiMartino, *MOJO*, August 1998

It's a Saturday night in Burbank, California, and perhaps two hundred invited guests are sitting in a circular arrangement of plush chairs, overstuffed sofas, even cross-legged on the floor. Wines and bottled water abound. At the centre of this velvet doughnut is a small, round stage, upon which stand Joni Mitchell and three, sometimes four, other musicians. Video cameras record every detail of this, the second of two private concerts, for a television special to be aired later in the year. Rosanna Arquette introduces Mitchell on both nights.

Joni's paintings are everywhere, hanging on the curtained perimeter of the circle and exhibited proudly on the curved pathway that led the small audience to their seats. Her friends are everywhere, too. There among her dazzling band – including drummer Brian Blade, pedal-steel guitarist Greg Leisz and trumpeter Mark Isham – stands bassist Larry Klein, Mitchell's former husband of ten years, whom she'll briefly and conspicuously kiss midway through her performance. And there in the audience is the familiar, greying figure of Graham Nash, her celebrated beau from earlier days. And tonight, the composer of 'Our House' has work to do.

Sure enough, Nash heads to the stage with a peculiar object in his hand, wrapped in what appears to be a disposable plastic bag. It is, says he, the trophy owed to Joni for her induction into the Rock and Roll Hall of Fame last year. The one she never got because she never showed up to claim it. 'You had your reasons,' Nash says, diplomatically, 'but I'm sure they're all fine.' Looking at Nash – bemusedly or begrudgingly, it's hard to tell – she grasps the object in its sloppy wrapper and deadpans that 'It's perfect in a garbage bag.'

One has to love Joni Mitchell, and these days one does. Since 1994's *Turbulent Indigo* netted the singer two Grammy awards – including album of the year – Mitchell has been on the receiving end of a nonstop series of honours, awards and the sort of accolades usually given posthumously to bluesmen most decent humans have never heard of. Among them: the Billboard Century award, the National Academy of Songwriters Lifetime Achievement award, the Canadian governor general's Performing Arts award, even Sweden's Polar Music Prize.

Such awards usually indicate a career nearing the end of its creative lifespan, but in Mitchell's case that's simply laughable. She's been *out there* in 1998 – touring with Bob Dylan and Van Morrison on a seven-date concert series verging on the historic, taking part in a memorable Los Angeles Walden Woods benefit (alongside an all-female cast including Sheryl Crow, Stevie Nicks, Björk, Shawn Colvin, Paula Cole and Trisha Yearwood) and completing *Taming The Tiger*, her sixteenth album. To be released thirty-one full years after she signed to Reprise Records in 1967, it is as fresh and vital as anything she has ever recorded and will not come packaged in a plastic garbage bag.

Sitting outside a restaurant she frequents in Brentwood – an area now famous for its association with disgraced celebrity athlete O. J. Simpson – Mitchell is chatty, warm, an excellent smoker and, frankly, among the most magnetic personalities I've ever encountered. She zigs and zags from subject to subject; she is highly opinionated and visibly proud of it. She talks about nearly everything, including her reunion last year with daughter Kilauren – after giving her up for adoption thirty-three years ago – and her own mother, now eighty-six and the subject of *Taming The Tiger*'s song 'Face Lift'.

So outspoken is Joni Mitchell that she and her publicist are discussing the downside of complete frankness. In these days of Lilith Fairs and tired topics like 'women in rock', the press – god bless 'em – continue to run familiar female names by Joni seeking assessment and, ideally, condemnation from the queen herself. Sheryl Crow? Alanis Morissette? Jewel? Even Rickie Lee Jones? Mitchell notes a previous reporter she'd encountered 'laid on me questions like, "What do you think of so-and-so?" and I deflected and deflected and deflected and finally said something. And I thought, If they cut *that* off and *that* off – and you know they will – he got the dirt. He *got* it.' She pauses. 'I'm getting a rep for that.'

So much for the mud-wrestling questions.

Dave: *It seems like you've been surfacing more lately. A conscious move on your part?*

Joni: No. I guess things started to take off in the last five years mainly because of the *Billboard* award. After that, it was a series of sort of copycat crimes, where people remembered me and I was the recipient of a lot of awards in a row. And then I won a Grammy – well, two Grammys, one for the artwork – which also pleased me very much.

I'm really a painter at heart and I can say this now since, you know, Kilauren has come along. Music was a hobby for me at art school, and art was serious. Art was always what I was going to do; I was going to be an artist. But the time that I went to art school was very disappointing – although I romanticised the time that Van Gogh went to art school. I thought that to go to the French Academy at that particular time – even though as a female I would have been considered an associate no matter how good I was – was the best education you could get. And yet in Van Gogh's letters to Bernard, he's begging him to get out of there, saying, 'They're providing you with subject matter – if they have their way, they'll make a mistress of your art and you won't know your true love should you come upon it.' He was begging him to get out and just paint from his heart at that time. That was an eye-opener to me – when I read that, I thought, I'm going to give *myself* the art education: I'm going to paint the way I want to, never mind the art world. So I went back to painting landscapes and my friends and cats and not making a mistress of it – stopping trying to be innovative and *moderne* and painting the kind of paintings that I can't afford to buy that I want to have in my house, you know?

The paintings on display on Saturday night were gorgeous.

People like that kind of painting. The art world will apologise for it if they write about it, you know what I mean? The art world is a funny world – I'm glad I never had to be a part of the gallery scene or anything.

Do you know Don Van Vliet, Captain Beefheart?

Yeah, he's a good painter.

He retired from making music in the early '80s, ostensibly to paint. I spoke with the man who handles his work professionally and he mentioned that it was tough for any musician to be taken seriously in the art world unless he devoted his time solely to art. He said it would take a minimum of ten years for him to be away from the music business to be taken seriously at all.

Absolutely. You're regarded as a dilettante. That's because – here's my opinion on that – America is far away from a renaissance spirit. I've seen shows passing through Rome, the poet as painter, Ferlinghetti's drawings on display. That's a renaissance culture: they understand it, condone it. Why shouldn't a poet be able to render? Not all of them can, but supposing they can? Don't rule it out.

You made that point very well on Saturday night when you mentioned what Georgia O'Keeffe said.

'Oh, I would've liked to be a musician, too, but you can't do both.' It's a lot of work, you have to give up a certain amount of socialising – but the way I learn anyway, everything that I admire sparks me: best teach it to me as admiration.

Funny, as a painter I have so many heroes. But as a musician I like one or two in each camp and then I don't like the rest. Like, I don't care for John Coltrane – many people think he's the greatest. Coltrane seems like he's on Valium to me. Charlie Parker, I see his greatness; then Wayne Shorter is a genius – he's a tributary of 'Trane, but he's got so much more breadth and mysticism and wit and passion and everything. So to me, Coltrane is kind of a stepping-off point to Wayne.

I have strong and strange opinions on things which are kinda controversial. As a painter I admire much. And it's been hard – like music, it's been hard to synthesise the many styles that I like. In art school I was criticised for painting in two or three schools at the same time. Music hybrids better than perhaps painting does immediately. I ended up kind of without a country – you know, musically speaking?

Do you derive the same degree of artistic satisfaction from painting as you do from music?

Yeah, as a painter there are so many painters that I bow to. I didn't like poetry, so the poetry that I made is the kind I like better. So I don't like a lot of poets, and that seems to annoy people, that I'm dismissive of a lot of what they think are great poets. I'm with Nietzsche on the poets. He went into a long harangue: 'The poet is the vainest of the vain, even before the ugliest of water buffalo does he fan his tail. I've looked among him for an honest man and all I've dredged up are old gods' heads. He muddies his waters that he might appear deep.' That's one of my favourites. I can see the filler in [poetry] – I can see, a lot of times, the effort. It wasn't honest enough for me a lot of times. It was tipping its hat always to the Greeks and classicism in a certain stylistic way. I like Yeats, I love Yeats – the Yeats poem that I set to music ['Slouching Towards Bethlehem'], though, I corrected . . . there were parts of it that I added; they let me do it, which was amazing. Because I think they sued Van Morrison for setting something. They just said, 'You have to put "adapted by".' And I think I did it pretty seamlessly because I understand his style – the third stanza is mine, and it's very much in the style of the first one, more so than his second stanza.

For that matter, onstage you mentioned Bob Dylan's covering your own 'Big Yellow Taxi'.

It's been so long since I heard it, but I don't think he ever mentions the taxi, he just goes straight to the tractor. It was on *Self Portrait*, I believe.

Actually the Dylan album, I think. But I wondered if you were as sensitive as the Yeats estate might be when someone was altering your own work.

Oh no, no. And I love Bobby. I think Bobby thinks of himself as not friendly. I think he just thinks of himself that way. But I'm very fond of him and over the years we've had a lot of encounters and most of the discussion has been about painting, actually. No, he can do whatever he wants as far as I'm concerned [*laughs*]. He's one of those people like Miles, you know? Even if he wasn't up to it that night – or I saw a performance where he just kinda cruised – whatever it was, I would always be curious about the next. Because he's kind of untouchable in a lot of ways.

And I love his writing – you know, not all of it. And I was a detractor in the beginning. In the beginning I thought he was a Woody Guthrie copycat. I never liked copycats and I just found out why from these horoscope books that just came out. I'm born the Day of the Discoverer in the Week of Depth. I really love innovators. I love the first guy to put the flag at the North Pole; the guy that went there second doesn't interest me a lot of times. Although some could say that Wayne Shorter is the guy who got there second but he took it somewhere. So Dylan went to Woody and you have to build off of something. Not everybody comes out of the blue as a genuine muse – a real cosmic muse. It used to be that's what music was – but now it's formulated. And, especially, it's become a producer's art, who's an interior decorator basically.

Does Dylan know that you were initially a detractor?

Oh, I don't know if he knows that or not, but you know, the thing that turned me around was 'Positively 4th Street'. It stopped me in my tracks, and I went, 'Oh, my God – that's just great. We can write about anything now.'

Because up till then, I was writing songs. And I wrote poetry in the closet because I didn't like it. I wrote it, I just rhymed, ha-ha. Rhyming Joan, I guess. But I didn't care to show it to anybody, or I did it in school on assignment because I had to. And I was praised for it but I just figured I got away with it. And songs I loved, stories I loved – I always loved stories from the moment I could understand English. Poetry was kind of like shelling sunflower seeds with your fingers – it just was too much work for too little return, a lot of times. I like things more plain-speak.

And the poems that I did like in school were very visual – and less diaphanous and cryptic. I think people like to say they understand it, but there's nothing really to understand. You can comb it and comb it for understanding and it may produce a lot of thoughts, but it doesn't get to the heart of the matter clearly enough for me. Most poetry.

In high school, my teacher loved T. S. Eliot and we studied 'The Love Song Of J. Alfred Prufrock' – which essentially needed a translation key to even begin to be deciphered by fourteen-year-olds. I'm not sure it should've been foisted on people who weren't willing and ready to explore it.

Not only that – but speaking as a poet, I wrote a song, say, 'Stay In Touch' on this album, and I know what I wrote it about. When my daughter and her boyfriend came, Teddy [the boyfriend] heard it and said, 'Kilauren, that song's about you.' Well, it was – it's about the beginning unsteadiness in a very passionate new relationship.

Any time I have a passionate new relationship, that song will come to life in a new way. If it's overly explained, you rob the people whose lives it brushes up against of their own interpretation and their own experience.

I know how a song falls differently against your life many times. To keep it alive it has to – you're bringing new experience to it all the time and it's not the experience you wrote it with, so it's open to interpretations. It's a kind of dead poet's society thing – tear those pages from your books. The songs shift around – either it means something to you or it doesn't. And that's one reason why I resent the 'Who is it about?', fixing it in time, 'It's about that over there . . .' No it isn't, it's a mirror – and it reflects you if you take the time to look as you pass it by.

I'm sure you've had people picking apart your songs on the autobiographical level, saying this line is about that person . . .

And they assume that – the new press. The new press is so irresponsible they print their assumptions without using the word. I don't think they know the word 'assume' exists. They print it as a bald-ass fact, 'When she wrote this, she meant this,' like bad poetry teachers.

I'm still living here and it's getting me in a lot of trouble, too. Especially if they name a person. 'Not To Blame' caused a lot of friction. Well, it's about men who batter women – and it has some details that are specific and some that apply to a lot of different situations. It's about the kind of guy who goes around battering women – and if the shoe fits, wear it, you know? [*laughs*]

But there's still a lot personally revealed, I think. On the new album, there are lyrics referring to radio stations playing 'genuine junk food for juveniles' and you're singing about 'a runaway from the record biz'. How do you view yourself as a record maker in the business of making records today?

The business – even the executives are kind of at the mercy of the Wall Street graph. The graph must go up. So it creates a kind of conservative poker playing. And they won't bet on any long shots. And among the long shots there are a lot of generalities. People over thirty, especially people over fifty. VH1, MTV – all of the outlets for music have been barred to me for many years, twenty years, for one reason or another. For mysterious reasons. In the beginning, when I first started, for the first five years I had no drums on my record, so I didn't go to AM radio, even in the time when I was a *young* artist. You only get about five or six years before they're sick of you in the business generally and they let you ride – they don't put any money or effort or interest into you, really. They just let you sit there like manure in the pasture, as a procurer of young artists at the label. But they don't help you get your product to market.

Has that in any way affected your art, your music?

No, it hasn't at all. I was accused of pandering on *Dog Eat Dog* – and my manager told Thomas Dolby, who'd been hired as a colourist, to give me colours and get away. And he was comfortable with that, or so he said – but behind my back, my manager thought that if Thomas was producing it would create some more excitement. And so they negotiated that and it caused a lot of trouble. And people said that I was selling out or pandering on that record. I wasn't.

What people don't know is I was a dancer – I like some disco. I don't belong to any camp. I like a little of this and a little of that – and at any moment, I could be inspired to go in any one of those directions.

No, I've always kept my painting pure and I've always kept my music pure, that's one thing. No matter how disturbed I've been. My predicament wasn't one in which effort worked any way. I was just *shut out*, period, after the *Mingus* album.

But, as you said, things have changed significantly since the Billboard *award. Take the Swedish Polar Music Prize – how exactly did that come along for you?*

They're trying to have a kind of Pulitzer Prize for music over there. It's fairly new. McCartney had been a recipient and Quincy Jones, and they have a pop and classical category.

Sounds like a wonderful idea.

Yeah, it was fun. I enjoyed the King, I really enjoyed his company, he was a character – kind of a hippie playboy guy.

Had you met any kings before?

No. He let me smoke, so that was good. I had to ask his permission, though. He smoked with me. He'd say he had to keep pace with me. So sometimes he'd say, 'Yes,' and sometimes he'd say, 'No.' Can I smoke now? 'No.' Well, when can I smoke next? 'I'll tell you.' And he had a silver cigarette case, and he'd say. 'OK, we will smoke now.' [*laughs heartily*]

How did you enjoy the Walden Woods benefit?

Oh, I loved it. I thought it was a beautiful night. People were talking about it for days afterwards. Weeks, of course, doesn't happen in this town. Maybe even weeks later I was still talking about it.

I've played with a big orchestra before, but never so comfortably. Maybe because I'm more comfortable – maybe because always I had to sing and play with them with very little rehearsal. This time I just had to stand up and sing, so I was liberated from having to plunk. And I loved the arrangement – I sang 'Stormy Weather' with sixty pieces. The most beautiful arrangement we could find of it. Frank Sinatra had recorded it several times, but this one – I forget the arranger's name, but we just copped it – you couldn't beat it, it was so gorgeous. And to feel all those strings come rising up around you, you know?

When I got to the hall that day, it was the first day that we went to our dressing room and we'd been rehearsing with a bit of the orchestra, the central kind of little jazz group that was the centrepiece of the orchestra. It was the first time I'd gone to my dressing room and there was a guy taking me up the stairs to my dressing room, and I was kind of huffing at the second landing and I said, 'Why would you put the oldest one on the third floor and the young ones all down on the stage? It should be the other way around.'

So I put all my stuff down and came back down to rehearsal and I played with this big orchestra. I went back up to my dressing room, we started to do make-up, and when I looked at my face I was glowing – and I realised I came up those three flights of stairs two at a time after playing with that orchestra. That's how incredible it was. So I have to do that again.

Tonight I'm going to record with Herbie Hancock, he's doing an album of Gershwin tunes. Stevie Wonder's going to be there too. I've got a choice of three songs. I think with Frank Sinatra's death and all, there's a resurgence of interest in that era. Of the eras of music, I would say I'm a swing-era baby. I love the swing beat. Even though my music doesn't reflect all the kinds of music that I love, it eventually will.

After watching you do Marvin Gaye's 'Trouble Man' on Saturday night, it struck me as odd that you've never recorded a complete album of cover songs.

I've never been able to. By contract. It was disallowed.

Would you like to do one?

I'm going to do one. I'd love to.

What you brought to that song was fabulous.

Oh, I love that song. I've played that song over and over – I'd only do the ones that I play over and over and over. I own them in a certain way because of my love of them. I love that song. I sang that at the 'Stormy Weather' concert also.

That was quite a group – how did you all relate to each other?

We didn't, really – aside from the duet that I did, there wasn't that much co-mingling. People came – they kind of kept us apart in case the fur would fly, I don't know. I saw Stevie [Nicks] because she was before me and Björk and I worked together. I love Björk. No, I think we were all a little out of our idiom – it was hard work, everybody was a little nervous, it was just beautiful. We're going to do it again in San Francisco in September, taping it there.

At the show with Dylan and Van, you all played so very well that I wondered if you felt you all rose to the occasion due to the company? I've seen Van play many, many times, yet when he played 'Moondance', it was as if I'd never heard it before.

I think we all did kick each other up. Bobby – I don't want to be indiscreet to Bobby, but it's beautiful what he said. I don't want to be a tattle-tale here.

We can go off the record, if you'd like . . .

Well, it's for his sake – and it's kind of a brag on my part. I treasure it, but it's not something I really can say publicly, I don't think – just as a person . . . [off the record stuff follows] . . . so anyway he greeted me after the show in Vancouver, he went on last that night and it was a difficult show for me because I'm not used to playing big sports arenas and there was a lot of milling, a lot of going for beer and a lot of talking really loud through all of the shows. It seemed to me that that crowd had come for the beer and the event itself – not to listen, just to be at it, you know? And I thought that was a shame. And you have three people that are really listened-to artists. It's OK if there's no lyrical text or something, but I assumed that this was gonna be a writers' tour so I picked a set for Bobby. And I think he did for me, too – because he put in one of the best line-ups of songs that I've seen him do for a long time. All of that you can quote me on.

But when he came offstage, he was there to greet me and it takes a moment to kind of recover – and I wasn't sure if it was a good experience. I thought we played well in spite of it but we weren't properly listened to. It was the first one, you know. Then I realised it was just the nature of the crowd. But Bobby was standing and he was very excited, and he said [*affecting Dylan's voice*], 'Oh, those chords, those chords – you've got to show me some of those chords. I love those chords that you play. We're gonna sound like an old hillbilly band when we go on.' I don't know whether that's indiscreet or not – what do you think? I'm so sensitive to it. I said, 'Bobby, you don't want to learn these chords. First of all, you have to learn tunings, and tunings are a pain in the butt. And you won't have nearly the fun that you're having now with your music.'

When I saw him it was almost as if he was taking songs that he hadn't written and making them his own, in a strange way.

Um-hum, um-hum – that's what I'm doing. Bobby and I played in Tokyo a few years back, three or four, I guess, and he called me up just before we went over and he said, 'I forgot how to *sing* – but I remember now, I remember now. The trouble is they want me to do all those Bob Dylan songs – and they're so heavy.' And that's exactly what I feel about my material. It's like Meryl Streep at a certain point decided to do comedy. I've done drama, he's done drama; we've done it very well. But we both have a sense of humour. His perhaps is more apparent in his writing than mine is. It's in there, here and there, there's a little bit of comic relief – you know, 'Drink up now, it's getting on time to close.' But people don't even seem to notice, they're so stunned by the drama of it all, you know?

And I started doing these cover songs with my hands free, like I say – the liberty in it is just exciting, you know? I'd like to make a whole show out of Gershwin. The songs that I write, you see, they're not really so much for singing – they're more dramatic. Like Bob's work, the prettiness of the singer, in the later work especially, is not the point – the point is to bring the words to life like a Shakespearean soliloquy. If you have to talk 'em, whatever it takes, you know? Whereas these old songs don't have a lot of words and there's plenty of time to ride the note and float and they're real singerly material, and I don't write stuff like that.

It seems to me that maybe around Hejira *time – not so much that you shifted styles per se, but . . .*

The poet took over the singer.

There were melodies that anyone could cover in some of your earlier songs and it would make perfect sense – they were gorgeous songs that existed unto themselves. And by no means are the newer songs inferior on any level . . .

The writing is superior, really – but, like rap, it's at the cost of melody to a certain degree. Although . . . it's more like jazz melody, it's conversational improvisation around a known melody. Except I don't really state the melody.

I had a difficult time trying to describe that when reviewing your show; I compared the speak-singing style to later Lou Reed . . .

It's the same thing that Bob does. The poet takes over. Maybe I guess Lou Reed, although I'm not as familiar with his material as Bob's. The point in the performance is to make the words come alive. Like, Ella Fitzgerald is a beautiful singer, she has perfect pitch and perfect time, but she doesn't illuminate the words – she just sings through it. Whereas Billie Holiday makes you hear the content and the intent of every word that she sings – even at the expense of her pitch or tone. So of the two, Billie is the one that touches me the deepest, although I admire perfect pitch and perfect time.

And you could have that at the expense of the read, but I don't think anybody could have perfect pitch, perfect time and colour the words, right? I'd sacrifice the perfect time and the perfect pitch to colour the words, but that's because I like the text. Dylan does that. He never reads the same thing the same two days in a row – and as a result, you can almost see his state of mind in the reading. And I respect that, I think that's emotional honesty and when you have this complex creature, the singer-songwriter . . .

Everybody's a singer-songwriter now but not everybody should be, not everybody can do all of these things and yet everybody does.

And that's why I think music has gone downhill. It used to take three – a great lyricist and a great musician and then a great singer. Like with Frank, and that's why that stuff is so enduring – because you had three gifted people doing it. Now you've got people, they're not really a great singer or a great writer or a great musician doing it, so the standards have dropped severely. And ironically, at the same time the standards dropped, the machines have increased. These people have twenty times the distribution, so the bad stuff is really everywhere.

The album that has one or two good songs, the rest being filler . . .

It's hard to write ten good songs. I know the fellow that runs my website said, 'You used to put records out once a year.' And I did for a long time – and I think that the standard of writing on them is pretty even. People listen to it and for one year they've got three favourites and then they put it on five years later and some of the ones they didn't even notice suddenly mean something because they're all about different themes. So either you've experienced that – and if you have, then you're closer to the songs, so you know.

But music now is so disposable. Like this new album – I'm very proud of it, I think the standard is high, I'm very proud of the composition, the tools were available. I play nearly everything and I guided everything into place on *Court and Spark* – even though I didn't play it, I sang it, and then they played it from that and it was pretty much as writ. *Hissing Of Summer Lawns* was a little looser – I let people stretch out and as result of that it had a jazzier flavour because they used their own harmonies instead of mine. People weren't really ready for jazz in pop music at that time – jazz-tingeing.

With those older things – lines like 'bombers into butterflies' – do you feel like that was a different Joni?

Yeah, there are some things that I'm prejudiced against in my early work. I think they're the work of an *ingénue*, that I'm miscast in them now. I don't do them for that reason. However, I saw this female impersonator, John Kelly, and he did a lot of my early work beautifully – from a spirit point of view, beautifully – and he's in his mid-thirties, I think. And in drag, to boot, and singing in a full tenor voice, some of them, not even imitating me, just singing them with all his heart. He sang 'Night in the City', which I think of as a childlike ditty and like I was a ghost at my own funeral. I saw the audience respond and I heard the song, it gave me some perspective on it that I never had. Not that in a [time] limited show I feel the need to include it.

What I felt when I put this show together, the necessity was to run by these songs that had become considered obscure and difficult. Any chance I get to air them and run them by people so they can make some new memories against these songs ... they're too good to kill, is the way I figure it. So I chose to use this run as an opportunity to revitalise them.

You, Dylan and Van Morrison seem nearly alone among your contemporaries, in that your newest work is treated by critics with as much respect and enthusiasm as your earlier material. You don't really seem to be as much tied into a time as others.

Well, they try to tie you to a time whether you're tied to a time or not. Like I've seen recently, 'that folk singer from the '60s'. I haven't been a folk singer since 1964 – and I didn't make my first record until 1967. When I started making my own music, that's not folk music – it has its roots in classical. The first music that I made that was my own, when I stopped singing folk songs, was rooted in Chuck Berry. 'Big Yellow Taxi' is rooted in Chuck Berry. In my pre-teen years, my best friends were classical musicians. And my parents, we only had five records in the house.

What were they?

'*Clair de Lune*'. My father had a Harry James record and a Leroy Anderson record, he was a trumpet player. And my mother had '*Clair de Lune*', Brahms' 'Lullaby', a lot of classicism, beautiful melodies. And I had personally, until I became a dancer and won records . . . because people didn't buy records like they do now. I've got a godson who lives in a trailer park who's got fifty CDs. These things are expensive. People charge now; they didn't when I was coming up. If you didn't have the cash for it you didn't get it. And I used to go down and take the records out of the brown paper and go in the listening booth and listen to Rachmaninov's 'Rhapsody on a Theme by Paganini'. It was like seventy-five cents but we couldn't afford it. I'd go downtown and put it on and listen to it and swoon, a couple of plays and put it back in the paper and put it back on the shelf. Like Russia or something, it seems like now.

I was wondering when I saw you get that Rock and Roll Hall of Fame award from Graham on Saturday night – was that staged or was that really the first time you received it?

No, he'd brought it the night before and, accidentally, a friend of mine, Chris, one of the boys who sang with me, broke it and the top piece came off of it, but he was scared to tell me – he was horrified, he went home and he couldn't sleep. But he did bring it in the garbage bag like that. So I laughed.

Graham has a very good attitude about the Rock and Roll Hall of Fame. My father would have the same attitude. Unfortunately I do not have a good attitude about the Rock and Roll Hall of Fame and you can say this. It was a dubious honour – in that they held me out conspicuously for three years. To go, 'Oh, thank you, thank you' – I mean, having conspicuously ostracised me for a few projects, how can I be gracious, really?

And the other complaint I had is that it was gonna cost about twenty grand to take my family – that they charge and they get a free concert out of you. It's exploitative, I'm sorry. Brian calls it the Hall of Shame and in a certain way I think it is. It's mercenary and they're putting everybody in – so the honour is dubious on that level. It's not really rarefied. The best records don't make that record of the year, the best records do not win the Grammys. The best do not win, so all this is perpetuating the falseness of the victors, you know? It's not correcting history as it should be. There's a lot that's in there that's great, but . . .

When you get these accolades do you feel, 'Good, I deserve it'? Embarrassed? Too little, too late? Or who cares – it's meaningless because the best things are never recognised?

Every one was different. Most of them fell short of honouring me. If I'm truly honoured, I should be humbled and most of them made me arrogant, because they didn't seem to know why they were putting me across, only that they should. And yeah, that kind of ticked me off. And then there were tailgaters too – people rubbing up and taking credit for things more than they're deserving of and that's always annoying too. And again my depth gets in the way. Because I know Graham just has a straight-ahead healthy attitude that it's an honour to be in there. And you know, coming from Manchester or whatever – I came from Saskatoon. It's more of a boondocky place than Manchester, really, although it is the centre of the North American continent, pretty much. It can have that claim to fame, I guess . . .

Yeah, I'm a deep thinker, so I thought a lot, 'What is honour?' I think about things like that. The governor general award – the governor general truly honoured me and I blushed like a schoolgirl when he gave me that award. And it was very sweet and it was kind of private, I don't need to repeat what he said. I enjoyed that but the applause was way too long and he kept saying, 'Get back up and take it.'

I don't really like a lot of applause. I'm not a natural performer, you know. I'm kind of ambiverted, in that I have hambone – I have enough ham to get up there, and enough introvert to be the writer. But of the two, I have no need to perform like a lot of performing animals do. Some people are just performing animals and need that, and don't feel comfortable anyplace else. But I feel very comfortable – well, Geffen said it years ago, he said, 'You're the only star I ever met that wanted to be ordinary.'

I was always a star. I'm not one of those kids that had a bad high school life. I was always invited to the pretty kids's parties – the doors were opened to the things that most people come to this business wanting. But I always chose my friends – my mother said, 'You have the weirdest friends', but I chose them with my heart.

I enjoy the car jockeys down here, you know – one guy brings the cars in like a matador – I enjoy village life, let's say that. This is my small town here; I know the shopkeepers and I tease them. I like that, I'm a small-town person.

Celebrity takes all of that away from you in a certain way. There's a tremendous pocket of adjustment where you either take drugs or kill yourself or something. You say you're not gonna change but everything around you changes and you eventually have to change. Everybody goes through that awful period. I'm kind of used to it, I'm comfortable with my celebrity, but I don't think anything much of it. But I'm like a mother about my art. I know what's good about it, what's exceptional about it, what's unique about it; I don't like it being compared to things that aren't unique. So that makes me seem kind of salty or rivalrous.

I love making music. There's still plenty to discover. I haven't hybridised all my interests yet. Cab Calloway started appearing in some of the music, there's many things that I've enjoyed, the crooning era – I'm going to make a record of '40s music to get that out of my system, so that lies ahead of me, the thrill with that big orchestra. It's the business I don't like, the pigeonholing I don't like, the pitting me against every female that comes along, favourably and unfavourably. That I've had to do because there weren't that many women in the business. I don't like the idea that they make us both put on the gloves, they prod one of them until they say something snotty about me, then hit me over the head with the snotty thing that they said, then get a rise out of me and start these artificial catfights.

Rather than thinking of me as a bitter old fogey like the young press would like to do, if they thought about it as a mature artist, if it was the old guild system, it would be respected that I knew something and that maybe my criticisms of these people who outsell me twenty to one, so they really are creating more public interest . . . but there are things, habits they have gotten into that aren't great art. False coming in the vocals, whining.

The '40s singers smiled and were elegant, they were drinking and having a high time, they really were more adult, there was a more graceful suffering going on. My generation was a generation of screamers, we were screaming over mountains of amplifiers – not myself per se [laughs], I was the only one on with an acoustic guitar, surrounded by the Who's amplifiers, usually (laughs). But generally speaking, my generation was screaming over loud electrical impulses, right? And their faces were all contorted and they were railing, but this next generation has a general tone – they're whiners. I think of Noël Coward: 'What's going to happen to the children/ When there are no more grown-ups . . . What's, what's what's going to happen to the tots?' They're not growing up, this generation, somehow, and they're malformed in a real insipid way, like blaming. And whining. And I just wish they had more character in general. And the over-sexed part of it all and the guns, you know – it's a degenerate era in the history of music.

But then there are things like the Lilith Fair . . .

I've been invited to play.

Are you going to?

Um, I'm contemplating. It was out of the question, because I just didn't want to play last year. This year I've had a taste of it and I had some enjoyment. I got sick out on this little tour, so I had to do three concerts in the state of delirium but I managed to stay on my feet, so it was a mixed pleasure. In spite of the illness, I enjoyed myself.

But in light of what you were saying before about false comparisons – because you're all women, say . . .

Yeah, I'm sick of being lumped in with the women. Laura Nyro you can lump me in with because Laura exerted an influence on me. I looked to her and took some direction from her. On account of her I started playing piano again. Some of the things she did were very fresh. Hers was a hybrid of black pop singers – Motown singers – and Broadway musicals, and I like some things also from both those camps.

That record New York Tendaberry ...

Beautiful record, beautiful. I love Edith Piaf and I love Billie Holiday, but there's no one of that stature among this crop that's come up ... would you help with this? Because otherwise I'm gonna spend this whole press tour with them pinning me and me having to deflect. Well, it's *nice*. Because some of it, it's like *culture*.

Like, if you look at children's toys. I have a grandson now. Toys are supposed to teach a child the culture. It's frightening to see these killer crushers, the destructive nature of the toys they're exposed to, the violent nature of the toys. This is very bad for culture. Now, art can reflect culture or it can deflect culture. I took the stance to sort through my own bullshit and *meshuga*, so to speak, for something that was useful to me – my own silver linings. If you could describe the quandary you were in accurately, with some saving grace, so that it was worth it to them to suffer with you or suffer with the character you're playing – like a good play it had some illumination to it. I don't see much illumination in the work that's coming up.

Could you give me an example of the first case?

Whose work in particular?

Yours or anyone else's.

Well, you'd have to ask different people. For different people it's different things. [The new lyric] 'happiness is the best face lift', for instance. I said that to my boyfriend one day and he said write that down – or it would've gone up into the air, you know? I think that's a useful phrase.

I got a letter from a guy once who had broken up with his wife. She had had an affair and he hadn't – they were about to get back together and he couldn't forgive her. And he was putting together a tape of everything they were listening to when they were courting – and they were going to the lake of their courtship. And he said, the funny thing was when they were going together I was *her* music and he was putting all of his music and her music together. But in the final wash, the only thing that was keeping him from blowing this relationship, because he was so mad at her, was 'You can't find your goodness because you've lost your heart'. And it was that line that was going over and over in his head, so that he didn't just tell her off when she got to the door – 'You had an affair and I didn't' [*laughs*] – and blow the whole thing that he was attempting to set up.

People are always telling me that I saved their life or I changed their life. And lately I've taken to saying, 'How?' Because I have a funny look on my face, they go, 'Oh, you hear that so much.' And I say, 'No, the funny look on my face is because I'm wondering, "How?"' Well, they always pull a different line. Some of them I wouldn't even think had that kind of power but it's a little phrase stuck in there somewhere that was just the thing they needed to keep from drowning at a certain moment. I think you'd find it would be different things for different people.

When I see contemporary songs quoted by contemporary music critics, they say, 'This is a great lyric,' and they'll isolate a line, and I'll think, What's great about that? There's no nourishment in that line. There's not even alliteration or linguistic colour, you know? 'Everybody's gay.' You know – it's a statement, but there's no art. I mean, OK, am I missing something, is it minimalism here? Is it Barnett Newman? Is it all distilled down to its simplest essence and therefore it's valid? Or do people just not know how to express themselves very well? Are they not thinking? Have they been praised too much in the school system, because the school system changed because they didn't want to give them an inferiority complex? So they gave them an A when they really shouldn't have had one? So they think that's good and now everybody thinks that's good? I mean, the standards have just dropped so far from Dickens, so far from Kipling. These are masterful thinkers and writers, rich in character . . .

If someone new emerged today and wrote songs with as much depth and meaning as, say, the material you wrote in the '60s, would there be – in marketplace terms – even an audience for them, one that wasn't tied to some weird nostalgia?

It seems like all we left this generation was shock value. And they're very, very concerned about bodily excretions, in terms of their art and what they say. It seems like that's all we left them or something. I heard there's a new singer-songwriter – you might know who this is – that someone was touting . . . 'Oh, this great new singer-songwriter,' and he's got a line, 'Strap on the dildo, honey, I want to get fucked in the ass tonight,' or something.

I was listening to Noël Coward last night – incredible, incredible craft, incredible wit, incredible social commentary with humour. Stylistically, the language is a bit more formal than certainly this generation would understand. But beautiful and correct and internal rhyme and so much skill and so much to say without being *heavy*. I think that's what happened to Bob and I: not to take a poke at drama and the dramatic song, because it's important and Piaf was one of my first childhood heroes – but I know within the context of my generation I was considered much too dramatic for most people's tastes.

What was the stereotype or misperception about you that bothered you the most?

I guess 'that folk singer'. Because it's so ignorant. The only thing I've taken from folk music in my art since I began to record is the long lines of the folk songs, to give you the space to put some text to it. A longer line than, 'Embrace me, da-dah-dah'. [Larry] Klein, from time to time, would provide me with the melody with short lines, and I'd say, 'Oh, let me parquet words to that just for the exercise,' like the Jimmy Swaggart piece, 'Tax Free'. 'Tax Free' had really short little lines, and I chose to collaborate with him on that just for the challenge – 'Front rooms/Back rooms/Slide into tables/Crowd into bathrooms'. But generally, 'I picked the morning paper off the floor,' that's long folk-line singing.

But my chords – nobody in the coffee houses ever played chords like those. And they're not jazz chords, either. Wayne Shorter came in on – what song was it? 'Ethiopia'? – and he said, 'What are these chords? These are not piano chords and these are not guitar chords – what are these chords?' And he waded into it like a champ. But harmonically speaking, I'm in my own kind of world.

Did you expect your audience to grow along with you?

I'd hoped. I didn't expect anything. One would hope that it would find an audience.

Do you feel that it has?

It's hard to say, because the last twenty years I've had no record company support, no radio support – the marketplace has been denied me, so I think a lot of those records, there's a bigger audience for it than it received. *Chalk Mark in a Rain Storm* really deserves a big audience, as big as anything the contemporary females have. It's not difficult music. I was disappointed that the company couldn't somehow or other – I was disappointed in the industry at large, that had closed me out from the marketplace, so to speak, that no one would allow me the normal venues that are open to announce that you have product out, with pride. Or that nobody saw. Except Janet Jackson saw it – and she touted it in her interview.

Was that a good thing for you?

Yeah, that was – the best review I got for that record was from Janet Jackson. Yeah. And it really pleased me, it touched me.

Do you think the market access you're talking about is more a function of age or sex?

Both. It's more than that. I'm a long-distance runner. Miles was a long-distance runner. And I'd have to look up his birthdate, but there was always that restlessness to never rest on your laurels and become a human jukebox. Miles, to the end, was moving forward, still searching and exploring, like Picasso. I belong to that restless camp, you know. Not everybody does. Probably because of the stars, something as simple as that – the moment you popped out [*laughs*]. Go figure.

But the industry, to answer your question more tersely, is basically designed to make of you something disposable. That's the way mercantilism in America works. And they get the new improved version of the product. The attention span in this country is shorter, I think, than most. In other countries, if something's good, they're loyal to it. But here, good or not, people get off at a certain point. It's because we're trained – even more so than ever, this batch of babies coming up with the TV – to fear not to be hip. Well, hip is a herd mentality, so anything too adventuresome, people are afraid to be the first or they'll stick out too much. And usually anything that's innovative is not hip and the copycat gets it all. Once they've heard it the second time, the copier gets the mass approval, because it's kind of familiar by that time. It's been run past them once already.

Another aspect in which you're sort of an uncelebrated pioneer is that in the early '70s it seemed like your private life was the subject of some discussion – but it's nothing compared to what's happening now to people selling ten million copies of each album. We're so familiar with every aspect of their lives through the media, it's as if they've given over their privacy as part of the deal.

It's become like movie stars. I wrote a poem when I was sixteen. Having written this poem, why am I in this business? But we had to write a poem, right? It was supposed to be blank verse. So I was getting my hair done for some kind of prom deal, because that's the only time we'd go to the beauty parlour in those days. And I was sitting under the dryer and they had stacks of movie star magazines. The reigning deities, the teenage idols at that time, were Sandra Dee and Bobby Darin, who were newly married. So the tabloids were full of the misadventures of their marriage. And I just felt so bad for them. And I remember thinking to myself, if somebody wrote this about me in the school paper, I would just die. So that's what triggered this poem that had to be turned in for assignment. It was called *The Fish Bowl*.

How could you end up in show business with that insight, you know? Because I knew it was a trade-off. Blessedly, when I entered into it, there was this brief time when it was viewed as collaborative – because our generation was all in it together – and you were even given the luxury of correcting an interview such as this.

I did an interview with Cameron Crowe and he was allowed – it was before it was them and us, the critic and the artist. I forget what's it's called – a *blow job*, isn't it? – when you write a nice thing about an artist or something. It didn't used to be like that. And people were allowed to write about an artist that they liked and say nice things. Anyway, Cameron came back with the piece and I read it over and I said, 'Oh, gee, I didn't really explain this very well – I missed a part and put in this and this and this.'

And he said, 'Well, Joni, you said that but I took it out.'

I said, 'OK, don't edit me internally – you have to pick your favourite paragraph because if you take it out in the middle, it's not going to make any sense because it's such a convoluted thing.'

So anyway, he was still living at home at the time. And he'd written a piece about Neil Young, who he adored, and he read it to his mother, whose opinion he valued. And his mother said, 'Cameron – why would you write a thing like this? You *love* Neil Young.' And he realised then that peer-group pressure among writers had caused him to put in some, I don't know, cynical or snotty things about this artist who he simply adored. That's when it began to shift.

Do you think the new artists who sell ten million records have their own sense of community in the us-versus-them sense or is it a different scenario altogether?

No. This generation seems to be the most celebrity-loving, celebrity-hating generation that ever lived. And nobody wants to do the mundane job. In my parents' generation, you got a job and you kept it. My father wanted to be a lawyer but he was a grocery clerk and then the store manager. You got a job no matter what your dream job was. That was your dream job. Then my generation, which was a more affluent generation – no war to deal with, no Great Depression to deal with – saw through and became very critical of the powers that be.

I don't know whether that's good or bad – like certainly the dope wars of Vietnam, the transparency of that, did not deserve the thwarting of the boys coming home. I used to play in Fort Bragg to soldiers, like Bob Hope. I figured I don't care whether it's an unjust war or not, soldiers need singers. So I disagreed with my own generation. I wasn't really of my own generation, either. I wasn't an anarchist, I wasn't a nihilist – I never really could find my politics.

The only thing from the hippie thing that I believed in, that I saw evidence of, the only positive thing that I carry on to this day, is the Rainbow Coalition. There we were, white middle-class kids, but we were treated like a grungy minority and we got a taste of prejudice which I thought was very healthy and should give us the empathy for all people, an insight that no other generation had. The other generations were very apartheid; my parents tried to teach me their ways, which were too narrow for me. Anything different was feared. To me, anything different was compelling and something to explore.

On that level, how was it for you being reacquainted with your daughter Kilauren? Has she turned out the way you thought a young woman of her generation might?

Her adoptive parents are very like my parents, so her rebellion, I think – and I'm just getting to know her, it's only been a year – is quite similar to my own. I was difficult to raise in my teens and she was too. Both of us wanted to stretch out and see the world. She took off at fourteen with her brother as a chaperone, and modelled quite extensively, 'til twenty-seven, all around the world. And she's going through a second rebellion as we speak, you know – against me, trying to shock me. Well, it's harder to shock me than it was the kids because they're more like my parents, you know? I loved the experience, everything, with the difficulty and all. We'll be fine, but it's an odd situation and there's much that has to be worked through. So I'm going on Saturday to see her. We had a bit of an awkward encounter and then we had a beautiful encounter, so we're going through everything intensely in a short space of time. But, yeah, there are a lot of things.

Surprisingly, there's less of a gap than there was between my mother and me. My mother thinks I'm *immoral*. I've searched diligently for a morality that applied to the times that I lived in. I keep saying to my mother, 'Think of me as a Catholic priest that drinks a little with the dock workers.' [*laughs*] I just don't want to get that *clean*.

Did she hear 'Face Lift'?

Yeah.

What did she think?

I think she's getting used to it. I keep saying, 'It's not our song, Mum, any more, this is so many people's story.' This is a story of mothers and daughters; I can say now that I have my own back. There are bad Christmases from time to time. There's a big moral breach. Before I was separated from my husband, my mother introduced us to the man who later became my boyfriend. But the divorce had not come through; as far as she was concerned I was living in sin, flaunting my Hollywood ways in their faces, in their town. Humiliating them. I said, 'Who am I humiliating you in front of? Your generation is all *dead*. There are no witnesses as far as I can see.' [*laughs*] My generation is not as intolerant of this. So that's a generation-gap song. The funny part of it is that she's eighty-six and I'm fifty-five or fifty when the song occurred.

One of the things that's marvellous to watch is Larry playing onstage with you even now.

He begged me, 'Joan, Joan, I'm jealous. You've got to take me on this tour. Who's playing bass?'

I said, 'The seat is open, I'm not cheating on you.' I played the bass myself on this last record but he came in and played the parts that I'd written – because sonically the keyboard that I was using wasn't quite right for a couple of songs. He played the bass part that I'd already transcribed. I was really tight on this record that it be my composition all the way down the line. Klein and I always had a broad ability to relate. Great discussions – that never went away. Playing music – that never went away. I said to Donald – Donald's my boyfriend – it's not like Klein and I are out of each other's life, we're just out of each other's hair [*laughs warmly*]. He said, 'Write that down, that's another song.'

Is it an odd thing for you – the boyfriend, the husband and then even Graham giving you that award the other night?

They're all wonderful men, though. Graham is a sweetheart – and we didn't part with any animosity. A lot of pain – there's always pain in pulling apart. Graham needed a more traditional female. He loved me dearly and you can see there's still a fondness and everything, but he wanted a stay-at-home wife to raise his children. And I said that I could – a rash promise I made in my youth – and then realised I couldn't. So it all worked out.

———

The conversation winds down and a surprisingly cool summer breeze blows, whisking lingering cigarette smoke up into the pure and oxygen-rich air of luxurious Brentwood. By any standard, this is good. And this encounter with the woman who penned *Ladies of the Canyon* is also good, a significant step up from our first – which took place in a Los Angeles theatre in 1991 and remains a conspicuous exhibit in my own Hall of Shame. Picture this: six-foot-four writer, watching Sting's *Soul Cages* tour, crammed into a seat with his knees pressed hard up against the seat in front of him. Writer shifts in discomfort, unavoidably tugging hard at the hair of the woman sitting directly in front of him. Said woman turns around and fixes the innocent but inescapably tall hair-puller behind her with a glare as cold as a Saskatoon winter.

'I gave you a look that would curl you?' Mitchell grins. She didn't think it was so funny seven years ago.

We descend the staircase leading down from the restaurant and enter a courtyard filled with luxury stores, designer fashion shops and Brentwood car jockeys who bring very expensive cars in like matadors. And in this paved paradise, can you guess where they keep them?

Part Six

Both Sides, Then (2000–2014)

Review of *Both Sides Now*

Gerrie Lim, *BigO*, April 2000

To put it mildly, the new year's most surprising new album has arrived. And it comes from Joni Mitchell, the woman who wrote 'Woodstock' and once defined hippie-chick chic, who then turned jazz chanteuse and then returned to invoke the blithe spirit of folk-rock fusion and who now gives us a new disc of old songs striving to push a point home.

And what point might that be? Why, simply that of the Great American Songbook. Cheekily titled *Both Sides Now*, after her best-known composition of 1967, this is a collection of old classics and standards, plus two of Mitchell's own songs. Call it something old, something new, something borrowed and definitely blue.

The meek and faithful among Mitchell's flock will be well and truly stunned. Here, there's not one strident strum of that carefully tuned acoustic guitar (its aural zenith already reached in *Miles of Aisles*, Mitchell's excellent live album of 1974). Neither is there any of that slap-happy Ibanez electric (showcased in 1979 on her other live album, the lovely *Shadows and Light*). And forget that Steinway piano, because she doesn't play any at all here (preferring to deploy the great Herbie Hancock instead).

All she does now is sing. The only remnant of her past is the confessional nature of the songs, and it's quite an improvement on the bloodless mess of her last album, 1998's largely forgettable *Taming The Tiger*. Clocking in at a reasonable 51:37, this new one begs repeated listenings and is best appreciated if heard all the way through.

The standards are classic songs that Mitchell began incorporating into her live shows of recent years. Themes of lost love now loom large amid the counterpoint of French horns, muted trumpets and soprano saxes (the latter played to perfection by Wayne Shorter). The album was cut in just three days in London, at Sir George Martin's famous Air Studios. Four songs were done with a 71-piece orchestra, four with a 42-piece orchestra, and four with a 22-piece big band.

The results are mixed. Mitchell bravely attempts 'At Last', the Mack Gordon/Harry Warren tune of 1942 best rendered by Etta James, and leaves you wondering why she tried. That old torch ballad, 'Stormy Weather', doesn't quite cut it either, not when compared to Frank Sinatra's austerely beautiful 1944 recording. Mitchell's reading may be note-perfect but lacks the extra edges that lend conviction, and her attempts to cop Billie Holiday seem a tad shallow.

But redeeming features abound. Aided by Mark Isham's searing trumpet, 'Comes Love' and 'Don't Go to Strangers' come uniquely alive. Rodgers and Hart's 'I Wish I Were in Love Again' is a jaunty experiment in wistful longing, as Mitchell shows us her love for the deft turn of phrase. How can anyone resist lines like 'The furtive sigh, the blackened eye/The words "I love you till the day I die"/The self-deception that believes that lie'?

And, ironically, the high point here isn't those old cover tunes but one of Mitchell's own songs. 'A Case of You', first heard on her brilliant 1971 album *Blue*, is rearranged with a brooding string section that makes it even more boldly evocative than the original. That's perhaps the most poignant statement of all, given that Mitchell has now forsworn writing new songs.

Both Sides Now is the first album in a new trilogy planned by Mitchell and her co-producer (and ex-husband) Larry Klein, the common thread being old songs spun anew in a symphonic setting. Way past the point of worrying about silly words like 'career suicide', Mitchell shows us that the hippie chick in her has rebelled in the smartest way possible, by crafting music so unexpected that it may take critics and fans years to recover. She challenges you to love the gamut of her self-expression, the whimsical and the sly – both sides, now.

Joni Looks at Life

Fred Goodman, *TV Guide*, 15 April 2000

'I never wanted to be a star,' Joni Mitchell says with a nervous laugh. 'If anything, I've been trying to get out since I got in.' It's a surprising remark, particularly delivered over lunch at one of the entertainment industry's posh watering holes, the Hotel Bel-Air near her Los Angeles home. But then, contradictions and confessions have always been coded into the DNA of the legendary singer-songwriter's creations.

At fifty-six, Mitchell is one of the most enduring musical icons of her generation – the author of such tie-dyed classics as 'Woodstock', 'The Circle Game' and 'Big Yellow Taxi' – and an artist whose musical impact will be showcased this month when TNT's Masters Series presents *An All-Star Tribute to Joni Mitchell* hosted by Ashley Judd. The artists performing on the show, timed to the release of Mitchell's latest album *Both Sides Now*, include Chaka Khan, James Taylor and Diana Krall.

That such a diverse group would sing Mitchell's praises is no surprise. Wynonna couldn't be more ardent. 'She's my hero. I've known her music since I was ten – I can remember being in my room, grounded, and she was my escape. When I went to the Lilith Fair last summer, I thought, We're all just Joni Mitchell wannabes.'

Adds *Tribute* producer Monica Hardiman, 'Elton John said, "I will do anything for her – I must be in the show."' And why not? After all, she is the only songwriter who can claim she named a president's daughter: Chelsea Clinton got her moniker from Mitchell's 'Chelsea Morning'.

Born Roberta Joan Anderson to schoolteacher Myrtle and grocery chain manager Bill in Alberta, Canada, Mitchell got a sideways start on the road to being a rock'n'roll pioneer. A commercial artist by training and an unrepentant chain-smoker, she says she began playing folk music in art school just 'to make money to smoke. I wrote poetry but didn't want anyone to know I was an egghead – I was a party animal!'

All that changed quickly, however, when Mitchell found herself pregnant at twenty. After putting her child up for adoption, she entered a doomed marriage with folksinger Chuck Mitchell. By the time she launched her career, Joni was a different person. 'I lost my daughter and I went down,' she says. 'I just began to sink as I was reeled up into the public eye.'

Still, the transformation fuelled the writings that would touch a nerve with listeners, especially young women, all over the world. 'I began to write because I made a bad marriage,' she says. 'Make a good marriage, God bless you. Make a bad marriage, become a philosopher. That is what I did.' (A second union, to Larry Klein, ended in 1992 after ten years, though he remains her producer and a close friend. Her steady for the last six years has been musician Donald Freed.)

Signed by Reprise Records in 1967, Mitchell moved to LA just as California was reaching its musical and cultural heyday. She recalls, 'A friend found an old book that said, "Ask anyone in Hollywood where the craziest people live and they'll tell you Laurel Canyon.

Ask anyone in Laurel Canyon and they'll tell you Lookout Mountain [Avenue]." So we went to Lookout Mountain.'

For Mitchell, who lived with Graham Nash in a bungalow that inspired his song 'Our House' and who has also been linked romantically with David Crosby, James Taylor and Warren Beatty, those early days were golden. 'When I moved [there],' she recalls, 'there were no sidewalks, it smelled of eucalyptus and the air was filled with the sound of young bands practising.'

Mitchell had her first big success in 1968 when Judy Collins's version of her song 'Both Sides Now', written when she was just twenty-one, became a Top 10 hit; it would take another six years before Mitchell achieved her own Top 10 single with 'Help Me' from her breakthrough album *Court and Spark*.

With a career that now spans thirty-three years and twenty-one albums, she has proved adventurous, working with jazz and world music long before most contemporaries. Her most recent reinvention is as an interpreter of pop classics. *Both Sides Now* pairs her with an orchestra for smoky renditions of such standards as 'Stormy Weather' as well as two of her own songs, including the title track.

Mitchell's private life has also come full circle: three years ago she was reunited with Kilauren Gibb, the daughter put up for adoption thirty-five years ago, and she is now a grandmother to Marlin, seven, and Daisy, nine months. Indeed, Mitchell prepped for *Both Sides Now* by listening to recordings of female jazz singers at a Toronto bistro during the weeks she was waiting for her granddaughter to be born.

Whatever trepidation Mitchell has about stardom, she admits to looking forward to performing her tribute show. In fact, one of the most intriguing aspects of the special is that, despite once being playfully described by David Crosby as 'about as humble as

Mussolini,' Mitchell has generally turned her nose up at homage, as the Rock and Roll Hall of Fame discovered in 1997 when she snubbed her own induction. 'If you're genuinely honoured, it humbles you,' she says, 'but when you're getting arrogant, those things begin to ring hollow.'

For Mitchell, who once again thinks of herself primarily as a painter, the show and an upcoming tour present a unique showcase. They're also sure to reawaken an old conflict: reaching a large audience versus maintaining privacy. After doing her best Ethel Merman imitation of 'There's No Business Like Show Business', she says 'I don't believe [the lyrics]. I'm not addicted to the roar of the crowd and don't understand why the show must go on.'

After a pause, she begins to sing 'I did it my way'. Mitchell is having a joke at her own expense but, as usual, mixes it with serious reflection. 'I learned early that I couldn't trust anybody's judgement but my own,' she says. Suddenly she brightens, the furrowed brow replaced by a playful, toothy smile. 'And even that only sometimes.'

Elton John, James Taylor Pay Tribute to Joni Mitchell

Frank Tortorici, SonicNet.com, 9 April 2000

NEW YORK – Posters adorning the walls of the Hammerstein Ballroom on Thursday said it all: 'Pop, rock, jazz and soul: one woman changed them all'.

A tribute to Joni Mitchell there honoured the singer/songwriter with a musical celebration featuring piano rocker Elton John, folk rocker James Taylor, recent jazz Grammy award winner Diana Krall and others.

The artists spoke of Mitchell's influences on music over the last thirty years and sang some of her best-known songs before the stage was cleared for an orchestra to back Mitchell on her late '60s signature song 'Both Sides Now'. Dressed in a grey, willowy dress with a regal auburn jacket over her shoulders, Mitchell sang the tune in the torch-singer mode she employs on her latest LP, *Both Sides Now*, on which the 56-year-old Canadian covers pop/jazz standards.

'She played guitar and was a singer/songwriter . . . and I was a little girl and there weren't too many of them,' pop singer Cyndi Lauper said backstage about how Mitchell had influenced her. 'I hoped that someday I could be a great artist like her. It's a privilege for me to be here.'

Country singer Wynonna and pop rocker Bryan Adams opened the tribute – produced by and scheduled to air on the TNT cable network on 16 April – with a rollicking duet on Mitchell's 'Raised on Robbery'. Lauper delivered a slow, moody version of 'Carey', from Mitchell's seminal *Blue* (1971). Wearing a shiny green top with a black jacket and pants, Lauper thrust her hands up at the sides of her face and swayed back and forth as she emoted. The cameras caught Mitchell in the audience tapping her toes to the singer's performance. Lauper was one of the night's few singers to reach the high-octave range that Mitchell had in her heyday.

Musical director/bassist Larry Klein, who is Mitchell's ex-husband, led a team of musicians equally suited to rock, folk, soul and jazz numbers. Jazz singer Cassandra Wilson offered a take on 'The Dry Cleaner from Des Moines', off Mitchell's controversial *Mingus*, which put her words to the music of jazz great Charles Mingus.

Before Wilson, British folk rocker and former Fairport Convention member Richard Thompson sang a faithful version of the song Mitchell wrote about the epochal 1969 music festival, 'Woodstock'. Wearing a black beret, Thompson delivered the line 'We've got to get ourselves back to the garden' with gravity.

Celebrity baby boomers in the audience, including talk show host Rosie O'Donnell and actress Goldie Hawn, were visibly moved. Rock group Stone Temple Pilots had been scheduled to perform the song but pulled out at the last minute.

Thompson later performed the most rock-oriented song of the night, 'Black Crow', from the classic *Hejira* (1976), highlighting his blazing electric guitar. John performed 'Free Man in Paris', Mitchell's 1974 ode to record mogul and DreamWorks co-founder David Geffen. 'I've played before the Queen of England,' the bespectacled veteran said as he gestured toward Mitchell from his piano. 'It's not so intimidating as having such a great musician there.'

John introduced a beaming Krall, who captivated the audience with 'A Case of You'. Far-reaching inspiration and first lady Hillary Rodham Clinton, via videotape, discussed President Clinton's and her decision to name their daughter after Mitchell's 'Chelsea Morning' before introducing pop/folk-rocker Shawn Colvin and country/folk singer Mary Chapin Carpenter to sing that song as well as perhaps Mitchell's most famous tune, 'Big Yellow Taxi'. Colvin addressed Mitchell: 'Joni, it's such an honour to be here . . . I don't know what I would have done without you.' Colvin returned later with Chapin Carpenter for 'Amelia', the song inspired by aviator Amelia Earhart, that had Mitchell, with eyes closed, swaying in her seat.

Taylor sang Mitchell's sad Christmas-time song 'River' before country siren k. d. lang received loud applause for her take on Mitchell's jazzy 'Help Me', from *Court and Spark*. 'She's a deep well,' Taylor said backstage about Mitchell, his early '70s' girlfriend. Lang said, 'A very sturdy standard has been set by Joni. It's a very proud thing to be a Canadian songwriter.' Lang said she would be participating in an upcoming tribute LP to Mitchell, along with such artists as Stevie Wonder and Sarah McLachlan.

After Mitchell sang, she remained onstage as most of the evening's performers were led by female a cappella blues/soul/jazz ensemble Sweet Honey in the Rock through 'The Circle Game', Mitchell's early singalong song.

'It's such a surrealistic event, you can imagine,' Mitchell told the audience at the sold-out show. The tribute, hosted by Wynonna's sister, actress Ashley Judd, also featured spoken tributes to Mitchell's music and paintings by actors Susan Sarandon and Laurence Fishburne, as well as crooner Tony Bennett.

Review of Show at the Chronicle Pavilion, Concord, Ca.

Joel Selvin, *San Francisco Chronicle*,
15 May 2000

Nobody sings Joni Mitchell like Joni Mitchell. Unfortunately, Joni Mitchell didn't sing much Joni Mitchell at her concert Saturday at the Chronicle Pavilion in Concord.

Most of the programme was devoted to a song-by-song recital of her entire new album of pop standards, *Both Sides Now*, backed by a full symphony orchestra. Drawing from the songbooks of classic vocalists such as Nat King Cole and Billie Holiday, singer-songwriter Mitchell took the chanteuse inside her out for a ride in front of an audience of more than eight thousand fervid fans who ponied up big bucks to see their diva.

Walking out in a glamorous, floor-length, soft pink silk gown, Mitchell looked resplendent, her trademark long blonde hair hanging over her shoulders. When the orchestra launched the full crescendo behind her at the end of the first refrain of 'You're My Thrill', a song associated with the redoubtable Holiday, there was a dizzying whoosh as the strings and brass combined in that extraordinary lift-off that only a symphony orchestra can provide.

Inspired by a performance with other famous female vocalists two years ago, arranged by the Eagles' Don Henley to benefit his Walden Woods Project, Mitchell went into the studio to produce an entire album of standards sung with a full orchestra. It must be heady stuff for the adventurous former folksinger, whose forays into jazz and other artistic experiments have endeared her to her most devoted fans as much as they have alienated her from the mainstream public.

On Saturday, she worked hard at stitching nuance and detail into her first few vocals, although the burnished consonants and little filigree on the end of notes ultimately came across more as quirk than style. She toyed with time, spitting out phrases like trumpet runs behind the beat. She practically smothered the songs with technique.

A lot of women in rock have tried this gambit – notably Linda Ronstadt, whose three albums with famous arranger Nelson Riddle revived her sagging commercial fortunes in the mid-'80s – but, sadly, Mitchell isn't even as good at this as Toni Tennille.

Mitchell's high-concept premise was that the songs she selected moved through the stages of the life and death of a love affair, a context so flimsy and ridiculous that even Mitchell broke character and dissolved into giggles introducing one of Holiday's most desolate numbers, 'You've Changed'. Just singing the old-fashioned pop songs probably would have been concept enough.

Most of the songs slogged along at the same elegiac tempo. Many were in the same key. The orchestra sounded fabulous – illuminated not insubstantially by trumpeter Mark Isham doing his muted Miles Davis thing and a swinging rhythm section of drummer

Peter Erskine and bassist Larry Klein, Mitchell's long-time musical director and ex-husband. Pianist Herbie Hancock turned up for a couple of splashy solos.

The dreary sameness of her standards was made all the more evident by the four Mitchell songs she gave the orchestral treatment after bringing her performance of the new album to a close with its unquestioned highlight, the symphonic treatment of her own best-known composition, 'Both Sides Now'.

After that, she dragged out the playful 'Be Cool' and gave it a kind of hip insolence. She swathed her Beethoven metaphor, 'Judgment of the Moon and Stars (Ludwig's Tune)', in a kind of Kurt Weill wash and let Klein pump propulsive electric bass into a daring reworking of her 'Hejira' before closing with an equally intense version of 'For the Roses'. Her encore was a superficial take on Marvin Gaye's subversive soul, 'Trouble Man'.

But the final four songs pointed to the reasons Mitchell's fans have followed her wherever she's gone. She knows the emotional interior of her own songs so well, she can wring them out under any conditions – solo on acoustic guitar or in front of a symphony. Her point of view is so specific and so unique to her writing that she is not only her own best interpreter but also best when singing her own material.

Review of *Travelogue*

Jaan Uhelszki, CDNow.com,
19 November 2002

O n Joni Mitchell's twentieth album [eighteenth not including
the two live releases], the high priestess of singer-songwriters
raids her own back catalogue, revisiting songs that she believes
have stood the test of time and her own stylistic transformations,
using the London Symphony Orchestra to accompany her.

This is not a nostalgia trip into the Wayback Machine, bringing
back winsome souvenirs like 'Big Yellow Taxi' and 'Chelsea
Morning'. Instead, this collection shows Mitchell as the self-
conscious and restless innovator, picking her way carefully through
the minefields of human relationships, leaving a trail of eloquent
breadcrumbs, as she describes the passing scenery with her
evocative and off-kilter imagery.

Back in 1974, Mitchell complained that she felt miscast singing
some of the songs that she wrote as a younger woman, so almost
30 years later it's no surprise that she has abandoned many of her
trademark songs for more sophisticated prescient fare. Included in
the two-disc set are songs like her Dylan-esque narrative 'Otis and
Marlena', the still topical and prophetic 'Amelia' and her end-of-
the-world tome 'Slouching Toward Bethlehem'. The anthemic

'Woodstock' has become a ponderous meditation on the meaning of life and purpose, as Mitchell, with the help of arranger Vince Mendoza (who worked with the chanteuse on her 2000 album of standards, *Both Sides Now*) changes both the emphasis and the pacing of the classic song that helped define a cultural revolution.

'I'm quitting this corrupt cesspool'

Dave Simpson, *Guardian*,
21 November 2002

Joni Mitchell has often been called the 'greatest ever female singer-songwriter', although she has been known to object to the use of the word 'female'. Many of her hits, including 'Big Yellow Taxi' and 'Woodstock', are legendary; her albums, such as *The Hissing of Summer Lawns*, classics. After thirty-five years in the business, the original woman with a guitar is one of few artists on a par with Bob Dylan. She has inspired Madonna, Prince and virtually every female singer-songwriter.

Which makes it all the more surprising that she has decided to walk away. Talking in the December issue of America's *W* magazine, Mitchell insists that her new album, *Travelogue*, will be her last. Calling the music industry a 'corrupt cesspool', the Canadian rages, 'I'm quitting because the business made itself so repugnant to me. Record companies are not looking for talent. They're looking for a look and a willingness to cooperate.'

The singer Kathryn Williams, one of several generations inspired by Mitchell, is distraught: 'She made me want to be a singer-songwriter. When she turns around and says she's had enough, it's so disheartening for everyone else.'

Mitchell's raging against the machine is nothing new. As Karen O'Brien, author of *Shadows and Light*, a biography of the singer, explains, Mitchell has threatened to quit before. This time, however, there's a difference. Following the *W* article, Mitchell stopped doing interviews. 'That's a worrying sign,' says the biographer. 'Her songs are her babies and she always promotes them. So she could actually mean it.'

The singer's ire seems to have been provoked by a spat with her last label, Reprise. According to sources close to the singer, the company was reluctant to release *Travelogue*. Irked, Mitchell took it to Nonesuch, an artist-friendly label which, ironically, is backed by Warner, the conglomerate that owns Reprise. The company won't comment on the situation but the row seems to have been the final straw in a three-decade-long battle between the music business and one of its greatest talents.

Emerging from the hippie/folk scene in the 1960s, Mitchell was initially offered what she called 'slave labour deals'. However, as the value of her songwriting ability dawned on executives, her manager Elliot Roberts negotiated a landmark contract with Reprise (she has recorded for other labels in between). Though unknown at the time, Mitchell was given total artistic control.

'She got the same deal with Asylum and Geffen,' says O'Brien. 'She's never even had a producer foisted on her – she always went into the studio without a producer. She's always had a lot more autonomy than any other artist.'

Despite this autonomy, Mitchell has long felt not just uncomfortable with the industry but also with her position within it. 'For Joni it was always about creative control,' says O'Brien, 'but at some point it will always come down to the bottom line. Even when she was on David Geffen's label, money fractured their friendship. At some point some MD is going to say, "When did we actually make some money out of Joni Mitchell? Oh, I remember: 1974." I despise that attitude, but that's how they work.'

Mitchell has become expensive to have around. For *Travelogue*, she re-recorded old songs with the London Symphony Orchestra, Wayne Shorter and Herbie Hancock. Although they are friends of Mitchell's and may have given her a preferential rate, none of this would have come cheap.

Furthermore, Mitchell's sales have never matched her influence and critical standing. Early in her career, she decided that pop hits were ephemeral and set out to explore other avenues, as with her 1979 jazz album, *Mingus*. And it won't have delighted Reprise that *Travelogue* includes none of her hits.

But just how much value does a label put on the creativity and credibility of a twentieth-century giant like Mitchell? Until recently, the big labels wanted to keep artists such as Leonard Cohen, Van Morrison and Bob Dylan because, while they might not enjoy the sales of the latest pop phenomenon, having them around was good for respectability and clout.

But times are changing. Execs have realised that if they have the back catalogue, they don't need the ageing artist. Warner's recent dropping of Rod Stewart was just as significant as EMI's reported eighty-million-pound deal for Robbie Williams.

In one of her last new songs, 'Lead Balloon', Mitchell describes meeting a corporate executive and opens with the words: 'Kiss my ass' She then talks specifically about running away from the music biz and the 'whiny white kids on the radio', and 'formula music, girly guile/Genuine junk food for juveniles' [Note: these two lines are actually from the song 'Taming the Tiger' rather than 'Lead Balloon'.].

More recently, she had a widely reported pop at Madonna: 'She has knocked the importance of talent out of the arena,' sniped Mitchell. 'She's made a lot of money and become the biggest star in the world by hiring the right people.'

'Joni's been quite unforgiving,' admits O'Brien, 'but then again, she'll rail against these "women in rock" features and then appear in the next one in *Rolling Stone*. So there is that ambivalence.' Similarly, while Mitchell berates Madonna and others' use of sexual imagery she once appeared on the inner sleeve of *The Hissing of Summer Lawns* in a bikini. Her justification: 'But I swim every day.'

'She's a very strong person and very sensitive,' says Rob Dickins, her former chairman at Warner. 'That's a great combination and a terrible one. There is an argument that she's done such a fine body of work, why should she put herself through a system geared to fifteen-year-olds? But if you have the creativity within you, it's very hard to stop it.'

It is possible that Mitchell's pronouncement is a Machiavellian way of drawing attention to *Travelogue*, but this seems unlikely. Dickins is particularly surprised at the timing: 'Nonesuch is not a corporate label and I would think that her experience there might be pleasurable enough for her to continue.'

In a recent interview in *Rolling Stone*, Mitchell was quoted as saying. 'I'll be glad if the industry goes down the crapper.' It's just possible that this final act of artistic defiance is her way of getting one hand on the flush.

Shadows and Light

Joni Mitchell is an enigma – anyone who knows anything about the legendary Canadian artist knows this. For nearly half a century she's been a major voice for her generation, her words and music having influenced countless singer-songwriters and inspired scores of young girls to pick up acoustic guitars. And yet Mitchell considers herself to be a painter first, a musician second. From her rare, sometimes combative interviews to her wholly individual style of acoustic guitar playing, Mitchell has always been nearly impossible to peg.

In the foreword to the new songbook *Joni Mitchell Complete So Far . . .* , Jeffrey Pepper Rodgers, *Acoustic Guitar*'s editor-at-large, writes that 'a guitarist haunted by Mitchell's playing on an album like *Court and Spark* or *Hejira*, for instance, can't find much help in the music store in exploring that sound; what she plays, from the way she tunes her strings to the way she strokes them with her right hand, is utterly off the chart of how most of us approach the guitar.'

Those words come from a piece Rodgers wrote about Mitchell for this magazine in 1996, and from that time until now her guitar style has remained as enigmatic as ever.

The operative words in that last sentence are 'until now'.

This new songbook, supervised by Aaron Stang, compiles 167 compositions from across Mitchell's rich and variegated songwriting career – early acoustic classics like the gauzy 'Michael from Mountains' and bright 'Chelsea Morning' (from her 1968 debut *Song to a Seagull* and its follow-up *Clouds*, respectively) through her prolific run of classic '70s songs such as 'Big Yellow Taxi', 'Woodstock', 'Carey', 'You Turn Me On, I'm a Radio' and 'Coyote', to her later jazz-based music and her occasional return to acoustic-based songs in the '90s and 2000s. Best of all, the book shows exactly how Mitchell plays these songs, with chord diagrams in the correct tunings and sections of tab for song intros and key instrumental passages.

Famous for her alternate tunings, Mitchell includes a tuning index here that's categorised into chord families 'based upon either similarity to standard tuning or quality (major/minor) of the open chord implied by the component notes'. Using Mitchell's numeric system, the index indicates what kinds of tunings she employs for specific songs (for example, standard for 'Urge for Going', double dropped-D for 'Free Man in Paris', major seventh for 'Help Me' and so on), as well as which songs require a capo.

Instructions make the process relatively easy to understand: 'Joni has devised a system of tuning notation using the letter name of the note found on the sixth string followed by five numbers representing the fret to which the next string will be tuned. Non-guitar songs in the book – such as 'The Last Time I Saw Richard' and 'California', which Mitchell played on piano and dulcimer, respectively – are not included in the tuning index, although the music for those songs has been arranged for guitar. ('California' also includes the dulcimer tuning and a line of dulcimer tab.)

While *Joni Mitchell Complete So Far . . .* is first and foremost a songbook, it also includes nine pages of photos, by photographer and former Modern Folk Quartet member Henry Diltz, mostly taken from the '70s and '80s. One shows her alone in a field playing a dulcimer, another has her sitting next to David Crosby in Laurel Canyon, picking on a Martin dreadnought, and another shows her onstage, playing a Gibson Dove, with saxophonist Tom Scott.

And then there's the foreword, 'My secret place: the guitar odyssey of Joni Mitchell', in which Rodgers, Mitchell and others use technical language as well as art metaphors to get to the heart of how and why she does what she does. 'When I'm playing the guitar,' Mitchell says, 'I hear it as an orchestra: the top three strings being my horn section, the bottom three being cello, viola – the bass being indicated, but not rooted yet.'

Joel Bernstein, Mitchell's longtime guitar tech, telescopes the evolution of her playing. 'Her first album has some very fine, detailed finger-picking – note for note, there are very specific figures,' he says. 'As time goes on, she gets into more of a strumming thing until it becomes more like a brush stroke – it's a real expressive rhythmic thing.'

Simple yet deep.

That's how many of Mitchell's songs have appeared to her fans over the decades. And though she may remain an enigma, *Joni Mitchell Complete So Far . . .* cracks open the window just a little bit more.

Captive on the Carousel of Time

Paul Sexton, *Guardian*, 19 March 2007

'I'm an uppity female,' Joni Mitchell says while sitting in the kitchen of her house in an upmarket neighbourhood of Los Angeles. 'In the media, there's no one like me. I'm as good as – and better than – most. But I'm not given my fair shake.'

Mitchell's house is big, warm and rustic, very much the abode of a working artist. A large pot of brushes sits out; a giant painting is propped against a wall. She looks healthy and serene, younger than her years, dressed in a casual smock and no-nonsense boots and laughs readily and infectiously.

When Mitchell announced her retirement as a recording artist in 2002, she did so spitting bile at what the music business had become. She bowed out with *Travelogue*, an orchestral revisiting of her earlier work, and quietly set about directing her creativity at her surviving passion: visual art. It's hard to reconcile that embittered woman of fifty-eight with the energised, feisty, funny sixty-three-year-old before me now.

'Here,' Mitchell says when I arrive, 'let me hug you.' I'm here as the producer of a two-part radio series in which Mitchell talks to her friend and fellow songwriter Amanda Ghost, whose R&B song 'Beautiful Liar', which she co-wrote for Beyoncé and Shakira, has raced up the US charts.

From the next room, I can hear the elegant strains of Mitchell's work in progress. Tentatively titled *Shine*, featuring a new version of 'Big Yellow Taxi' and due later in the year, it will be her first album of new songs since 1998's *Taming the Tiger*.

The prototype singer-songwriter, five times a Grammy winner and inducted into the Rock and Roll Hall of Fame in 1997, has no doubts about her place in the annals of music. But her absence from the mainstream has bred an endearing uncertainty. As a fumbling icebreaker, I say, 'That sounds great, even from the next room.' She looks genuinely delighted.

Mitchell makes frequent eye contact, smoking prodigiously. She talks about the 'pornographic pigs' of the modern music machine who care only about 'golf and rappers'. It's a subject she can now tackle with a hearty laugh, no longer bothered by music executives' belief that her sell-by date has been reached, and delighted to be embarking on her busiest and most productive schedule for more than a decade.

The newly inspired Mitchell has lately immersed herself in *The Fiddle and the Drum*, a ballet based on her songs and art by the Alberta Ballet Company in her native Canada. From merely advising on which of her songs to use, she has progressed to designing the set and collaborating with choreographer Jean Grand-Maître.

Amanda Ghost talks to her as an informed fan and fellow sufferer at the industry's hands. They became friends when Ghost, a Londoner of Spanish and Indian parentage, was signed in 2000 to Warner Brothers by Andrew Wickham, who had signed Mitchell to the same company about thirty-two years before. 'We're the bookends of Wickham's collection,' Mitchell jokes. 'What happened in the middle is what I want to know.'

In that time Mitchell became universally garlanded as the most eloquent songwriter of her generation. But it was soon clear that the profundity of her work would burst out of the stifling restrictions of mainstream pop-rock. She wrote the precociously world-weary 'Both Sides Now' as a mere twenty-one-year-old, much to the disdain of her then husband Chuck Mitchell. 'I was married to a man who had a degree in literature, who knew I'd never read anything and basically thought I was stupid,' she says. 'He married the package and thought he'd Svengali a brain into it. He married what he was pretty certain was a dumb blonde. When I wrote "Both Sides Now", he said, "What do you know about life? You're only twenty-one." Well, I had lived quite a bit. I'd survived quite a few diseases.'

Mitchell had polio as a child but says she had 'terrific' teenage years. 'I wasn't like Janis [Joplin]. I didn't come to rock'n'roll to be popular. But the worst thing that could befall a woman at that time was to have a child out of wedlock, and I'd gone through that and been tortured in the hospital. By the time I was twenty-one I had experienced a lot of life.'

After the success of 'Both Sides Now' and other compositions such as 'Woodstock' and 'Big Yellow Taxi', it wasn't long before Mitchell tired of what she describes as the 'hit-making rat race'.

'The company said, "Come on, Joan, write us a hit," and I said, "I thought the idea was I wrote you a song and you make it a hit."'

When Ghost arrived three decades later, little had changed. Warners tried to make a 'sex-bomb pop chick' out of a substantial songwriter and lost interest in the process, leaving her disillusioned and her career in neutral. Ghost says she practically had to mount a 'prison break' to get to where she is now. Clearly seeing her younger self in Ghost, Mitchell says she was insulted to find that, after briefly allowing herself to be milked as a source of revenue – notably around the time of 1974's double-platinum *Court and Spark* – she was then effectively written off, regarded almost as a specialist taste by the time of 1979's *Mingus*.

'It was my time to die,' she says of the 1980s. 'The bosses were looking, thinking, Oh, she's getting old now, she's just about thirty-seven. They want to dispose of you and get a fourteen-year-old in there.'

By the late 1990s, Mitchell had simply had enough. 'I came to hate music,' she says. 'I listened only to talk shows for ten years.'

Her rebirth came about, improbably, when she asked her management if they could arrange for her to compile a CD for Starbucks' Artist's Choice series. 'I listened to everything I ever loved, to see if it held up, and much did. So I put together one that starts with Debussy then takes a journey up through Duke Ellington and Billie Holiday and Miles Davis and then Louis Jordan. That joyous music was conceived in such terrible times – and it was such a great relief to the culture at the time. That's the trouble with now. Now we've got a horrible culture, horrible times and horrible music.'

But Mitchell is determined that, concerned though she is about the state of the world, her return to recording does not come across as embittered heckling. It shouldn't. Pieces such as 'Shine' and 'If' (inspired by Rudyard Kipling) resonate with bruised but unbroken optimism, not to mention an absolute refusal to be classifiable: one moment she's jazz, the next classical, then occasionally pop.

'A real artist is going to like a little bit of this and a little bit of that, and it's going to take an entire life to assimilate them into something new,' Mitchell says. 'It's not going to happen when you're young – and this is a youth-driven market. It's like painting: everybody knows, or they used to, that it takes a long time to distil all this. You don't become a master until you're in your fifties and sixties.'

If she sometimes suffers compared with her contemporaries, Mitchell has found a way of enjoying it. She seems to know her value, laughs readily and has rediscovered her creative centre. Privately, she does a mean impersonation of Bob Dylan, too, delivered as a hazy drone. 'I'm not considered a poet,' she says. 'Dylan is, Jim Morrison is. In a way, that's a good thing, because I don't like poetry, for the most part. I'm with Nietzsche: "They muddy their waters that they might appear deep."

'I'm a frustrated filmmaker and my favourite compliments have always come from the black community. This girl came up to me in the green room at the Grammys and said, "Girl, you make me see pictures in my head." To me, that's better than poetry.'

Review of *Shine*

Barney Hoskyns, eMusic.com,
November 2007

J oni Mitchell declared in 2002 that she was done with the music biz and would never, ever, make another album. I can't have been the only fan not to have believed her. For bless her, Dame Joan does love the sound of her own voice.

On the Starbucks-spawned *Shine*, that nicotine-scorched voice holds forth – as it has done since 1985's *Dog Eat Dog* – on the many ills that beset our world, its musical backdrop her favoured spare setting (since 1994's *Turbulent Indigo*, anyway) of piano, percussion and twittering soprano sax. Huskily it wails and rails on all the Big Issues: war ('Strong and Wrong') and the environment ('This Place'), more war ('Bad Dreams'), more environment ('If I Had a Heart'). Mitchell gazes down from her LA eyrie and likes not what she sees.

Most of the time the spiky self-righteousness is redeemed by the mournful melodicism: there are magical passages on 'If I Had a Heart' and 'Hana', on 'Bad Dreams' and 'Night of the Iguana'. But the revisiting of the 1970 ecology classic 'Big Yellow Taxi' is a mistake and the closing adaptation of Rudyard Kipling's famous poem 'If' (with Herbie Hancock on piano) drones on interminably.

Joni's last truly great song may have been 'Man from Mars' on 1998's *Taming the Tiger*, her last great performance the stunning re-arrangement of 'Amelia' on 2002's *Travelogue*. Nothing on *Shine* touches either of those peaks.

How Joni Mitchell
Got Her Groove Back

Robin Eggar, *Rolling Stone* (Germany), May 2007

Joni Mitchell is lost in her own music, eyes closed, head still, an American Spirit burning between her fingers. A scarcely sipped glass of red wine sits next to a bowl of cooling soup. The song is 'Shine', the putative title track of an album that was never meant to be, since in 2002 Joni announced her absolute final retirement with an attack of stiletto-sharp bile on the record business.

She looks just like Joni Mitchell should look: ageless, elegant and passionate, the same as she has always done, stepped straight from the cover of *Hejira*, a little more lined perhaps but nowhere near sixty-three (both her parents are going strong in their nineties). Joni is in the Hotel Arts in Calgary, Alberta, a few days before the world premiere of *The Fiddle and the Drum*, a ballet of ten Mitchell songs choreographed by Jean Grand-Maître, the artistic director of the Alberta Ballet. It's her first serious collaboration with anyone since Charles Mingus back in 1979, and she's loving every minute of it. The ballet received such a rapturous reception that they are already discussing a follow-up.

Joni inhabits a simpler world, without computers, voicemail, mobiles, email and superstar demands. Until Grand-Maître loaned her his home stereo, she was listening to the mixes of *Shine* on the bedside CD radio alarm. She happily hitches a lift in my rental car and – though desperate for a cigarette – obeys the 'no smoking' stickers. The only visible extravagance is her understated but expensive clothes and exquisite jewellery. To rehearsals she's wearing a jaunty green beret decorated by a diamante lizard which she admired at Graham Nash's sixtieth birthday party, whereupon Nash hassled the owner into giving it to her.

For someone without a current record deal and espousing a worldview that has been in direct conflict with prevailing political and business orthodoxies for the past twenty years, Mitchell is in creative overdrive. She says she's working a triple shift, doing the work of three twenty-year-olds, and she loves it. She's just closed her first-ever art exhibition, 'Flag Dance', sixty pieces of anti-war mixed-media art inspired when her TV went on the blink and started spewing out negative images in green and black (some of the images were adapted for the ballet's set design). And there's her first album of new material in ten years.

On the title track 'Shine' she sings: 'Shine on the dazzling darkness that mends us when we sleep/Shine on what we throw away and what we keep.' Joni has already discarded some fifty rhyming couplets for the song, leaving essence of Mitchell, a melody and a voice of such beauty that they make you cry, counterpointing lyrics that make you weep with frustration and anger at the state of the world.

She sparkles at night, when the stories and reminiscences, brought alive by her extraordinary painter's eye for detail and setting, unfold. She doesn't mention her daughter Kilauren, adopted when she was twenty-one, with whom she was reunited a decade ago and enjoys a difficult relationship, but refers fondly to her grandsons.

And she smokes.

Conversation with Joni Mitchell is a spiralling, fractured thing. It is the way she creates her songs, paintings, maybe even lives her life. Imagine a bright blue sky slowly filling with clouds of ideas, some an intriguing way off in the distance, others denser, storm-bringers. Over time the clouds dance and spin, some vanish, until the rest coalesce. They circle faster and faster, attaining tornado speed until there is this tightly focused twister tail, powerful enough to rock the foundations of a house.

It's hard to keep up but it's a thrilling ride.

––––––––––

Robin: *How did you get involved with the Alberta Ballet's production of* The Fiddle and the Drum?

Joni: It just happened at a time when I was already very busy. I had a few phone conversations with Jean and I liked what I heard. I am very intuitive. He came down to visit me and told me about his idea. It was called *Dancing Joni* and was somewhat autobiographical. It isn't the set I would have put together, so I told Jean that I wasn't interested in escapist entertainment when the planet is at red alert. We're busy wasting our time on this fairytale war, when nobody's fighting for God's creation.

I was preparing for an art show of about sixty pieces and I had a model of my installation on my pool table. The paintings were eight feet high, they were all war and torture and revolution. Jean liked what he saw and said, 'I want to put this with the ballet.' I said, 'Not with this ballet, but I could put together a ballet for you.' I was in the process of recording, which I hadn't done in ten years. So I already had two very big projects going on.

I came straight out of retirement into doing the work of three twenty-year-olds. I really burnt myself out physically but emotionally it was very uplifting. I realised I wasn't ready for retirement, for gardening and watching old movies, which is what I'd been doing for ten years. I pulled together a lot of material and designed a set that would take the war images from 'Flag Dance'. The set is hanging above their heads, which is unorthodox. We worked through the budget problems and because we would not be able to rear-project we had to project over the dancers' heads on to a circular screen.

Then, like I didn't have anything else to do, I made a moving video for the screen. [Chuckles] I even made a little cameo in the 'Beat of Black Wings' dressed as a black soldier . . . plus I get to say the curse words in the song.

There are two new songs included in the ballet, a reworking of Rudyard Kipling's 'If' and 'If I Had a Heart'. Were they written especially for the ballet?

I was already writing the album – which would have been the whole ballet but I have only just finished it now and couldn't get it in time for Jean to choreograph. But it did include those two pieces.

You announced in 2002 that you were sick of the cesspool that passed for the record business and that you'd had enough of it. Forever. So what changed your mind?

I really believed I was never going to make another record. I convinced a lot of people and, oops, here it came. I was trying to keep my legs crossed and it was like a late birth. They all come out that way. It's like they're writing me.

What made you quit?

I have taken a year off here and there before. *For the Roses* . . . that was one of my first swansongs. Some parts of the job – the creative processes – I loved, some I didn't like at all. I like a certain amount of attention but . . . it got more and more difficult to be a public person. The public person became more and more of a hostile witness. My work is deep, it's all there and you can't get any deeper, so there were aspects of the job that became repugnant to me. I started having nightmares about it, and when it hits your subconscious like that it's time to quit.

Was there any particular event that sparked those nightmares?

I did a VH1 interview and I ended up sitting for five hours on a stool answering questions. After that I felt so miserable, so drained, that I went to bed for three days. I just didn't understand why I felt so awful. I got up and Klein [ex-husband producer Larry Klein] was watching TV so I took the remote off him and started channel-hopping. For some reason I stopped it on Larry King, who was talking to this soldier who been a prisoner in the first Gulf War. He'd also been a prisoner in Vietnam and explained how they tortured people differently there. They'd sit you on a chair and fire questions at you for hours and hours until you'd tell them anything they wanted. That way I knew what had happened to me. What are the chances of that, eh?

What inspired you to start recording again?

I've had a small place up in British Columbia for years. It's where I wrote *For The Roses* and it's always been the place I feel most comfortable and secure. Plus I can smoke there as much as I want [laughs]. I just started playing this instrumental piece on the piano. I had a guitar there but after ten years off you have to go through a little pain. I had no calluses left and I bled at first. On the piano your chops will be down but there's no physical pain.

Suddenly I had four piano songs. It started off piano-dominant, as *For The Roses* had. I worked alone in a room with Dan Marnien [engineer on *Night Ride Home*, *Turbulent Indigo* and *Taming The Tiger*]. I am kinda profuse with ideas and I had to train Klein to either leave the room or zip it so he didn't disturb the experiment. I am back in the ideal creative situation for me where I try every idea that I have and, while they don't all work, Dan let me try them all. My instincts were really tweaked this time and things fell together. The earlier piano stuff was harder, it took more experimentation with the orchestra, but once I got my palette the later work came together quickly. Many of the other songs are synth-based. A lot of them fell together once I knew where the colours were. Sometimes the synth would roll up to a colour – 'church ooze' – which is just what I need. There was a high degree of synchronicity and, as the project went on, it gathered a magical steam.

It is much less dense than my last albums. I had to go through density. I would have made *Chalk Mark in a Rain Storm* denser but Klein stopped me. I was seeing it graphically. Wherever there was a hollow I'd put a musical figure in it that had two hollows in it like a W, and in those two hollows I'd plant another figure with a hollow in it and then put the cherry on the pudding. It was a very painterly approach to music. Painters, who understand layering, liked it. Many times they would follow a horn line or follow one colour for a while. A lot of people thought it was eccentric. I still quite like it. This time it is not as wordy as it has been. That was another experiment – how many words could I get in a line – and then Paul Simon started doing that and when I heard him doing it I thought, This is a bad idea. Woe be to the imitators.

You seem to enjoy setting poetry to music. 'Slouching Towards Bethlehem', your adaptation of W. B. Yeats's 'The Second Coming' [from Night Ride Home*], is one of the highlights of the ballet. What made you choose Kipling's 'If'?*

Synchronicity. In the middle of writing the album, Val [Broadway dancer Charles Valentino] read it to me over the phone. I said, 'That's perfect for the ending of the album.' I had to do a little rewrite on it. That was the fifth song and the first guitar song. Then they decided to whittle down this mountain behind my sanctuary and sell it to California as gravel for McMansions, so along came the second guitar song. The rest were coughed up by this wonderful colour box, a five-year-old Yamaha synthesiser.

My guitar has always been very orchestral: even on the first album it is not folk music, it is semi-classical, very easy to orchestrate – songs like 'Marcie' are more like Schubert than folk music. I don't know Schubert that well but the *New York Times* seem to think there is something similar – though the only thing I can think of is that he set a lot of popular German poems to music, which I have done a little bit with 'The Book of Job' and the Yeats poem. It was called folk because that was what it looked like – a girl with a guitar. I am not a folk singer at all. I have an appetite for Debussy. My childhood roots were in Rachmaninoff, Tchaikovsky, the 'Nocturnes', the 'Moonlight Sonata', 'Clair de Lune' and 'Variations on a Theme by Paganini'. That was what made me want to make beautiful music, which I don't think is either masculine or feminine. I took one year of piano lessons, but they used to hit me with a ruler. I didn't like that too much. It made me quit.

Classical music today is underwater elevator music, bad Brian Eno. I love *Music for Airports* – he is the champ of classical composition – but at this point they are all doing this electronic horizontal stuff. It's a weird direction because of its sameness. It's a copycat crime. I guess it always was, except for Debussy . . . there was no one like him.

What inspired 'If I Had a Heart'? It is such a beautiful ballad that the impact of the lyrics – 'Holy earth/How can we heal you/We cover you like blight/Strange birds of appetite/If I had a heart I'd cry' – take a while to come through.

During the ballet we projected seven night photographs of the earth from every angle onto the screen. It's frightening to witness what an electronic blight we are. Ever since I saw those pictures of North America at night I turn lights off at night. All of that energy is sucking from nature; the man-made has taken over the natural world. All over the globe, war is accelerating. We need that energy diverted into saving the planet while the planet is trying to shake us off its back. It is our host and we are this bacteria, this infection. We insist on wounding it more and more. War is ridiculous at this time and then to add insult to injury by calling it a holy war is just obscene, ignorant and tragic.

This album is about the war of the fairytales, possibly the end of our species from this macho I-got-a-bigger-bomb-than-you-have instinct. This spaceship we are all riding on is dying: somebody tell the captain to stop punching holes in the walls. We have atrocious leadership everywhere, mankind at its most diabolical.

Why do you hate critics so much?

They hold you in your decade. You are supposed to stay neatly in your decade and then die. From my sixth album on they were dismissive while I knew I was still growing. It was an extraordinary rejection of good work. Everything was compared unfavourably to

Court and Spark until *Blue* surpassed it in sales. *Blue* was not a hit out of the chute either, but once the sales got bigger that became the masterpiece. It was all contingent on sales; my later work did not sell and the press did not help me in any way. *Dog Eat Dog* was literally repressed and taken off the market for twenty years. I just recently got it reinstated. People called it negative but they had their heads in the sand. It was getting more like Russia, where people were getting more and more ignorant and buying the propaganda. Somebody had to say something but it didn't make me very popular, so the album got dumped. From then on I felt like Gauguin and Van Gogh. I knew the work was progressive but it was not selling, not receiving respectful attention – the general consensus was thumbs-down. I know enough to know when I am doing good work, but fools were reviewing it. I'd see the crap they'd elevate. They'd pit me against three-chord wonders who weren't saying anything. It was my time to die. It wasn't rational but it finally killed my interest in doing it. I couldn't face any more stupidity. I don't care for fame and fortune, but the rejection of my later work was too extreme. Everything about the business was ignorance. The company would say, 'You didn't give us anything.' Nothing! Didn't they listen to the songs?

Now there is a reprise coming around. Prince always says *Hissing of Summer Lawns* is his favourite album. People who came in from there carried on and the earlier work that was so hallowed they never got into. It depends where you got in on the ride. I never wanted to be a human jukebox: when Bob and Van and I went out on tour [in 1998], they were playing their hits. I was advised to do mine and went, 'No way.'

Personally I always thought your earlier stuff was a bit girlie.

I was girlie – 'twee', as the English might say. I got more tooth later. One of my favourite compliments was from a blind black piano player who said that my work was raceless and genderless. I considered that a true honour coming from him. I set out to get rid of the girlie part to give it strength. I think I accomplished that as a writer. You can't tell that a girl wrote my later work. It doesn't have a feminine perspective.

Are you frustrated by this lack of recognition for work that has got better as its sales have declined?

They [the critics] didn't like the harmonies and general musicality of the direction I was going in. It is not jazz, it is outside the laws of jazz, totally original music that is now being studied in music schools, my harmonics. The great jazzers Herbie [Hancock] and Wayne [Shorter] know and accept me as a member of the academy; the lesser jazzers go, 'Where is the downbeat?'

What made you start writing political songs?

I got stung by Reaganomics. He levied an unjust tax against me for not having a producer, which made me look not slave enough and seized money from my bank account. I fought two courts and I won, but it cost a lot of money and the lawyers picked a lot off me. That was my life savings.

I was a girl, so I was underpaid compared to men's wages. I had two points on my first record, two pennies on *Blue*. That's, excuse me, 'N-word' wages – actually it's less than that. My N-friends [chuckles] were appalled. Basically, they robbed me. That awoke me as a political animal and I wrote *Dog Eat Dog*. A lot of the songs I wrote at the time were a warning which people may be ready for now but they weren't then. It was dismissed as negative and sophomoric. That tells you something about an American culture that says once you are past first year of college you shouldn't be worrying about the world. You are supposed to grow up and go with the programme.

On your last recordings your voice had lost a lot of its range.

I had lost some of my voice. It was severe. I'd go to hit a note and there was nothing there. I used to have three octaves and people blamed it on my smoking. I went to a throat specialist who assured me it wasn't and said it had to do with my digestion partially. I also had nodes from singing rock'n'roll.

I went to do this lecture – on how to instil a love of nature on Earth Day in San Francisco – to the Commonwealth Club, which is one of those groups of very wealthy people who buy presidents, the power behind the throne. I was a bit nervous, as what I was going to say was going to be more than slightly unorthodox, critical of the western mind in general and psychology in particular. They sent me a masseuse, who turned out also to be a chiropractor, as a gift. After she worked on me she said, 'Are you having problems singing? No wonder your larynx is compressed.' She gave me a Styrofoam block to realign my spine that had been damaged from polio and, as it had gotten worse, my neck was pokey.

I'd had it straightened out by a Chinese healer who regenerated my back so the nerves came back to life. Neil Young, who caught polio in the same epidemic as me as a child, had the same injury and he went the western way, they struck a metal pole in his back and charged him thousands of dollars. Still a bad idea as this Chinese guy regenerated the nerves in my back for two hundred dollars. He gave me some exercises to maintain my joints; I had been doing them for a couple of years, which put my shoulders back.

One shoulder was out from playing acoustic guitar: that took me about two years to stop it rubbing the socket. As everything went back, some of my high end came back. I am singing well on this album, certainly better than on the two before.

People always like to blame it on my smoking. I have smoked since I was nine so it obviously didn't affect the early work that much. My voice isn't completely back as my sinuses are screwed up. Maybe that is from smoking . . . or the LA air. I have progressed as a singer, my stroke is better, my phrasing is better. I have learned a lot. I am closer to the singers I love. I never imagined I'd be able to sing like Edith Piaf.

Do you have a record deal for the new album?

Because the corporations bought up a lot of record companies, they became a conglomerate. My Warner's catalogue descended to Rhino Records to exploit. Robin [Hurley of Rhino] came to me with an album tentatively called *The Best of Joni Mitchell.* I said to him, 'I wouldn't call it that. I'd call it *Boss's Choices*.' It was all singles but I had no say in their release and I don't think it is my best work. Robin and I developed a relationship. We did some creative recycling and I worked on the package. I figured, Why don't we make it interesting enough so that people who don't have those songs will want to acquire it because it rounds up a theme?

We did *Dreamland*, then *Songs of a Prairie Girl*, which was for the Saskatchewan centennial and has all the songs that refer back to my time there. We intend to do a couple more but as I didn't think I was going to be doing another album I took off time to do these other projects. I don't have a contract for my new songs, since my deal with Nonesuch ended. My manager is looking at it because the business has fallen apart and there are a lot of ways to approach it to enter back into the game. Everything is in a state of flux in the world right now. Newspapers are struggling against the net as information-givers, trying all their tricks to stay alive. I understand that. Record companies are drowning, trying to get artists back by giving fair deals – what a concept!

But you might have to play the media game.

I know, but I don't give good soundbite. Some of the stuff I am thinking about, especially now, is awfully deep, you can't speak of it flippantly in a good soundbite. The project I am working on now is as serious a work as I've done. I am a wordsmith and so careful to try and be clear even if it is clear in a surrealistic way, to get the images right.

You don't like people reducing what you say to soundbites.

It doesn't go very well. It dumbs it down. It breaks my heart, it's the hardest thing about this job for me. I know it is not easy, it takes up a lot of space to explain things correctly. Condensed down oversimplifies it, it doesn't bother other people but it does bother me. I find it difficult when they put quotations around things you didn't say that have been edited and the point has been missed.

Do you think that what people find hard is that your melodies and voice are so pretty that the message in the lyrics doesn't fit with what they are hearing?

Somehow the music makes it more palatable than my usual irritated tone in conversation about it. Maybe if I had developed a crusty old character like Bobby [Dylan], I could have got the lines across better theatrically. But he didn't succeed, tried to tell everybody certain things but couldn't get it across. According to himself.

It is a bit of a problem with straight white males. Gay men don't have a problem and neither do black men. The white straight male is afraid of emotionality in himself and is liable to be caught off guard because my chords are sneaky. There is a fear to go there in case you cry like a girly-girl. I have a big black audience, fans who are warriors all round the world. The second-in-command of the Crips in LA is a three-hundred pound black man and he is a fan. They are emotional people who do not fear to listen to me.

Is there anything you wish had turned out differently?

I don't indulge that much in wishing. I've always kept the carrot pretty close to the nose, just inched my way forward. I don't look back much. I'll indulge in reminiscing with old friends.

What about your autobiography? It was announced years ago.

I am still circling it, trying to find a way to approach it. They paid me five/six years ago and they're getting a bit chompy. Recently I had the idea for *Cats, Characters and Dreams . . .* disjointed vignettes. In a linear biography I could get bogged down in verbosity, which makes a boring book. I tried to tell stories to people but I didn't find myself scintillating. It seemed artificial, flat.

Stories I remember I store like film, they don't need embellishment or exaggeration. When I am in a story that is happening all around me, I become alert and soak all the dialogue. I am a really good listener, I scoop it. I have a gift of chronology so I would remember exactly how things unfolded, but I am losing my ability for new memories – not so much the older ones, they are kinda locked in.

I remember too much, that's the problem. I wasn't a druggie long enough.

Contributors

Loraine Alterman was for a period the New York bureau chief of *Rolling Stone*, as well as the US correspondent for *Melody Maker*. She has also written for the *New York Times* and many other publications. She lives in New York City.

Colman Andrews wrote extensively for *Phonograph Record* in the early-to-mid-'70s, as well as for *Creem* and other publications. Today, he is an internationally-known food writer and editor, and the vice-president and editorial director of TheDailyMeal.com, a food and drink mega-site.

Jacoba Atlas wrote for *Melody Maker* in the UK and also for *Circus*, the *Los Angeles Free Press* and *KRLA Beat* in the US. She is an Emmy and Peabody award-winning writer and producer, with extensive experience as a broadcast executive at NBC News, Turner Broadcasting, CNN and PBS.

Johnny Black is a frequent contributor to *Q, MOJO* and other magazines and a leading scholar of rock history and minutiae. Drawing on his vast archives, he has helped to compile numerous 'Time Machine' and 'Eyewitness' features for those magazines. Based in Wiltshire, he also hosts his own local radio show.

Caroline Boucher left *Disc and Music Echo* in the early '70s to work as an in-house PR for Elton John at Rocket Records (replacing Penny

Valentine, who became head of A&R). She is married to music business lawyer Robert Lee and writes about food for the *Guardian*.

Stephen M. H. Braitman is a former writer for the *Los Angeles Times* and other publications, and a music appraiser who works with companies such as Gracenote.

Mick Brown is a freelance writer and broadcaster who has written on music and other cultural affairs for a wide variety of publications including the *Sunday Times, Rolling Stone* and *Crawdaddy!* He is a regular contributor to the *Telegraph* magazine and the *Daily Telegraph* in London.

Geoffrey Cannon was the first ever regular rock critic for a UK daily national newspaper, the *Guardian*, between 1968 and 1972. Subsequently he wrote for *New Society, The Listener,* the *Los Angeles Times,* the *Chicago Sun-Times, Creem, Rock et Folk, Melody Maker, Time Out* and many other publications. He has lived in Brazil since 2000.

Barbara Charone wrote for *Sounds, NME* and *Creem* among other publications before becoming one of the most respected publicists in the music industry.

Martin Colyer is a co-founder of Rock's Backpages, and the site's design director. He is a freelance designer, living in London.

J. D. Considine has written for many US magazines and newspapers. From 1979 to 1996, he wrote for *Rolling Stone* and then wrote for *Musician*. He was on the staff of the *Baltimore Sun* from 1986 to the end of 2000, leaving to become managing editor of *Revolver* magazine. He later became jazz critic at *The Globe and Mail* in Toronto.

Karl Dallas was a contributor to *Melody Maker* from the 1950s to the 1970s. He also wrote for *Musical Opinion*, the *Daily Worker* (later, the *Morning Star*), *The Times*, the *Independent, Sounds, Kerrang!, Schlager* (Germany) and other international magazines. He passed away in 2016.

Dave DiMartino is a former editor of *Creem*. He has worked for launch.com in Los Angeles, and is the author of *Singer-Songwriters: Pop Music's Performer-Composers, from A to Zevon* (Billboard Books, 1994).

Ian Dove is a former contributor to *New Musical Express* who has spent most of his career in the US. He has written for *Billboard*, the *New York Times* and other publications.

Robin Eggar has been the *Daily Mirror*'s rock and pop writer and has freelanced for national and international newspapers and magazines including the *Sunday Times, Esquire, You* magazine, *Marie Claire, The Times*, the *Daily Mail, Us* magazine, *Cosmopolitan, The Face, Time Out*, the *NME*, the *Observer, The Word*, the *Sunday Mirror* magazine and *Rolling Stone*.

Todd Everett has written for *Daily Variety, The Hollywood Reporter* and *Cash Box*, edited magazines (*Record Review, KIIS – The Newspaper* and *Ampersand*) and for several years was the entire pop music staff of Los Angeles's second-largest circulation newspaper.

Helen FitzGerald wrote about Dublin's punk scene for *VOX* fanzine, then moved to London in the early '80s to freelance for *Sounds* and *MasterBAG*. In 1983 she joined *Melody Maker* as a staff journalist, writing for *MM* from 1983 until 1989.

Ben Fong-Torres is one of the legendary names of rock writing. One of the first writers and editors at *Rolling Stone*, Ben worked for the magazine for many years, writing seminal profiles of the leading rock figures of the late '60s and '70s. He is the author of the Gram Parsons' biography, *Hickory Wind* (Atria, 1991), *The Hits Just Keep On Coming: The History of Top 40 Radio in America* (Backbeat Books, 1998) and the Little Feat biography *Willin'* (Da Capo Press, 2013).

Jerry Gilbert wrote for *Melody Maker, Sounds* and *ZigZag* in the '70s, also producing regular bylined columns for the *Daily Mirror* and *Midweek*. He still writes widely on folk and other genres.

Fred Goodman is the author of numerous books including *The Mansion on the Hill* (Crown, 1997) and *Allen Klein: The Man Who Bailed Out the Beatles, Made the Stones and Transformed Rock & Roll* (Eamon Dolan/Houghton Mifflin Harcourt, 2015). He lives in White Plains, New York.

Michael Gross, who began his career contributing to *Circus, Rock* and other music publications, is the author of the new *Genuine Authentic: The Real Life of Ralph Lauren* (Harper, 2003) and the *New York Times* bestseller *Model: The Ugly Business of Beautiful Women* (William Morrow & Co, 1995). He is also a contributing writer at *Radar* and a contributing editor at *Travel & Leisure* and has written for the *New York Times, Talk, George, New York, GQ, Esquire* and *Vanity Fair.*

Nicholas Jennings is one of Canada's leading music journalists. As the long-time critic for *Maclean's* magazine, Jennings has interviewed and written about Joni Mitchell numerous times. His acclaimed book *Before the Gold Rush* (Viking Canada, 1997) is the definitive account of Toronto's fertile music scene in the '60s.

Mark Kemp has written features, columns, essays and reviews since the late '80s for *Option, Rolling Stone,* the *New York Times,* the *Charlotte Observer, Harp, Paste, Business North Carolina* and many other publications. He has served as music editor of *Rolling Stone* and vice president of music editorial for MTV Networks.

Larry LeBlanc is a Canadian music journalist and recipient of the Walt Grealis special achievement award. He has written for numerous publications including *Rolling Stone, Guitar Player, The Globe & Mail* and *Maclean's*. He is currently a senior writer at the weekly US entertainment trade *Celebrity Access*.

Gerrie Lim has written for numerous publications, including *Billboard, LA Weekly, LA Style, Playboy, Details, Harper's Bazaar, Elle,* the *Wall Street Journal* and the *San Diego Union-Tribune*. He is currently the international correspondent for the adult internet trade magazine AVN Online.

Kristine McKenna is a Los Angeles writer whose work has appeared in publications including the *Los Angeles Times* and *NME*. Along with two volumes of collected interviews, she's published books on various aspects of alternative culture including first generation LA punk, radical hippie group the Diggers' and the West Coast beat community of the '50s.

Stuart Maconie is a journalist, broadcaster and author who has written for *Q, The Word, Elle, The Times,* the *Guardian,* the *Evening Standard, Daily Express, Select, Mojo, Country Walking, Deluxe* and was an assistant editor for the *NME*. He hosts a daily radio show on BBC6 music and is the author of several books including *Cider with Roadies* (Ebury Press, 2004) and *Pies and Prejudice* (Ebury Press, 2007).

John Milward has written about music and popular culture for more than thirty-five years, contributing to such publications as *Rolling Stone,* the *New York Times,* the *Philadelphia Inquirer,* the *Los Angeles Times,* the *Boston Globe, USA Today* and *No Depression,* among many others. He is the author of *Crossroads: How the Blues Shaped Rock'n'Roll (and Rock Saved the Blues)* (Northeastern, 2013).

Tom Nolan wrote for *Cheetah*, the *LA Times* and *Rolling Stone* in the '60s. He has subsequently written for the *Wall Street Journal* and been a contributing editor to *California* and *Los Angeles* magazines. Nolan's acclaimed biography of crime writer Ross MacDonald was published by Scribner in 1999 and *Three Chords for Beauty's Sake: The Life of Artie Shaw* by Norton in 2010. He lives in Glendale, Los Angeles.

Betty Page, real name Beverley Glick, first started writing for *Sounds* in 1979 and went on to make her name as the music journalist who championed the New Romantic movement, conducting the first major interviews with Spandau Ballet, Duran Duran and others in the early '80s. She subsequently became editor of *Record Mirror*. In 2011 she qualified as a life coach and is now freelancing at the *Telegraph* while building her coaching practice.

Ian Penman wrote for *NME* in the late '70s and early '80s and has subsequently written for *The Wire*, the *London Review of Books* and other publications. A collection of his best pieces, *Vital Signs*, was published by Serpent's Tail in 1998.

Sandy Robertson was features editor of *Sounds* and subsequently associate editor of *Penthouse* in the UK. He was the first UK writer to interview/pick up on Madonna, REM, Meat Loaf, Kirsty MacColl and Aimee Mann.

Wayne Robins has been writing about rock since 1969. In the 1970s he wrote for the *Village Voice* and *Rolling Stone*, but especially *Creem*. He subsequently wrote for *Newsday* and *New York Newsday*. He lives with his wife and two of his three daughters in Queens, NY.

Steven Rosen has written for dozens of publications, including *Guitar Player*, *Guitar World*, *Rolling Stone*, *Playboy*, *Creem*, *Circus* and

Musician. He is the author of such books as *Wheels of Confusion: The Story of Black Sabbath* (Music Sales, 1996), currently in its third printing, and acts as West Coast editor for the Japanese magazine *Player*.

Ellen Sander was *Saturday Review*'s rock critic in the mid–late '60s and also wrote on rock for *Vogue, The Realist, Cavalier, The LA Free Press*, the Sunday *New York Times* arts and leisure section and others.

Joel Selvin was chief music critic for the *San Francisco Chronicle* and author of landmark books such as *Summer of Love* (Dutton Adult, 1994), about the Haight-Ashbury scene. Selvin also contributes to *MOJO* and other publications.

Paul Sexton has been writing about music and avoiding a proper job since he started with the – now occasionally lamented – pop weekly *Record Mirror* while still at school in 1977.

Ben Sidran has recorded more than thirty solo albums and produced recordings for such noted artists as Van Morrison, Diana Ross and Mose Allison. Sidran has authored two books on the subject of jazz, *Black Talk*, a cultural history of the music, and *Talking Jazz*, a series of conversations with inspirational musicians. His latest works include the memoir, *A Life in the Music* (Taylor Trade, 2003), and the groundbreaking text, *There Was a Fire: Jews, Music and the American Dream* (Unlimited Media Ltd., 2012).

Dave Simpson has written regularly for the *Guardian*, as well as for *Melody Maker, i-D, Uncut* and many other publications. He is the author of *The Fallen: In and Out of Britain's Most Insane Group* (Canongate, 2008).

Wesley Strick began his writing career as a rock critic and journalist, contributing articles and reviews in the late '70s to *Circus, Creem* and

Rolling Stone. He has also written award-winning screenplays as well as a wide variety of Hollywood films and has served as an advisor at the Sundance Screenwriters Lab since 1995.

Adam Sweeting is a former features editor for *Melody Maker* and wrote for *Q* in its early days. Currently he writes regularly for the *Guardian*, *Uncut* and other magazines.

Frank Tortorici is a corporate communications director for a major business research organisation who has moonlighted periodically as a music writer. He was a contributing editor to Sonicnet/VH1.com for more than four years and was a contributing editor to Addicted to Noise. He has written for Preamp.com and Katrillion.com.

Jaan Uhelszki was one of the illustrious gang of writers who made *Creem* magazine a household name in the '70s. She has subsequently written for *Rolling Stone, Uncut*, and many other publications.

Michael Watts was *Melody Maker*'s US editor in the early 1970s. He's since been an editor at the *Financial Times*, the *Independent*, the *Evening Standard* and *Esquire*. He now writes for *Wired* and anyone else who'll have him.

Susan Whitall has been writing about music since she joined *Creem* in 1975. She became editor of that magazine in 1978 and left in 1983 to become a feature writer for the *Detroit News*. She is the author of *Fever: Little Willie John's Fast Life, Mysterious Death and the Birth of Soul* (Titan, 2011).

Paul Williams' '60s magazine *Crawdaddy!* marked the birth of rock criticism as we know it. He subsequently wrote many acclaimed books from *Outlaw Blues* (Entwhistle Books, 2000) to *The Twentieth Century's Greatest Hits* (Forge Books, 2000). He passed away in 2013.

CONTRIBUTORS

Richard Williams is the former editor of *Melody Maker* and former-chief sports writer for the *Guardian*. His books include *Out of his Head* (Outerbridge and Lazard, 1972), about Phil Spector and *The Man in the Green Shirt* (Bloomsbury, 1993), about Miles Davis. *Long Distance Call* (Aurum Press, 2000) collected some of his best music pieces.

Dave Zimmer has been a music journalist and rock historian since the late '70s. He is the author of *Crosby, Stills & Nash: The Authorized Biography* (St Martin's Press, 1984). Since 1990 he has worked as a communications director for MCA Records, Universal Studios, Seagram, Vivendi and, most recently, the Penguin Group. A native Californian, he currently lives in West Orange, New Jersey, with his wife and son.

Index

INDEX

INDEX

INDEX

INDEX

INDEX

INDEX